9556655

Recapitalizing AMERICA

Recapitalizing AMERICA

Alternatives to the corporate distortion of national policy

S. M. Miller
and
Donald Tomaskovic-Devey

Routledge & Kegan Paul
Boston, London, Melbourne and Henley

First published in 1983
by Routledge & Kegan Paul plc
9 Park Street, Boston, Mass. 02108, USA,
39 Store Street, London WC1E 7DD,
464 St Kilda Road, Melbourne,
Victoria 3004, Australia, and
Broadway House, Newtown Road,
Henley-on-Thames, Oxon RG9 1EN

Phototypeset in 10/12 Sabon
by Input Typesetting Ltd, London
Printed in the United States of America

Library of Congress Cataloging in Publication Data

Miller, S. M. (Seymour Michael), 1922–
Recapitalizing America.
Bibliography: p.
Includes index.
1. United States – Economic policy – 1981 –   .
2. Great Britain – Economic policy – 1945–   .
I. Tomaskovic-Devey, Donald, 1957–   . II. Title.
HC106.8.M54 1983   338.973   83–6658
ISBN 0–7100–9941–X

Contents

Preface ix
Acknowledgments xiii

Part One Misunderstanding America 1

1 Accepted wisdoms 3
2 The Great Transformation 14
Power and trade 14
Corporate changes 20
Inflation 26
Industrial changes 28
    Deindustrialization 29
    Services and employment 30
Political changes 33

3 International trade: the real British Disease? 35
Exports 36
Imports 37
Balance of payments 38
Recapitalization is inadequate trade policy 40
The real British Disease 46

4 Productivity: producing confusion 51
The myth of productivity decline 51
    Overselling productivity 54
    Labor costs 55

The politics of productivity 56
A better diagnosis 59
Productivity, wages, and inflation 61
Productivity and employment 64

5 **Investment panacea** 66
Wicked government? 67
Taxation and profits 67
Government spending 69
Regulation 71
Capital crowding 73
Wicked business? 74
Uneven investment 74
Profits and investment 76
Non-productive investments 77
Managerial incompetence 81
The non-rational market 86
Investment lures 88

6 **Can recapitalization provide the jobs?** 93
Employment 95
The service sector 95
Small business 97
High technology 98
Defining high technology 99
Employment increases 101
Output and jobs 103
Job location 106
Upward redistribution and recapitalization 108
Dim prospects 112

Part Two Moving beyond Reaganism and liberalism
117

7 **Old beginnings: contradictions and tensions in
bureaucratic liberalism** 119
The limited role of taxes and transfers 122

Keynesian macro-economic policy versus industrial policy 125
Political mood 126

8 **Progressive departures** 129
Macro–micro 130
International trade 131
Job-centered growth 134
Towards a new GNP 138
Direction without bureaucracy 139
"Planning" as politics 143
Work relations 146
Taxation and revenues 150
A participatory social sector 152
Beyond liberalism 155
    The basis of compassion 155
    The "moral majorities" 157
    Sharing and caring 160
The politics of creativity 162

9 **Breaking political boundaries** 164
Toward coalition 165
The 1930s vs. the 1980s 166
Coalition cracks 168
The labor question 169
Democratic realignment? 172
"After the ball" 173
Backward America 174
Politics as education 176
Where are the grass roots? 178
Starting up theory 180
Notes 184
Index 205

Preface

This book deals with such topics as Reaganism, deindustrialization, economic crisis, and industrial policy. We believe that most of the current American political, social, and economic discussion of these topics (with some notable exceptions) is mired within the ideological and political framework of recapitalizing America – the magical belief that increasing the power and profitability of private capital will solve the cyclical and structural problems of a faltering economy. The task of this book is to identify, criticize, and go beyond the accepted wisdoms of recapitalization.

This book was begun long before Reagan became President of the United States or Thatcher Prime Minister in the U.K. One of us (Miller), moving between the U.S. and Britain, began to sense in the mid-1970s that changes were occurring in the acceptability of the welfare state and that the diminution in the rate of economic growth was changing the prospects of employment, government revenues, and business, as well as popular opinion about greater governmental activity and the desirability of economic (and social) equality. Business leaders were mounting an organized campaign to convince citizens and politicians that business needed help – relief from regulation, access to capital funds, and lower taxes. In a number of articles, most published in *Social Policy* magazine, many of these issues were raised around the theme of the recapitalization of American capitalism.

In 1980, we turned to refashion these articles into a book. Before we could finish, Reaganism was on the scene, and what we were discussing in terms of the future became the present. We discarded most of the work of the past and started afresh to analyze the roots and destiny of Reaganism, which we characterize as reactionary recapitalization.

We emphasize two neglected elements in the discussion of recapitalization and industrial policy.

One is that Reaganism (and Thatcherism, for that matter) did not suddenly appear. For some time in the 1970s business groups were pushing for reduced taxes and an invigorated pro-business orientation by government. While arguments and proposals varied somewhat, the general push was clear. Recapitalization is a general ideology which preceded and transcends Reaganism and Reaganomics; Reagan and his radical right initiatives are only one variant of pro-business recapitalization. Critics who concentrate (as most do) on the harshness of Reaganism or the misadventures of supply-side economics will miss the overriding social transformation embodied in recapitalizing America. Ignoring recapitalization makes the nation more susceptible to its variants – less harsh than Reaganism, but no more appropriate to current needs. The belief that neo-liberal or moderate recapitalization is significantly different from the discredited Reagan approach is dangerous. Marx was wrong: when tragic history is repeated the second time, it is not farce but the wastage of the scarce commodity of opportunity. Naming the beast as recapitalization – increasing the importance of business and capital – and recognizing Reaganism as only one variant of it should make people more sensitive to the dangers and potential of the present period.

The second point is that economics and politics should not be technicized. Terms like "industrial policy" and "high technology," those whirlwind responses to the successes of Japan, mask the political issues of who bears the burdens of economic and social policy changes, who benefits, and who is to decide on the policies pursued. Our concern is to recognize the political and distributional implications of economic issues, not to remove these questions from intense scrutiny. That is why we are concerned with the politics as well as the economics of alternative policies.

We sense the possibilities of new political formations occurring which could pursue alternatives to the deeply flawed policies of recapitalization. In our discussion of these possibilities readers may not readily grasp "where we are coming from." We do not see ourselves as liberals, certainly not neo-liberals, nor as old or new left radicals. We think with liberals that social programs are important and accept much radical (and conservative) criticism of past and present programs as heavily bureaucratic and not empowering their beneficiaries. But unlike many radicals we do believe that the New Deal and Great Society were steps forward. Nor are we radical decentralists, despite our concern for community empowerment. For we believe that the federal government has not only a broad economic role to play but also that it is necessary that it act to prevent discrimination, promote equality, and monitor local performance. Like those of the old and new left we believe that liberal Keynesian policy, even if politically possible, is not able to deal with the current structural difficulties of the American economy. But we do not have confidence in saying that planning and nationalization of industry would automatically or axiomatically solve these problems. The United States must learn how to plan effectively and democratically. This will take time and activism on the part of subordinate groups. Premature plunging into such efforts will yield unfortunate results certain to hinder further development.

We believe strongly that values and sentiments are important, that material forces and interests do not alone determine what people prefer and support. There has been an erosion of support for greater equality, although the harshness of Reaganism has begun to stir humanitarian feelings. Programs have to be conducted in ways which win popular support, and interpreted in ways which make sense to people. A more caring society depends not only on legislation and administration but more basically on our acceptance of and concern for one another. Developing feelings of caring is an important political act.

We do not have a simple single name for what we propose, nor a convenient political label for its supporters. "Communitarian" and "progressive" are terms that appeal to us, but phrasing is not the important issue. The weakening of party affiliation and the growth of social movement participation suggest that many Americans are searching for new ways of living and new ways of conducting civic life. Working on concrete issues within a broader outlook is what is immediately needed.

Our contention is that the many variants of recapitalization misdiagnose the economic ills of the United States and misprescribe for them. The present political likelihood is that less harsh variants will supplant ineffective Reaganism, for the "accepted wisdoms" of the day are captured by recapitalist thinking. It is important to break away from misleading analyses and faulty remedies, to begin to think in terms of alternative strategies which will not increase the disturbing domination pursued by big business. Political motion *is* occurring; our hope is that by analyzing the faulty premises and prescriptions of recapitalization and industrial policy, and by outlining new approaches, we will contribute to an economics and politics of alternatives.

SMM
DTD

Acknowledgments

We thank the following for encouragement, example, advice, or information. None is responsible for what we have wrought with their aid.

Frank Riessman, Roy Bennett, Bob Kuttner, Mike Miller, Colin Greer, Peter Dreier, Michael Harloe, Barry Bluestone, Bennett Harrison, Peter Marris, Sol Levine, Frances Fox Piven, Martin Rein, Bert Gross, Dick Boone, Peter Cove, Susan Friedman, Ralph Milliband, Michael Ansara, Susan Eckstein, Michael Useem, Jean Baker Miller.

A German Marshall Fund Fellowship to Miller was important for his work on the book. We appreciate the typing of Michael Coury.

Special thanks to Barbara Tomaskovic-Devey, who helped out even when she had more important things to attend to.

Part One

Misunderstanding America

Chapter 1
Accepted wisdoms

The post-World War II era has ended in the advanced capitalist nations. Economic growth was the norm during the decades between the end of the war and, say, 1973, when the Middle East oil price rise made obvious what had already begun to be sensed – that the era of economic expansion and a growing social sector would not easily continue. After the extraordinarily prolonged and strong expansion of the 1960s, the U.S. entered the 1970s on a wave of attack on social expenditures and social policies. Business criticism of the active state grew as economic growth slowed and the federal government promulgated environmental and social regulations. A newly fashioned ideology of "neo-conservatism" gained wide currency, contending that government was doing too much and too badly in efforts to overcome discrimination and inequality. The intellectual analysis of neo-conservatism was soon joined in its attack on the role of the state in economic and social life by the well-organized offensive of the Radical Right social movements.[1] The 1980s began on a Reaganite note which greatly extended that departure from the liberal ideology of the 1960s which had argued that much could and should be done to shape the United States into a more fair society.

The key phrases of "reindustrialization," "revitalization," "Reaganomics," "productivity," "supply-side economics," and "industrial policy" resounded. They belong to the family of buzz words that capture great attention and then quickly die, replaced by new clichés. But the assumptions, ideas, arguments, and proposals behind these words are hardy. They have become the "accepted wisdoms" for business leaders, most economists, and commenta-

3

tors. They were heard before reindustrialization, industrial policies, and productivity emerged to cover-story glamor in *Newsweek* and *Time*. They continue to shape public understanding and political debate. They are gravely flawed as diagnosis of and prescription for the American political economy.

The sudden introduction of Reaganomics should not obscure the fact that its basic tenets had been urged for some time. Nor should the failures of the Reaganite version interfere with the awareness of the continuing importance of these premises in molding policy and politics. Similar efforts will supplant it, perhaps softening its edges, but working in the same vein. For the fundamental doctrine – of contracted welfare state and expanded business freedom – is widely accepted, among liberals and neo-liberals as well as more conservative citizens and leaders.

Reagan's supply-side economics and Carter's revitalization/reindustrialization thinking are variants of a more general approach that was hawked throughout the 1970s. While Carterism and Reaganism differ on important points, they share a common core about the importance of *private* investment in restoring America's economic greatness.

Carter's revitalization plan, like Reagan's supply-side economics, proposed to cut business taxes in order to increase investment and boost productivity and exports. Revitalization differed from supply-side economics in its intent to have some targeting of tax cut benefits in order to have some direct stimulation of investment. It also refused to abandon as much of the liberal legacy of social programs. Reaganomics is a socially harsh, free-market variant of the underlying thinking of Carterism.[2]

In the 1970s the core of what we call recapitalization, which we discuss shortly, assumed various faces. Most notable then was the poorly documented assertion of David Rockefeller and other business and financial leaders that the U.S. faced a "capital crunch," a long-term shortage of capital funds for investment, that would block future economic growth. Heavy taxation was stripping business of funds for investment. Worsening the situation, the charge went on, was that governmental borrowing was "crowding out" or absorbing loans that would have been made to the private sector, depriving the latter of vital investment funds.[3]

In the 1980s liberals, such as Senators Paul Tsongas

(Democrat–Massachusetts) and Gary Hart (Democrat–Colorado) and investment banker Felix Rohatyn, mainly offer somewhat different means to the same goals of increasing private business investment.[4] The essential character of calling for boosting big business has varied little. The bedrock of the diagnosis is that American productivity is declining; the prescription is to decrease taxation in order to increase incentives in order to promote productivity.

Our contention in this book is that this current wisdom is flawed and that the Reaganomic prescription for American ills is grossly inadequate for restoring America's economic strength in the post-post-World War II world. But first let us outline the basic ingredients of this view of America's needed changes.

According to current wisdom, a strong domestic economy is necessary to restore the U.S. to its dominant role in the world economy. And that *Number One* world role is essential in the rehabilitation of the domestic economy. The Number One economy is the Number One world power and vice versa. But even weaker military powers move towards a deep change – constricting the public sector (read the welfare state) and strongly aiding the ailing private sectors. At stake is the well-being of working classes and marginal populations as the long-term direction of capitalist economies is reformulated.

In several countries, but most clearly in the United States and the United Kingdom, big business and banking interests, supported by influential economists and policy analysts (with support from inflation-weary middle-income groups), have been laying out the terms of that reformulation. That reformulation or, better, restoration, had five major objectives in its Reaganite design:

1 reducing taxation on corporations and the well-to-do in order to promote profits, and thereby investment and productivity;
2 contracting the public social sector in order to offset the decline in tax revenues, decrease federal deficits, and reduce inflationary pressures;
3 increasing the role of manufacturing, especially exported goods, within the private sector;
4 reducing inflationary pressures by not permitting the domestic

economy to grow quickly and relying on slow increases in the money supply to dampen inflationary periods;

5 decreased governmental regulation of business and industry; reduction of antitrust action, especially against export-oriented firms; contraction of environmental, occupational safety, and consumer protections.

Underriding these proposals to make the U.S. more "competitive" in the world market is the long-run intention to dampen wage increases to keep down labor costs. A basic premise is that the United States must expand exports in order to "survive." The expectation is the continuing expansion of international trade. The goals are to expand American exports, especially in the manufacturing sector, and to reduce imports by underselling goods manufactured in other countries.

Even though many proposals about industrialization do not specifically mention the promotion of exports (or the curbing of imports), the export–import issue is central. The belief is that a weak nation economically in world trade will be a weak nation politically. The militarily weak nation will be troubled economically. The long-term American need is defined as expanding exports and contracting imports.[5]

The means to these restorationist goals involve the growth of capital investment in manufacturing and its auxiliaries, e.g., power plants. The purpose of this outlay is to increase productivity. Since only some services can be exported, an export-oriented strategy requires the strengthening of manufacturing and allied activities.[6] Its basic objective is to restore American manufacturing to a more competitive place in the world economy by increasing productivity. It is this setting of expanded international trade which shapes the basic elements of recapitalization and makes it more acceptable than the simple, long-expressed, conservative argument for untrammeled private enterprise.

The reorienting of capitalist functioning away from an expanding public sector to strong support for expanding the private sector is a response to "the crisis of capitalism," a term employed by both left and right analysts. Whether the economic difficulties of the day warrant that appellation is less clear. To be sure, a general air of uncertainty and decline prevails. One does not have to believe, as does Marxist Ernest Mandel, that capitalism is in the downward phase of the long (Kondratieff) business-cycle to be pessimistic about economic prospects.[7] For contemporary capitalism is in trouble, acutely in Britain and Italy, less so in the United States, and much less so in Japan and West Germany.

But thanks to slower growth and continuing inflation, business-oriented slogans against "big government" are popularly compelling. This apparent mutuality of interest across classes and its corollary attack on public spending has even made headway in Denmark and its rumblings are heard in Sweden. Uncertainty, especially around inflation, has made many middle- and working-class Americans resonate to some of the themes of the recapitalization approach, particularly to the complaints about taxes and the character of public social expenditures. Underlying the apparent mutuality of interests among moderate-income persons, the well-to-do, and large corporate and banking interests is a deep-seated dissatisfaction with government performance.

Carter's revitalization or reindustrialization or Reagan's supply-side economics are misleading or, at least, inadequate terms to convey what is being demanded.[8] A more appropriate term is *the recapitalization of capitalism*. We use recapitalization in a physical, economic, and ideological sense. One effort is to increase the amount of physical capital or investment (capital formation) in industry in order to promote productivity. The second is to increase the role of private economic capitalism (reprivatization) in American society by reducing the domestic activities of American government, lower taxation of corporations and the well-to-do, decreasing social expenditures, and by contracting the regulation of industries. The third drive seeks to teach ideological lessons – expect less of government, there are no entitlements. Less government then means more capitalist activity.

In the reactionary Reaganite variant of recapitalization, the way to the twenty-first century is through the eighteenth. Adam Smith's 1776 guide, *The Wealth of Nations*, was to lead the way to a new era – that of restoration of an unregulated capitalism that never was. The Reagan policies are unique in their intense pursuit of recapitalization objectives. They have sought to turn growth with welfare statism to growth without an expanding social sector.

But the Carter revitalization proposals also intended to do much of what Reagan attempted, though on a smaller, less radical, less swift scale, and with many fewer inroads into the welfare state. Carter's acceptance of the investment approach as the solution to American economic ills was strong. Reaganomics *appeared* to be a great break because of its almost total reliance on the invisible hand of the market to accomplish its investment, productivity, and export goals and its efforts to dismantle social programs rapidly while spectacularly expanding military outlays. The general outlook on how to promote long-run development of the American economy differed little from the outlook of Carter and leaders of other capitalist countries. None the less, the differences in means and attitudes towards social programs and the character and subsidies (tax reductions) to business are significant enough to speak of moderate, neo-liberal, liberal, as well as reactionary variants of the recapitalization of capitalism.[9]

The recapitalization of U.S. capitalism is the *accepted wisdom* of the 1980s. Even as the harsh, free-market, anti-state policies of Reaganomics fail, recapitalization, with its goals of private corporate investment and productivity growth, is likely to remain politically compelling. Recapitalization is larger than the Reaganomics and supply-side radicalism that polarize current political debate. Recapitalization should be understood as the fairly entrenched ideology that it is, so that when Reagan et al. disappoint, another more moderate recapitalization variant is not blithely accepted by a relieved electorate, only to fail again.

The moderate business variant of recapitalization concentrates on investment by increasing corporate tax deductions for depreciation on equipment and buildings. The less targeted Reaganite reduction of personal income taxes is not a central theme in the "moderate" recapitalization approach of big business. Unlike supporters of "supply-side" economics, the more traditional business leaders are concerned with narrowing federal budget deficits. In general, they would rely on fiscal policy to a greater extent than do the Reaganites. Many big business moderates advocate a less drastic and less unsettling curtailment of public social expenditures than the reactionary recapitalists pursue. While seeking to dampen wage increases, many would seek some accommodation with unions rather than head-on collision. In foreign policy, they are less bellicose than the militant ideologists of Reagan who so inflamed domestic and world opinion in the opening days of the Reagan Administration. In short, they are moderates, seeking goals similar to reactionary supporters of recapitalization but more flexible and more willing to compromise than the Reagan extremists.

The neo-liberal variant overlaps with the moderate business stance. Neo-liberals prefer a higher degree of targeting in tax incentives to promote investment. While they would accept reductions in public social expenditures to balance the budget, they would not make such large cuts as the moderate recapitalists and attack the reductions sought by the reactionary camp. Indeed, the size of the Reaganite cuts made some neo-liberals more supportive of social programs than they had been. The neo-liberals' main difference from the moderates is that they campaign for an active governmental role in the promotion of investment. They seek to promote industrial "winners" – and some would aid "loser" firms and industries – by resurrecting some version of the Reconstruction Finance Corporation (RFC) of the 1930s. The new RFC would lend to firms which had difficulty borrowing in the private capital markets. Most advocate "industrial policy," active intervention by the federal government to promote particular industries, especially potential "winners."[10]

The liberal variant is not always easy to distinguish from the neo-liberal. Liberal recapitalists seek to promote investment *and* employment. They would strongly support a high degree of tax targeting on investment. They would concentrate personal income tax cuts on low-income households and seek to maintain the progressive elements of the tax system. They promote active industrial policy by government. In particular, they seek to aid sick industries, in addition to promoting winning sectors. "Planning" is not a negative but a positive term for them, in contrast to those in the reactionary and moderate camps and to many neo-liberals as well. They would accept wage-price controls, as would some neo-liberals, as intrinsic to the dampening of inflation. Many liberals and some neo-liberals advocate high spending on rebuilding the infrastructure (e.g., highways, ports, bridges, sewage systems, transportation) of America. One reason is that these basic facilities are wearing out; another is that extensive public works programs would generate jobs. They espouse an active Keynesian fiscal and monetary policy of growth to spur employment.[11]

Unlike the other variants, liberals do not believe that the struggle against inflation is the prime requirement for economic recovery. They focus on employment. They seek to maintain public social expenditures and are largely uncritical of the operation of the programs. This position contrasts with that of the other three variants who object to major features of social programs.

Accepting these perspectives has aided the spread of other recapitalist ideas which liberals reject. What makes recapitalists of many liberals despite important differences is that they basically accept the diagnosis that the United States's difficulties revolve around low productivity and that the remedy lies mainly in promoting private sector investment.

Many liberals dislike being lumped with neo-liberals and vigorously disagree that they overlap in outlook with the more conservative variants.

In the recapitalization scenario, accomplishing the more-export, less-import goal requires moving the economy into a further capitalistic direction. Reactionary and moderate recapitalization seek a social–political change away from a large social sector and an active government influencing the behavior of enterprises. Even liberal recapitalization foresees a limiting of the welfare state, although some of its adherents advocate a more direct governmental role in influencing capital investment.

The export approach requires keeping down prices of U.S. goods to make them more competitive. How? Productivity is the panacea. In the 1960s liberals offered economic growth as the all-win, cost-free game that would improve the conditions of all. In the 1980s *productivity is the recapitalist cost-free game*. It is charged with improving the competitiveness of American exports without depressing wages, thereby increasing employment and real incomes. A most pleasant hope.

Over time, however, as productivity solutions disappoint, keeping down labor costs by limiting real wages will be the preferred way of most recapitalists for increasing the competitiveness of U.S. products. This will be done by the "discipline" of high unemployment rates which frighten workers into lowering wage expectations, limiting union power through governmental pressures, mandatory or "guideline" wage controls, slower minimum wage increase, and/or the creation of Third World-type production platforms (in the guise of urban enterprise zones) within the U.S.

The logic of recapitalization is that government intervention in the market and excesses of consumption by American workers and the poor, at least relative to real economic growth, undermined the economic base of the United States. At the same time Japanese and European competitors (except Britain) have expanded their productivity and threaten to bury the American economy with imports. The gradually developed national consensus about recapitalization asserts that the U.S. has ruined its once invincible economy (1945–69) and must now act to make it great once more by freeing private enterprise to recreate its historic role of stimulating growth. This reindustrialization diagnosis has been actively and avidly constructed by politicians, the media, academics, and of course, big business.

For most recapitalists the only alternative to imminent demise is to forgo individual consumption (through wage restraint and cuts in social services) in order to lower production costs and raise profit levels. (Liberals object to this view, but the logic of the emphasis on productivity leads to this emphasis.) The resulting capital would then be productively used to reindustrialize the United States.

The recapitalist road to a healthy American economy is swift improvement in the rate of productivity. If more is produced per labor hour, then U.S. goods will be cheaper. An overall increase in productivity, regardless of in which industries it occurs, is the solution to America's economic ills. Providing more funds to business through lower taxation will result in high productivity. This process of renewed or revitalized investment in industrial capital will enhance the ability of U.S. exports to compete internationally. If this process is not followed, the argument runs, the future is threateningly bleak: a long and inevitable economic decline will occur, throwing many workers out of work and leading to the (further) collapse of some of our greatest industries.

Government is depicted as the dangerous dinosaur in most recapitalist variants, while big business and the well-to-do are relegitimated in American society. In the reactionary variant

inequality is described as a positive condition, one to be encouraged, for the privileged are the savers who provide the funds for
investment which spurs the productivity of industry. Indeed, for
the first time in many years, inequality has been heralded as a
desirable goal. This feeling fuels "the social issue" – the attack on
abortion, the contention that blacks and minorities are ripping off
welfare systems, and that government and the counter-culture have
endangered the family.

Large corporations claim the right to pursue their special interests on the basis of the improvidence, incompetence, arrogance,
and corruption of government. Big business versus the state is the
order of the day. Once business was willing to accept, tolerate, or
compromise on the welfare state; now it seizes the opportunity to
roll it back. Among many U.K. and U.S. economists, the sanctity of
private sector priorities is revitalized and has achieved widespread
appeal.[12]

The aim for most recapitalists is a consensual policy of contained
wage increases, less social spending, lower corporation taxation,
and more private investment. An *unavoidable* dictum is promulgated: recapitalization measures are absolutely necessary. No alternative way to economic well-being is possible. Not ideology but
economic practicality and imperatives require this course.[13]

We do not have to wait for the future to conclude that the
recapitalization approach is likely to be successful. For, in one
respect, it has already proved a great winner. The recapitalization
and neo-conservative scenarios have had enormous and profound
success in shaping public opinion and debate. The widely touted
decline of New Deal/Great Society liberalism, its supposed intellectual and political bankruptcy, is an important development. The
distrust of government and the savior-like confidence in productivity are important beliefs. Conservative recapitalization in both
the U.S. and Britain has had considerable success (despite Reagan's
over-kill) in attacking social programs and in "throwing money at
the military."

Certainly, the Keynesian economists of the 1960s had a simple
view of the economic world and an arrogant understanding of
what they could fine-tune. But the attack on this outlook is not
only on the efficacy of means but on the worthiness of goals.
The aims of greater equality and less poverty are repudiated in

recapitalization – and widely shared, perhaps with less dogmatism, by many others. In this view, only those who espouse recapitalization in its reactionary or moderate dress have good sense; all others are utopians who would defeat the achievement of their own goals because they would impede the turning around of the economy.

The closing down of alternatives and options has been an enormous success. For some issues do not enter public discussion at all or, if they do, are easily and airily dismissed as not politically acceptable. The recapitalization adherents have succeeded in narrowing the debate and framing the variables which can be discussed. Spurring the private sector to invest is the major goal. Although liberal and conservative recapitalists differ on protecting the poor and social programs, they often converge in their basic interpretation of what the economy needs while disagreeing on the degree to which government should try to "target" investment. A very limited set of policies (promoting present-day U.S. firms) is now the main method of prescribing for the course of the American economy.

It is our contention that all variants of recapitalization policies will fail to reach their politico-economic goals because of their faulty diagnosis (discussed in Chapters 3, 4, and 5) and because they ignore the complex changes in the U.S. political economy of the last twenty years, the topic of Chapter 2.

Chapter 2
The Great Transformation

What is behind the push for recapitalization? Obviously, the desire to increase profits through reduced taxes is always there for U.S. business. What was special about the 1970s and early 1980s was the deep, unsettling feeling that the U.S. was undergoing great changes domestically and internationally. Improving "productivity" was offered as the solution to the American "crisis." Since both conservative and liberal variants of recapitalization do not grasp the nature of these changes, their polemic will yield unsuccessful policies. At best they deal with productivity as a symptom, largely ignoring the issues which led to its visibility.

Although put forward as nationally necessary and apolitical proposals, pro-productivity policies are attempts to restore business profitability in a new economic and political context. That context is the Great Transformation of the U.S. and world political economy over the last few decades. The recapitalization solutions fail to alleviate the strains produced by these structural rather than cyclical changes.

In this chapter we discuss four components of the Great Transformation: power diffusion and the internationalization of trade; changes in corporate behavior; inflation; and industrial changes.

Power and trade

The major transformation is the loss by the U.S. of its world hegemonic position. Clearly, the United States dominated the post-

World War II world; it was Number One. Here is a simple indication of this supremacy: in 1950, the U.S. produced about half of the production in the world as measured by economists (the Gross National Product); twenty-five years later, U.S. production was only a little more than a quarter of world output while West German and Japanese output expanded spectacularly. Certainly, U.S. production in this period increased mightily in absolute size, but the U.S. is no longer the unrivaled economic colossus of the world.

American military and political might was dimmed by the desire to intervene in Third World situations around the globe and the growing inability to dictate outcomes of these military, diplomatic, and economic interventions. Viet Nam is only the most dramatic case of U.S. failure. The long imprisonment of Americans at the Embassy in Iran further signified the waning of American power. The U.S. is no longer alone in its military strength; the USSR now is in an amorphous "parity position" with the U.S. The independent policy and politics of many Third World nations and the loss of U.S. control over the United Nations are further evidence of U.S. decline.

Certainly, recapitalization is in part a response to this loss of dominance. A curious psychological number-oneism was converted into public policy as the restoration of U.S. economic and military dominance of the world became a policy objective.[1] Number-oneism is the irrational urge of the U.S. to dominate the world. The efficacy of world dominance could be questioned when dominance was a real possibility. Now when that dominance is beyond the reach of U.S. economic and, probably, military policy, a number-oneism objective can be disastrous. Instead of remaking the world in its image, the U.S. is now participating in the world as a more nearly equal partner. Its economic and military preeminence no longer go unquestioned. The development of a multipolar political world has paralleled the loss of U.S. economic hegemony.[2]

"How the mighty have fallen" is the way that many Americans regard these changes. And as with the reaction to the Chinese Revolution in 1949, domestic scapegoats may be sought. Restoration of past glories and power is often an effective appeal for politicians with little else to offer.

The more realistic response is that U.S. dominance could not have been expected to last as long as it did, for it was largely the aftermath of the special conditions of war-devastated countries and a war-improved American economy. It is our contention that the U.S. has to learn how to live with its shared world power and to reconcile itself to a narrower span of American interests.

The U.S., in aggressive and stumbling pursuit of restoration of worldwide supremacy, cannot adequately address its severe internal problems such as unemployment, inflation, depressed regions and industries, and cultural divisiveness. One reason is that a nation can only address politically one major problem at a time. Second, high military expenditures distort the economy. A less militaristic and expansive foreign policy is necessary if the U.S. is to begin to face realistically the charge of recasting domestic structures and policies.

The new, difficult context includes the growth of many strong trading nations, the proliferation of multinational enterprises, the instability produced by international capital mobility, and a deep and general international economic interdependence. Factories in several countries often have a role in the various stages of industrial production which lead up to a final product. "The world car" is the term applied to the truly international character of production of some automobiles: a car has so many parents that no country can be considered its birthplace. Imports in many fields, especially from Japan and Third World export platforms like Hong Kong and South Korea, have wiped out or forced the contraction of a few American industries and firms (e.g., automobiles, steel, and consumer electronics). The growth of multinational firms has been spectacular. With their ability to shift capital, production, and employment from one country to another, they have outmoded the nation-state. The quantitative expansion of world trade is truly a transformation, profoundly reshaping domestic economies, even that of the U.S.

For many Third World nations, particularly heavily indebted export platforms such as Korea and Brazil, declines in the world market or in the price of key commodities can trigger international payment problems. For nations to keep exports high, domestic wages and consumption must be limited. This is as true in Japan, Great Britain, and now in the United States as it is in the Third

World. The difference is that in the Third World curtailing consumption can mean starvation and/or political instability. While international trade-based instability may lead to redistribution or consumption modification in the industrialized West, in the less affluent nations such as Brazil, Poland, or El Salvador privation and political turmoil are likely outcomes and influence American military and foreign policies.

The U.S. is now much more vulnerable to the vicissitudes of world trade. The OPEC-engineered oil shocks of 1973 dramatized this vulnerability. By then the changed world economic scene was already apparent in the decline of the dollar, negative U.S. trade balances, and the contracting share of U.S. exports in world markets.

Export-dependent national economies are highly sensitive to fluctuations in the world market. In the past the U.S. has been largely insulated from these fluctuations because of its small involvement (relative to overall economic activity) in the export/import market. Recently, as U.S. imports have zoomed, particularly in strategic commodities such as oil, steel, automobiles, and as agricultural and capital goods (except automotive) exports climbed, the U.S. has become more vulnerable to shifts in the world economy. Foreign trade has doubled as a percentage of GNP in the post-war period. The U.S. is, however, still much less dependent on the world market than are other major capitalist nations.

Nevertheless, U.S. social, economic, and political structures are internationalized as goods and capital are exported to and from the United States.

This internationalization of the U.S. political economy is not a minor occurrence. Increased economic competition from abroad has weakened the ability of a number of U.S. industries both to sell domestically and to export their products. The increased economic interdependence of the nations of the world has left the United States increasingly vulnerable to world trade cycles, world inflation, and specific international economic and political crises (e.g., the Iranian revolution).[3]

The result of this changed world political economy is the loss of U.S. economic and political influence, domestic industrial and employment weakness in the face of international competition (e.g., autos), and a psychological sense of loss in the U.S. body-politic as international prestige and power decline. Internationalization of U.S. social structure implies that the U.S. can no longer be treated politically or economically as a closed system. The strength of the U.S. economy depends to a large extent upon its ability to compete or co-exist with other economies. The U.S. is now shaped by the international context rather than being the determinant of that context.[4]

Internationalization makes uncertain what is the national interest, particularly for the U.S. The interests of large, internationally oriented enterprises and smaller nationally oriented firms collide. Even the utility of analyzing the world in terms of nation-states is questionable as giant industrial and particularly financial firms transcend national boundaries. If IBM, Exxon, and Chase Manhattan Bank are now citizens of the world, in terms of profits, operations, and long-term interests, the appropriateness of treating them as U.S.-based entities is undermined. Although IBM, Exxon, and Chase Manhattan are certainly influenced by the internal U.S. economy, they move their activities among nations in order to maximize post-tax profits. National interests of the U.S. or the host nation where they ply their interests have little to do with the decisions they make.

Wallerstein's analysis of the world capitalist system is especially striking in this regard. He suggests that the competitive nature of the world capitalist economy does not allow, over the long term, a single-nation world empire. U.S. dominance in the post-war period approached the control implied by world empire. The political and economic cost of the *pax Americana* was too high and is now eclipsed. Wallerstein also suggests that as U.S. world dominance declines or is eclipsed, U.S. control over U.S.-based multinationals will decline.[5]

In addition, the entire world has been drawn closer together in a precarious web of international dependence. World trade increasingly brings all nations into a more intimate interdependence. Interdependence does not imply stability or solidarity. One country's (e.g., U.S.) high interest rates may lower inflationary forces there but disturb another economy as capital flows out (e.g., Germany) to the first nation to benefit from its interest rates. Each nation struggles to export unemployment through its exports (e.g.,

Japanese vs. U.S. auto industries). Stagnation and inflation are now world-level phenomena, independent of any one nation. International currency flows, particularly international debt, have rendered the entire world banking system perilously unstable. In addition, many once self-sufficient nations are now dependent on other countries for their food (e.g., Italy, Poland, and much of the Third World). Many nations are export dependent. Japan, South Korea, and West Germany must keep up their exports in order to provide domestic employment. Other nations, such as Brazil, Mexico, and again Poland, are forced by their foreign debt to export in order to earn the foreign currency necessary to pay their debts to western banks, often at the cost of domestic consumption. Other nations such as the U.S. and Great Britain find domestic employment threatened by foreign imports.

The result of international interdependence is world-wide political and economic instability. Nations must choose between "beggaring their neighbor" (decreasing imports and increasing exports in order to increase domestic production and employment) and beggaring their citizenry (reducing wages and/or public programs) in order to survive in the web of international trade. The recapitalization path of maintaining free trade for export expansion does both: it beggars a nation's citizens by changing the tax structure and decreasing public expenditures so as to transfer income from consumers to potential manufacturing investors; and it beggars other nations by trying to increase domestic production and employment by invading other countries' markets.

World economic trends, particularly the growth of international trade, affect deeply American production and employment. The U.S. is threatened currently by an international web of perilously imbalanced trade dependence. Economic growth and higher personal income in the U.S. lead to increased demand for imports such as cars from Japan or machine tools from Germany. As a result, American workers may not benefit from domestic growth. On the other hand, the expansion of American output may not be accompanied by demand for American exports or by an expansion of productive capacity in U.S. export-oriented industries, an important objective of current economic policies.

Which industries expand as the economy grows and changes is important and uncertain in competitive, complex, international markets where prices, interest rates, currency exchange values, and trade policies interact. Conventional economic policy approaches pay attention only to the rate of growth in the volume of production; that outlook is now inadequate.

The present world need is for some way of regulating world trade. Expanding foreign trade increasingly strains the internal economics and politics of most nations. Multinational banks and corporations fear, however, that any restraint on free movement will spread and adversely affect them. Consequently, there will be great debate in many countries. Obviously the U.S., and world bodies like the OECD and IMF, will grapple with protectionism, selective controls, quotas – issues inimical to the needs of multinational capital and the present recapitalization ideology. We shall return to this issue in Chapter 8.

Corporate changes

Domestically, the behavior and organization of major American corporations are undergoing serious changes. While they furnish about 17 per cent of U.S. employment, the largest corporations (*Fortune Magazine's* largest one thousand), especially those in the manufacturing and finance sectors, tend to dominate the economy and economic policy through their control of capital and productive assets and their political pressure. The private giant corporations and banks that dominate the economy have changed their tactics and through short-sighted and irrational behavior present a major risk to the U.S. economy.

TABLE 2.1 *Assets of the 200 largest U.S. manufacturing firms as per cent share of all U.S. manufacturing assets*

	1950	1960	1970	1975	1980
200 largest	47.7	56.3	60.4	57.5	59.7

Source: *Statistical Abstract of the United States, 1981*, Table 917, p. 541, U.S. Government Printing Office, Washington D.C.

The increasing concentration of industrial activity in the U.S. is well-known and represents a long-term corporate change. The current debate about its significance revolves around questions of the political power and/or profit benefits of concentration. The concentration of national economic activity in a relatively small number of corporations leads to both political power for those corporations and increased profitability for firms in oligopolistic industries.[6]

The real significance of the large corporation goes beyond any deviance from pluralist theories of the democratic state or from neo-classical economists' expectations of competitive and self-clearing markets. Concentration raises fundamental questions about the ability of big business to influence the nature of social structure. More important than oligopoly pricing and political pull in Washington is that the largest corporations are the institutionalized repositories of major economic assets. National wealth, savings, investment, non-agricultural exports are concentrated in these corporations; their great power is to dispose of this institutionalized property. If a Chrysler were to fail, then a large chunk of national savings and investment would go with it. A Chrysler-type failure would destroy or weaken not only its own productive potential and capital investment but also the lives of its workers, their communities, and Chrysler's creditors and stockholders. Corporations with the power to fail or act irrationally or shortsightedly are a grave danger to the nation as a whole. Concentration gave the few men who controlled the U.S. auto industry tremendous power over the entire U.S. economy.

Another indication of the threat of corporate and financial instability is the sudden realization in the early 1980s that private U.S. banks have dangerously overextended themselves through loans to high-risk nations such as Poland, Mexico, and Brazil and other countries having grave difficulties repaying their debt. The U.S. government's penchant for paying the debts of foreign governments who cannot meet their obligations to U.S. banks is merely another Chrysler-type bailout, this time of the banks and without any political discussion.[7] If large banks suffer great losses, the stability of the entire financial system is endangered. Poland, Mexico and now Brazil are the most striking examples of U.S. government intervention to rectify excessive private investment risks.

Concentration is changing the American social structure: concentration narrows the range of decisions in the economy while expanding the impact of decisions. The investment patterns, product, employment choices, and managerial foresight of firms and banks such as Ford Motor Company and Franklin National Bank, a casualty of the 1970s, affect the fate of the U.S. transportation industry, balance of payments, government tax receipts, and many other economic realities. Decision-making by an industrial company or bank revolves around its profitability or stability. But its ramifications stretch beyond that corporation. New institutional forms of concentrated capital such as conglomerates and multinational enterprises perversely affect the stability of U.S. social and economic structure.[8]

Conglomerates and large multinational forms of the corporation are a basic transformation in the nature of production. Pursuing their own stability or profitability, the largest firms have contracted important national products (e.g., steel by U.S. Steel) and regions (Detroit by the auto industry). This transformation of size, activity, and locality is intimately linked to the process of internationalization. The basic transformation is that the scale of capital accumulation made possible by the modern oligopolistic firm and industry has produced new levels of capital mobility within a nation and among nations. Capital flows swiftly from area to area, dislocating and disrupting markets and regions. Region and product are negotiable when capital is large and fluid. The development of easy means of transferring capital has promoted quick and short-term capital movements. Increasingly, capital and credit-rich firms buy entire corporations rather than invest in new productive facilities. Similarly, foreign investment takes precedence over domestic investment when labor, taxes, or transport are relatively cheaper in non-U.S. locales. Conglomerates at home and multinational investment abroad are two examples of U.S. corporate capital pursuing mobile investment patterns which do not benefit the U.S. economy. No or few new jobs or taxes are generated through these uses of capital.

Multinational and conglomerate investment by the largest U.S. corporations has helped deplete manufacturing investment by siphoning funds for other uses. International investment by U.S. firms does produce some capital returns to the United States economy but few if any jobs. Conglomerate investment, on the other hand, merely represents the transfer of ownership of existing firms with no new productive facilities. Conglomerate investment may produce diversified and stable profit portfolios for individual firms; for the economy, the outcome is essentially a destruction of investment capital. The cost of conglomerate takeovers in 1981 was more than twice as high as the outlay for such takeovers a year earlier. It was the largest corporate takeover year in terms of both cost and number of transactions in U.S. history. (Chapter 5 provides the data on the impact on domestic productive investment.) Industrial production concentrates in fewer corporations; capital funds are diverted from new physical investment; employment does not expand nor prices decline.

Aggravating low domestic investment in manufacturing is the surge toward speculation in the U.S. economy. Speculation, not production, is the way to profits for many investors. A high and growing percentage of corporate capital funds is devoted to the purchase of financial assets by corporations rather than utilized for investment in physical capital. Conglomerate activity is itself a form of speculation because capital is used to buy capital in the hope that with no additional physical production a profit can be made. The boom in the 1960s and 1970s in real estate prices was partly a response to inflation but also partly a broader effort to seek speculative gains. Activities in real estate, stocks and commodities, and the growing reliance on borrowed funds to finance consumption and investment increase the importance of speculation in the American economy.

Conglomerates, international investment, and speculation have strengthened the importance of the financial sector in the economy. Major investment banks and insurance companies play a dominating role in domestic corporate financing as well as lending vast sums to foreign nations. "Playing around with money" is replacing production as the main source of wealth in the transformed 1980s. Corporations, banks, and wealthy individuals are finding investment in money more attractive than investment in production. High interest rates have led to the spectacular growth in money market instruments in the U.S. In 1981 money markets offered a higher return to investors than did most productive investments.

Speculation is not a minor occurrence in the U.S. economy; it is a *fundamental* part of the economic environment and activity.

Thorstein Veblen's distinction between industrial capital and finance capital is on target today though he applied the concepts at the beginning of the twentieth century. For Veblen, industrial capital and its managers are involved in producing a real product, e.g., an automobile or a computer. On the other hand, finance capital and its managers seek to manipulate balance sheets, currency exchange rates, stock market prices – all transactions without real product.[9]

The problem in the U.S. today is that financial activity is increasingly important in the economy. In addition to the growing activity of the financial sector, the manufacturing sector through speculative investments has often and increasingly eschewed its production possibilities. U.S. Steel is probably the worst offender in this regard.[10] The financial tail of the industrial body has now become its head with perverse results for the health of the American economy.

William Abernathy and Robert Hayes, both of the Harvard Business School, have extended this criticism to the inner workings of U.S. management. They argue that U.S. management, especially at the top, has become increasingly dominated by people with a financial background. These supposed captains of industry are more interested in short-term balance sheets than in turning out a product. In Veblen's phrase, they are "captains of finance," even though located in an industrial corporation rather than in a financial institution. They have a money orientation, not a product outlook. The result is that play-it-safe, short-term profit decisions push out long-term investment, new products, new markets, and new technologies. Abernathy and Hayes assert that American business is managing its way to economic decline.[11]

Speculation is rampant in the American economy. Doing well economically is less and less a function of entrepreneurial skill and hard work; the "successful" are increasingly those who can ride speculative booms and avoid taxation. Not new products but financial gimmickry produce wealth.

The results are most disturbing: funds for real, physical investment are reduced; interest rates are kept high; productivity is not improved; jobs are not generated; hard work seems a silly anachronism if the buck can be made through "funny money," wheeling and dealing in shady operations, and the lucky break. As underlined in the trial of Bert Lance, head of Office of Management and Budget in the Carter Administration and former head of a Georgia bank, making big money in America is often built on speculation and constant flirtation with bankruptcy (and not infrequently by skirting illegality). This situation is not a salutary climate for productive economic activity.

The possibilities of an unhinged economy, tailspinning into disaster, grow as the level of credit and borrowing increases. The chance of major financial and banking collapses cannot be dismissed as the figments of doomsayers even though the Federal Reserve System has made it clear that it will attempt to move rapidly to prevent crises. Not only are savings and loan associations overextended and forced into mergers by the governmental regulatory body, but major banks carry large domestic and foreign loans of dubious quality. In particular, some enormous loans to Third World countries may result in defaults and weaken the key money center financial institutions. Bankers, once regarded as the conservative stabilizers of economies, now play big-stake dice with "other people's money" and threaten economic stability.

Without some control over funds to limit speculation, the economy will be twisted and physical investment crippled. Certainly, a non-productive trickster economy will not produce a consensus, a willingness to work hard for the common objective of improving the economy and society, which some observers of Japan believe is a major reason for its post-World War II success.[12]

Speculation distorts and disturbs the American economy. The difficulties of this economy will not be overcome if the speculative mania continues to grow. Speculation is also a source and a consequence of inflation.

High inflation rates produce a fertile environment for speculation. In turn, speculation tends to raise commodity and real estate prices which the consumer experiences as inflation. Unless some form of government influence or control over the investment process is instituted, speculation will continue perversely to transform the U.S. economy.

Inflation

Inflation and inflation fears shape American policy and politics. This world-wide enduring phenomenon became the central focus of economic management in the capitalist nations in the late 1970s and into the 1980s. Policies to contain it have been largely inadequate. Centered on money supply issues, they have resulted in high interest rates, low rates of growth, and high unemployment rates. The term "stagflation" had to be invented to cover the once unusual circumstance of a low-growth, stagnating economy suffering from rising prices. Traditional liberal Keynesian policies of expansion are difficult to carry out because it is feared that inflation will follow. No longer does an assured economic growth facilitate the expansion of social programs which transferred cash and other resources to the needy and retired. New thinking about the unemployed and the poor is needed.

Inflation has altered the terms of international trade. The country with inflation higher than the world rate finds its money devalued and its goods therefore easier to export. The country with a very low inflation rate may have its currency revalued and find that its products become more expensive in world markets. An industrial nation's attempts to combat inflation produce distortions in world capital markets. For example, the U.S. reliance on high interest rates to restrict the money supply in the early 1980s led non-U.S. investors to flock to U.S. high interest rate markets, thereby draining capital funds from their own countries. At the same time, high interest rates in the U.S. block consumption and long-term investment and produce deep recessions and sputtering or no economic growth.

How inflation is handled is crucial to the long-term development of the American economy. A stop-go economy with short expansion and long recessions is not conducive to long-term investment. High interest rates to combat inflation not only encourage speculation rather than productive investment, but also squeeze out smaller firms (the source of most new domestic employment), dampen innovating activities and prolong and deepen recessions.

One source of world inflation is the tremendous growth in the world price of oil over the last decade. But oil prices cannot absorb all the blame. For prices continue to rise even when oil prices are stable or even declining. Slowing the rate of price increases becomes a great achievement even though it does not lower the level of prices. Even when inflation has been dampened – as in the U.S. in late 1982 – the fear of its re-igniting shapes policy decisions.

Inflation is in part due to changes in the domestic price structure. Overall, competitiveness has been reduced. Oligopolistic pricing has become manifest in recent years as prices increased when demand fell in auto and many other fields. As Lester Thurow has pointed out, all of the price shocks are in one direction – up. The inflexibility of prices in the face of declining demand and their apparently inexorable rise make economic policy much more complicated and difficult than is commonly understood.[13]

Monetarist policies which attempt to control the money supply in order to restrict inflation assume that inflation is made possible by the availability of money. Although this may be true, the choking of the money supply and consequent reduction of demand produces small declines in oligopolistic pricing. On the other hand, the traditional liberal policy of stimulating demand may increase prices more than production, especially if economic stimulation follows a monetarist limiting of the money supply. Oligopolistic pricing certainly contributes to inflation. Effective economic policy cannot assume a simple competitive market.

Shifts are also occurring in relative prices, what economists call "the structure of prices." The high American standard of living was due in large part to the low cost of food and energy. Their inexpensiveness permitted income to be spent on other commodities and lowered costs of production relative to other nations. High cereal exports (which reduce domestic supply), increasing producer costs, and government price supports are raising food prices. The great increases in energy prices since 1973 drain funds from other expenditures, change life-styles (e.g., house temperature; house and car size; car use) and swell the cost of production of most commodities. At the same time, high interest rates and speculative investments greatly raise already high housing costs. American health care is controlled by an unregulated and extremely inflationary medical establishment. The great rise in food, energy, housing, and health costs forms the core of the inflationary experience for most U.S. families.

Inflation and fears of it are a new reality for U.S. social and economic structure. Just as economic growth is visited unevenly upon different levels in the social hierarchy, inflation does not affect all evenly. Those working in declining industries, poor unorganized jobs, or ascribed discriminated statuses bear the brunt of inflation.

Inflation is linked to the other transformations of the U.S. political economy. Internationalization opens the U.S. to world inflationary pressures; speculation, an attempted escape from inflation, is itself inflationary; and oligopolistic pricing is a basic source of inflation in the economy.

Wage gains by American workers may also contribute to inflationary pressure as corporations raise prices to cover higher wages. It is only those corporations, however, in sheltered markets that can raise prices irrespective of demand factors. This was the pattern in the auto industry before the Japanese car invasion. Since organized workers are only a small part of the total U.S. workforce, they are unlikely to play the determinate role in the entire national inflation that is often attributed to them.[14] Union wage demands tend to be pegged to inflation rather than prior to it. Wage push may aggravate inflation but inflation exists independently of union wage demands. The 1979–80 period is a good example of this pattern. Inflation was rampant as the average real wage of American workers fell.

Industrial changes

The restructuring of the American economy is occurring. The content of overall economic activity is altered as some industries grow and others decline or stagnate and the rewards and risks of capital ownership become international in scope. On the individual level the expanding industries alter the very nature of employment (and unemployment) and conflict with much of the popular view of industrial change.

Three sets of processes are transforming U.S. industry: the deindustrialization of U.S. manufacturing, especially heavy industry; the development of a service economy; and the rise of high-technology/knowledge-based industries. Together these transformations are altering the nature of employment and political power in the U.S. We discuss the first two below; the high-tech change we examine in Chapter 6. At this point we simply assert that high-tech has been given undue prominence in both the popular and political media and that it does not possess great employment potential.

Deindustrialization

Deindustrialization refers to the economic decline of American heavy industry. Certain industries such as textiles, steel, automobiles, and consumer electronics, once large employers of unionized workers, have experienced real decline in either or both U.S. market share and profitability. Part of this decline can be explained in terms of the pressures of internationalization of production and capital. The rise of foreign competition has invaded the markets and profitability of some U.S. industries such as steel and autos. Competition in tandem with capital mobility has led some U.S. industries (automobile, consumer electronics, and textiles) to produce some or all of their products overseas where labor, taxes, and sometimes transportation (to the international market) are cheaper. In addition, increased capital mobility and differential profit opportunities between industries have encouraged large firms to diversify into new products, often through conglomerate activity, rather than to reinvest in their primary products. Good examples of conglomerate activity which neglects the primary product include the steel, rubber, and railroad industries.

Deindustrialization has had its largest consequences in the United States in terms of regional changes in employment and tax base. Older urban centers in the U.S. Northeast and Midwest became less attractive places in which to invest in the late 1960s and 1970s due to relatively older factories, high wages, high taxes, and high energy costs. As Bluestone and Harrison have shown, plant shutdowns and disinvestment resulted.[15] Capital flowed elsewhere – first to the suburbs, but more recently to the U.S. Southwest and overseas. This regional deindustrialization, of course, mirrors the industrial decline of the heavy industries that were once the backbone of the Northeast and Midwest and of the U.S. economy in general.

Regional shifts within the U.S. are leaving older industrial regions undercapitalized. They are prey to fiscal crises in governmental budgets. As industry moves out, high unemployment and poverty populations are left behind and burden the local tax base.

The deindustrialization of U.S. manufacturing industry, in addition to its regional consequences, has made the U.S. increasingly open to foreign imports and negative trade balances. Unemployment is increased. Over the long run, the U.S. has to pursue deflationary policies to close the trade gap if it is unsuccessful in increasing exports.

Politically, deindustrialization has weakened the power of unionized workers and their organizations such as the AFL-CIO. "Givebacks" of gains won in previous collective bargaining contracts, the loss of cost-of-living allowances, or small wage increases reduce real wage improvements. The decline in employment in once high-paid industries means a contraction in the number of "good jobs" available to those without higher education.

Services and employment

Capital has not only moved out of urban centers to southern or overseas manufacturing plants. Within the urban centers and in the U.S. economy in general, investment and employment are shifting from manufacturing into services. This important trend has been overshadowed by the glamor treatment given to high technology.[16]

Services are like a gas, expanding to fill available space. Real estate, banking, and law and accounting firms service manufacturing on an enlarged scale. The crucial middle sectors between manufacturing and consumers, such as transportation and wholesale trade, are also expanding. Services to consumers are an increasing part of the economy, and include, among others, retail trade, restaurants, and entertainment.

Comments on these changes abound; understanding lags. "Postindustrialism" is an inadequate term for what is occurring. Daniel Bell in his well-known post-industrial thesis sometimes characterizes these service/tertiary industries as providing high-knowledge employment.[17] The reality is that most service jobs are low paid, heavily filled and held by women and minorities, and generally non-unionized.[18] The service industries are populated by small firms that tend to be unstable. Competition is fierce and employment unstable. Unfortunately, most service jobs are not the best of employment. The media focus on the high-paid professionals in new high-technology firms while most jobs are created by very small firms in traditional, low-capital, low-wage service industries. These industries produced most of the new employment in the U.S. over the last decade, as shown in Table 2.2. The amazing spurt in employment in the 1970s – almost 19 million jobs were added to the economy in that period – was mainly in trade and service industries. Further, the one thousand largest *Fortune Magazine* industrial firms furnished almost no additional jobs in that period. Conglomerates and mergers occur at a feverish, accelerated pitch but do not promote employment. Small, low-technology, service firms and industries are the backbone of American employment expansion. Small firms with fewer than twenty employees produced over half of all new employment in the 1970s.[19]

Small service-oriented firms are notoriously low-wage, low fringe benefit companies and experience considerable economic instability.[20] The expanding employment fields of service industries burden the public transfer system with the need to supplement inadequate incomes from private employment.

An additional problem with the growing importance of service industries in the U.S. economy is that most services cannot be or are not exported. While services replace manufacturing jobs to some extent and in some regions, they do not replace lost exports or balance increased imports that result from industrial decline.

TABLE 2.2 *U.S. employment growth by sector, 1970–80 (in thousands)*

	1970	1979	1980	New jobs
Agriculture	3,566	3,455	3,470	–96
Mining	515	865	940	425
Construction	4,814	6,299	6,065	1,251
Manufacturing	20,737	22,137	21,593	856
Transport and utilities	5,317	6,406	6,393	1,076
Trade	14,996	19,672	19,727	4,731
Finance	3,942	5,779	5,860	1,918
Services	20,266	27,275	27,983	7,717
Government	4,473	5,056	5,240	767
Total employment	78,626	96,944	97,271	18,645

Source: *Statistical Abstract of the U.S., 1981*, Table 658, p. 390.

The structure of American industry has changed drastically. Despite the spectacular increase of more than 19 million additional jobs in the 1970s, unemployment was high and real wages did not improve. The U.S. economy is highly segmented, with an inadequate supply of good blue-collar and white-collar jobs and an expanding supply of low-paying service jobs. High-paying professional jobs are limited in number and restricted to those with specialized training, while high-paying jobs in mass-production industries, open to those with less education, are declining. Employment in non-defense fields may contract or stagnate as recapitalization-inspired policies reduce public social expenditures, particularly harming women, who are heavily concentrated in the human service fields. Employment demand in the expanding high-technology and defense fields cannot grow fast enough to provide employment for many would-be workers.

More important is that current trends are likely to result in a shortfall in the total volume of jobs produced in the 1980s. Even if economic growth were spurred by recapitalization, would jobs be generated? Will increased productivity requiring less labor time per unit of output be more than offset by rising demand so that additional workers will be needed? Productivity-oriented growth is unlikely to lead to additional jobs, especially if growth rates are deliberately kept low in order to retard inflationary forces and if the United States does not fare well in international export competition.

The U.S. has an underachieving economy in terms of usefully employing workers. In 1982, over 16 million adults in the U.S. were unemployed, had given up actively looking for work, or were involuntary part-time workers. In recent years the unemployment rate has shown an increasing trend towards a larger percentage of the U.S. labor force being unemployed at any one time. In 1982 the U.S. unemployment rate hovered around 10 per cent, up from about 7 per cent in the late 1970s, 5 per cent in the early 1970s, and 4 per cent in the late 1960s. A shockingly high level of 6.5 per cent is now being propagandized into acceptability as the "normal," frictional rate of unemployment – as something to live with, not to do something about.

"Jobless growth" is the likely distasteful discovery of the 1980s as "stagflation" was of the 1970s. Just as economists were surprised to learn that high price increases could accompany an economy in recession, so will many of us be sadly educated to experience an economic expansion which does little to meet the employment needs of society. An Organization for Economic Cooperation and Development (OECD) report has concluded that jobless growth will characterize many of the capitalist countries as technology-inspired productivity surges are linked to anti-inflation, slow-growth policies. Or, in a modified form, the service-based employment of the 1980s will lead to jobs offering meager rewards. A combination of generally high unemployment rates and low-paying jobs is likely. This situation would be a major catastrophe for the United States – if it is permitted to occur.[21]

Political changes

The great American economic transformation has produced political shifts. Big business has been relegitimated and politicized by the economic problems of the U.S. In addition, traditionalists with their reliance on God and free trade have gained political power as population and economic activity shifted from the more liberal Northeast into their southern strongholds. At the same time the allure of liberal solutions waned in the face of the purported failures of Keynesian policies and of the bureaucratic welfare state. Welfare state measures are criticized as ineffectual and resented by the tax-paying citizens who are experiencing declining real incomes. The Democratic Party has lost much of its strength as traditional southern allegiance wanes, northern liberal states suffer from economic decline, and the AFL-CIO is diminished in both political and economic power. The general feelings of economic insecurity and danger that have arisen from the great transformation of the U.S. political economy led to a powerful call for change. But the decline of liberal power and liberal policy legitimacy made the reactionary variant of recapitalization politically viable in the 1980 election.

The U.S. is no longer the bright and shiny economic colossus of the 1950s and 1960s. U.S. exports and politics no longer dominate the world, U.S. families and workers no longer experience a rising standard of living, and the future looks shaky. The old policies, old analyses of U.S. politics which rely on free markets with some Keynesian demand management, whether of the Reagan supply-side or liberal demand-side variant, will no longer work. Inflation, international competition and integration, and a new U.S. industrial structure are producing new problems in a new context. They demand new answers.[22] The last three chapters of the book discuss some answers and the routes to them.

In the next three chapters we evaluate the recapitalization diagnosis and policies in light of these transformations in U.S. industrial and social structure.

Chapter 3
International trade: the *real* British Disease?

Much of the recapitalization argument hinges upon the inability of American manufacturers to compete on the world export market. *Newsweek* made explicit the link between the current economic alarm and world trade: "Much of the new emphasis on productivity, in fact, stems from the foreign invasion of the U.S. market and the apparent inability of U.S. manufacturers to counterattack."[1] In a characteristic recapitalization vein, this story blames U.S. government policies. Anti-trust efforts, bribery, and military sales restrictions are charged with obstructing real improvement in U.S. manufacturers' ability to export.

The recapitalization analysis has always centered upon other nations threatening U.S. manufacturing dominance. In addition to distorting the economic significance of exports, this view leads to a winner- and loser-orientation. Politically this is transmuted into the simplistic demand of recapitalization – that the U.S. be Number One. There are too many areas (exports, living standards, defense, sports) in which to be Number One. The U.S. and its people would be better off concentrating on achieving collective economic and social health rather than vainly pursuing the strengthening of national pride.[2]

The problem with recapitalization discussions of exports is their failure to place exports within the context of world trade. U.S. exports are treated as independent factors to be expanded through policy-induced productivity surges. International trade is much more complex than this. Domestic consumption, foreign production by U.S. firms, foreign resistance to U.S. exports, and the promotion of exports *to* the U.S., intervene in the simplistic productivity-export equation.

Exports

Recapitalization-inspired programs are most often presented in an ominous context of crisis. The political discussion of international trade is no exception. U.S. vulnerability to foreign, particularly Japanese, imports is pictured as emblematic of the loss of U.S. competitive ability in the world market.[3] Has American ability to export declined? Yes, and more no.

The most commonly used indicator of the viability of American exports is American exports as a percentage of world exports. On that indicator, the U.S. suffers: the U.S. share of world exports of manufactured goods has declined in recent years. In 1960 U.S. exports comprised 25.3 per cent of all world exports. By 1981 that figure was only 11 per cent.[4] Although the U.S. has undoubtedly suffered in terms of world market share, how has this decline affected the domestic U.S. economy?

During this period, American exports absolutely and as a percentage of total U.S. economic activity soared. In 1960 the United States exported $28.9 billion worth of goods and services, roughly 5.7 per cent of that year's Gross National Product. By 1980 U.S. exports had grown absolutely to $223.9 billion or 8.9 per cent of GNP.[5] Absolutely, *exports increased more than seven-fold*. Relative to overall economic activity, their importance expanded more than 50 per cent.

U.S. exports have not declined; they have not even stagnated. What happened was that U.S. exports expanded extraordinarily, but other nations also increased their exports both to the United States and to other countries. True, the U.S. share of the world market declined in some fields, but share is less significant than absolute growth. A decreasing share of a greatly increasing market is a gain in terms of production, employment and (likely) profits. The emphasis on share is both dangerous and misleading.

Imports

The import side is more negative. Since 1976 the U.S. has imported more goods than it has exported. This is the root of the prevalent concern about U.S. competitiveness. Here the primary import culprit is energy, specifically oil imports, which have soared since the price rises of the early 1970s. Oil imports represented 32 per cent of the dollar value of all imports in 1980. Absolute crude oil imports, measured in barrels per year, rose from only 811 million barrels in 1972, worth $7 billion, to 1,975 million barrels, worth $62 billion, in 1980.[6] Increased imports of high-priced oil obviously do not benefit the U.S. balance of payments. In fact, as Table 3.1 shows, the cost of imported oil has been much higher than the deficit on merchandise trade in every year since 1974.

TABLE 3.1 *Merchandise trade balance and cost of imported oil, 1974–80 (in $ million)*

Year	Merchandise trade net balance*	Imports of petroleum products
1974	−5,343	26,609
1975	9,047	27,017
1976	−9,306	34,573
1977	−30,873	44,983
1978	−33,759	42,317
1979	−21,346	60,482
1980	−25,342	78,919

* Trade of goods only; services, capital flows excluded.
Source: *Economic Report of the President, 1981*, Tables B-101, p. 347, and B-102, p. 348.

Although oil imports had been gradually rising before 1973, it was only after the OPEC-inspired price doubling in 1973 and the attendant profit potentials that the U.S. petroleum industry accelerated the importation of OPEC oil. Oil imports rose because domestic oil was regulated at cheaper prices than imported oil, and the petroleum industry systematically substituted high-priced OPEC crude for cheaper American oil. The refusal to adequately regulate the oil industry has allowed a few corporations to increase unilaterally U.S. dependence on imported oil. Their profits have been astonishing and distorting. In 1981 28.3 per cent of all manu-

facturing sector profits were collected by the oil industry.[7] Reduction in the use of oil, development of domestic energy sources, and
restrictions on the importing of high-priced foreign oil would do
more for the U.S. balance of payments than increasing the productivity of U.S. manufacturers.

The impression given by Table 3.1 is, of course, incomplete.
While the U.S. has consistently run a trade surplus in some manufacturing sectors, a deficit has occurred in consumer goods as well
as raw material (oil) trade. In particular, the importing of foreign
automobiles accounts for about one-third of the trade deficit in the
consumer goods sector. Interestingly, the reliance on market forces
advocated by recapitalization proponents will most likely exacerbate the strains that the automobile and petroleum industries have
put on the U.S. balance of payments. Free markets increase the
power of the very concentrated and basic petroleum industry. The
U.S. auto industry, on the other hand, without some protection
from the free market will, at least in the short run, lose an even
greater market share to imports.

Balance of payments

The U.S. balance of payments cannot be adequately discussed solely
in terms of the relation of exports to imports. Reducing corporate
taxes to promote exports will not necessarily have that effect.
Foreign investment by U.S.-based firms competes directly with U.S.
exports. Private multinational corporations make investment decisions on the basis of where their capital investment will earn them
the greatest rate of return. Often it is cheaper to manufacture goods
in the area of eventual consumption or where labor costs are low.

Multinationals do not operate in terms of the interests of the
domestic U.S. economy. Exports of U.S. manufactured goods are
not a necessity for them. For example, in 1980 total U.S. manufacturing expenditures for plant and equipment were $115.8 billion.
In the same year capital expenditures by majority-owned affiliates
of U.S. multinational companies totaled $47.8 billion dollars, 41
per cent of the value of all capital investment in the U.S.[8] Another
way of looking at domestic versus foreign activity is to compare
asset levels. The dollar value of the productive assets in the U.S.

that accounted for U.S. exports in 1980 was roughly $246 billion. U.S. private assets and investments abroad in 1980 were $513 billion, or 2.1 times as large as U.S. investment for export.[9] Foreign investment by U.S.-based corporations competes with domestic investment for capital and markets.

U.S. inability to export is not as obvious and straightforward a problem as Americans are led to believe. Exports have not declined; they have soared. Concurrently, however, imports (particularly of oil and consumer goods) rose dramatically. U.S.-based corporations are also locating production overseas rather than exporting from domestic plants.

Some imported consumer goods (e.g., stereos, cameras), on the other hand, do seem to have an increasing competitive advantage over domestically produced consumer goods. Of course, this should be no surprise nor of much concern to capitalist free market advocates. Ever since Ricardo, comparative advantage has been their favored theoretical model for explaining (and regulating) international trade.[10] The loss of comparative advantage in an environment characterized by free markets does, however, mean the loss of jobs.

The U.S. total balance of payments is not as alarming as the manufacturing balance of trade. This is because the U.S. receives profits and interest from investments, loans, service activities, and the like. In fact, for most of the last decade the U.S. balance of payments was actually positive (1970, 1973–6, 1979–81).[11] The balance of payments picture makes discussions of U.S. trade weakness seem overstated or one-sided.

When we put U.S. exports and imports in a world context, the mixed and fluctuating nature of world trade becomes apparent. As Table 3.2 shows, the U.S. is not alone in its occasional deficit trade situation. The OECD countries as a whole ran significant trade deficits in 1979. In that year the U.S. did not run a trade deficit for the first time since 1976, while Germany's and Japan's current accounts were in the red.

U.S. current account strength (exports greater than imports) in 1975 and 1979 was the result not of superior U.S. marketing but of recessions in the U.S. which reduced imports, especially of consumer goods, coupled with still strong national economies overseas. German and Japanese consumption of all goods including

TABLE 3.2 *World trade and current account balances, various areas; 1965, 1970, 1975, and 1978–81*

Area and country	1965	1970	1975	1978	1979	1980	1981*
	World trade balance ($ billions)						
Developed countries**	−6.9	−9.6	−27.7	−34.1	−89.1	−135.5	−113.4
U.S.	4.3	0.8	4.2	−39.4	−37.0	−32.3	−31.4
Japan	0.3	0.4	−2.1	18.4	−7.5	−10.9	8.5
West Germany	0.3	4.3	15.2	20.7	12.2	4.9	12.5
OPEC	4.2	7.6	58.8	47.3	111.0	161.9	106.8
Non-OPEC (developing countries)	−6.0	−9.9	−45.1	−42.2	−49.9	−74.5	−82.8
	Current account balance ($ billions)						
Developed countries (OECD)	3.8	6.7	2.4	9.8	−30.7	−72.7	35.0
U.S.	5.4	2.3	18.3	−14.1	1.4	3.7	8.8
Japan	0.9	2.0	−0.7	16.5	−8.8	−10.7	5.5
West Germany	−1.6	0.9	4.0	9.2	−5.3	−16.4	−8.5
OPEC	−	−0.5	27.3	4.0	62.0	110.0	60.0
Non-OPEC (developing countries)	−	−8.0	−30.0	−23.0	−38.0	−60.0	−68.0

* Preliminary.
** OECD plus South Africa and non-OECD Europe.
Source: Table B-107, *Economic Report of the President*, U.S. GPO, January 1982, p. 353.

U.S. exports continued at non-recessionary rates. U.S. exports stayed the same, imports declined, and the current account looked good. Similar phenomena occurred in Japan and West Germany in 1976 and 1977 as the U.S. economy expanded and they experienced recessions. The effectiveness of one nation's pro-export policies depends on the economic capacity (and policies) of other nations. The U.S. alone cannot determine the export fate of its output.[12]

Recapitalization is inadequate trade policy

The need to increase U.S. exports has not been clearly established. U.S. exports have risen dramatically over the last two decades. U.S. imports, particularly of oil and consumer goods, have also swelled.

The recapitalization argument is that the U.S.'s declining share of world trade is a cause of economic stagnation. Only if the U.S. failed to export would this be a measure of economic stagnation. The more serious problem for U.S. world trade is the inflationary impact of high-priced OPEC oil and the employment impact of foreign-produced cars.

Distorting the economy, imposing heavy burdens on those at the bottom to keep wages and transfer payments low, is not the solution to specific import problems. International trade challenges are not system threats undermining American capitalism; they are difficulties concentrated in particular areas and should be addressed in terms of their specific characters.

Exhortations to expand exports should not be accepted uncritically.[13] Expanding world trade makes the U.S. more susceptible to international economic imbalances. The more dependent the U.S. is upon other nations' economic strength, the less the U.S. can influence and control its domestic economy. Our discussion of U.S., Japanese, and West German trade balances highlights the critical and delicate interdependence resulting from international trade. When U.S. recessions are counterbalanced by Japanese and German booms (and vice versa), demand for U.S.-produced goods is kept up during recessions. U.S. employment and production are kept from dropping still further during that recession by foreign demand. The U.S. fulfills the same function for Japan and Germany when their business cycles dip. When all three nations are in recession at the same time as in the early 1980s, much deeper and longer recessions are the rule.

Domestically, exports are a mixed blessing. Increasing exports undoubtedly increases the number of domestic jobs created compared to the employment impact of overseas investment by multinational companies. But, investment in export-dominated fields such as defense and high technology does not create as many jobs as does investment in manufacture for domestic consumption. In 1977, although 6.3 per cent of manufactured goods were exported, only 5.1 per cent of the jobs in the manufacturing sector were export-related. Thus, exports employ 11 per cent fewer workers per value of product than does production for domestic use.[14] In many ways it would make sense to promote investment in U.S. energy production, including coal and solar technologies, in order to cut costly oil imports rather than responding to oil-inspired balance of payments problems with increased exports.

There is, of course, an alternative to raising exports in order to balance the United States's trade. That alternative is to limit imports. In an aggressive international market that cannot be done by raising protectionist barriers without the threat of other trading nations following suit.[15] But the inroads of imports upon employment and the reliance on exports for economic well-being are both destabilizing. Over the long run, insistence on free trade and capital movements will conflict with domestic employment and standards of living as well as short-run political pressure for strengthening threatened industries. This tension will necessitate negotiation, if not outright conflict, with U.S. trading partners over the distribution of world trade. We discuss this issue in Chapter 8.

Another approach to limiting imports does not directly challenge U.S. trading partners. It is the imposition of deflationary economic policy by the U.S. government. A slow-growth economy limits demand for imports. The short-run growth in unemployment that results from this type of policy was visible in 1975 and 1979 and then again in 1981–2; in the long run the slow-growth and restricted domestic consumption policies of recapitalization may have the same effect of limiting imports. If slow-growth policies continue to be pursued, they will probably help the U.S. balance of payments by limiting domestic consumption if foreign demand for U.S. exports is unaffected.[16] But lowered U.S. demand for imports may affect the capacity of other nations to absorb American imports. Recapitalization plans characteristically call for limiting domestic consumption in order to strengthen business profitability. The implications of this course of action are that certain groups (the poor, small businesses, domestically oriented manufacturers) would suffer because of the lack of capital and expansion, and others (established large business, exporters) would prosper. What is "the national interest" will not be uncontested in this zero-sum game.

What are the prospects of export expansion in today's world? First, it is not at all likely that capitalist nations as a whole can simultaneously expand their exports and reduce their imports. "Beggar thy neighbor" policies in which countries seek to handle their problems by burdening other countries with them – selling goods to them but limiting purchases from them, what has been called "the exporting of unemployment" – are not system solutions. Keynes[17] called for a reliance on domestic forces to produce full production and employment rather than

> selling the interests of one nation against that of its neighbors. International trade would cease to be what it is, a desperate expedient to maintain employment at home by forcing sales on foreign markets and restricting purchases which, if successful, will merely shift the problem of unemployment to the neighbor which is worsted in the struggle.

Keynes's analysis of the mid-1930s still applies. Capitalism as a world-system cannot overcome its tensions and contradictions by each country becoming more competitive in international trade. For one country to gain, others must lose and suffer the consequences for their inferior accomplishment in the international scene. The national interests of the Big Three – the U.S., Japan, and West Germany – and the other capitalist nations do not easily coincide. The weaker are likely to be exploited by the stronger, via the International Monetary Fund, the Bank for International Settlements, or other dominant forces.

In a similar fashion, within a large capitalist nation, it is doubtful if smaller, non-multinational enterprises can benefit from free trade policies which permit imports without restriction. This is particularly true if strong anti-inflationary policies curtail their main domestic demand and high interest rates restrict their access to capital funds.

Even if export-oriented policies were successful in increasing the ability of U.S. manufacturers to market competitive products on the world market, there is no assurance that the U.S. share will expand. The world market is no longer made up of weak nations which the United States economy can dominate and control. As we discussed in the preceding chapter, the world situation has become much more complex. Major trading competitors have developed effective market economies which will not meekly accept U.S. claims for export dominance. Similarly, Third World nations are no longer passive recipients of U.S. "aid," as some of our exports have been termed in the past. Resistance by other nations to bold U.S. export initiatives can be expected.

For example, when initiatives were taken to protect the U.S. economy from future oil stoppages by creating the Strategic Oil Reserve, the mature power of its trading partners became apparent. Saudi Arabia effectively stymied attempts to create an adequate U.S. oil reserve simply by threatening to raise prices if the U.S. government continued to fill the reserve. In terms of limiting any export initiatives, this is an extreme example because of the importance of oil; but other producer cooperatives in the Third World, as well as import restrictions by both developed and developing countries *and* direct competition, can and may significantly impair U.S. export expansion.

Domestically, we must remember that the U.S. is not a monolithic economy made up solely of multinational and/or exporting giants.[18] Government policies that enhance the export ability of the largest firms may actually harm small and medium business by limiting available investment capital. If small firms cannot get capital because of the expansion of large firms, their prospects will deteriorate. Also, as U.S. products become more competitive abroad, they also become more competitive at home. The success of large manufacturing corporations will accelerate the process of economic concentration and the process of big-business domination of the U.S. overall economy. The limiting of consumption by American citizens in order to fund manufacturing expansion limits the demand for small service businesses.

Big business might not be indictable merely for being big, but the adverse consequences of the increasing strength of this sector of the economy may be seen in unemployment statistics. Big business tends to be more capital intensive than small businesses. Thus, it has higher productivity but *lower employment* per unit of output. In an era of slow growth, high productivity/low employment firms lead to unemployment.

More important, perhaps, is what happens to the dollar in international exchange markets and related occurrences. Some of the effects are very complicated: for example, the rise in the Japanese yen relative to the U.S. dollar in 1977 and 1978 was intended to make U.S. goods cheaper in world markets compared with Japanese goods. On one hand, the rise in the yen increases the dollar cost of Japanese products: on the other hand, it means that the materials that Japan must import to manufacture its exports have cheapened – they cost less than before. The result is that the rising price to U.S. consumers of buying goods from Japan because of the depreciated dollar is partially offset by the lower cost of materials to Japanese producers. Thus, the more expensive yen has not reduced Japanese sales to the United States and other countries except where the Japanese government has deliberately limited exports.

Another difficulty is that higher physical productivity has to be translated into favorable international value. Commodities are bought not only on the basis of their direct cost, but, for example, on the quality of the product and its appropriateness for particular purposes. Increasing output per worker does not assure all the needed qualities for effective competition, as Britain has discovered with complaints about the meeting of delivery dates, quality of commodities, and the like.

Exports will not increase simply because a U.S. president wills them to increase. The U.S. economy is merely one very large slice of the world market. U.S. exports have to compete not only with exports from Europe, Japan, and Third World export platforms, but also with various nationalistic trade barriers, fluctuations in the values of national currencies, and even international investment by U.S.-based multinational industrials and banks. In the world market comparative advantage does not go to the nation with the highest productivity or lowest wages but to the corporation that has favorable exchange rates and capital mobility to exploit effectively technology, labor costs, and local regulations.

Recapitalization policies rely heavily on export growth. If productivity is raised and inflation is controlled through restriction of the money supply, demand for high-productivity goods, at least at first, must come from outside of the U.S. Slow growth coupled with large investments in productivity-enhancing technology will result in unemployment unless exports expand mightily.

In turn, pro-export policies orient mainly to the needs of U.S. big business. But big business does not have a pro-American outlook. Chase Manhattan Bank, IBM, W.R. Grace are not corporations with obligations and allegiances solely to the United States and its peoples; they are international capitalist firms within a world capitalist economy. Capital and employment move competitively between domestic and foreign profit opportunities. When Mobil and Exxon and the other U.S. oil companies had to choose between $25 per barrel OPEC crude and $9 per barrel (controlled) U.S. crude for supplying the U.S. market, profit, not patriotism, triumphed and led to the accelerated importation of high-priced crude.

If U.S. exports are to grow, and they may, it will not be a simple reflection of productivity increases, but the result of international political and economic alignments. The U.S. problem has not really been exports; it has, if anything, been imports, particularly of oil, and foreign investment by U.S. multinational firms. Foreign investment by U.S. multinationals, while limiting domestic employment and U.S. exports, has also helped U.S. balance of payments by importing into the U.S. their capital returns on foreign investments.

In sum, a pro-export policy is not an imperative – unless the restoration of U.S. economic dominance overrides all other considerations. Alternative ways of improving the trade balance picture are possible. Nor is there any certainty that a greatly increased share of world exports can easily be accomplished. The prices of pursuing such a policy can be considerable. Even if achieved, high exports are unlikely to solve problems of unemployment. A faulty, constricted analysis leads to ineffective prescriptions.

The real British Disease

As the poorest performing economy in the industrialized West since World War II, Great Britain is used as the perfect example of how the U.S. should not develop. The British Disease to many Americans is creeping socialism. Strong trade unions, a powerful Labour Party, and an unusually active welfare state (in American eyes) have led some to the conclusion that the sickness in the British economy is the result of too little free market capitalism and too much domineering, inefficient state control of the economy.

Although this analysis of Great Britain's economic problems predated U.S. insecurities over economic functioning, the translation to the present recapitalization era has been fairly direct. The implication is that if the United States does not take hold and promote business, it too will suffer the long-term decline of Britain, the sad transformation of John Bull's Albion from dominating world power to second-rate status.

The reactionary and moderate recapitalization variants take as given the capitalist maxim that the less the government interferes in the economy, the better the economy will perform. This has led to very similar sets of economic policies in Great Britain and the United States. The Thatcher experiments of 1979–81 in tax and social service cuts coupled with tight control of the money supply are mirrored in the Reaganomic programs of 1981–3. Admittedly, differences exist in the economic health of the two nations and the specific implementation of their recapitalization policies. Overall, however, they are guided by the same understanding of the sickness of capitalism as caused by the infection of governmental involvement in the economy.

Our view is different. Although we agree that the liberal bureaucratic welfare state has definite limitations and problems (discussed in Chapter 7), it is not the source of contemporary economic problems. The great transformation of the world and U.S. economy is at the root of present needs to recapitalize U.S. capitalism.

The *real* British Disease is not the welfare state but international trade dependence. International trade dependence and capital outflow weakened the internal British economy early in this century. Britain was able to dominate the economies of its colonies and dominions and thrust its exports on them. Operating in largely protected markets, Britain fell behind technologically. A major factor was that investment at home was low. Starting in the last half of the nineteenth century, British capital invested in its dominions, particularly Australia and Canada, and in the U.S. and Europe. American railroads were built with Britain's capital; the development of the Argentinian and Canadian economies largely depended on British investors. Domestic British investment was limited. Thus, Great Britain began a long relative manufacturing decline while its large firms and investors benefited from continued income from foreign investments.

The *real* British Disease was and is international trade dependence followed by export stagnation, as once secure markets broke free. The difficulties are aggravated by capital flight as national capitalists become world capitalists investing their accumulated capital wherever they are likely to get the best rate of return. Taxation and high-priced labor in Great Britain may have contributed to the decline in comparative advantage and the attractiveness of foreign investment to British capitalists, but it was international trade dependence and capital mobility that underlay British stagnation.

The translation to the present-day U.S. case is fairly direct. Large U.S. firms have diversified internationally and are less dependent upon the internal health of the U.S. economy than U.S. workers are. The U.S. is becoming less attractive as a place to invest capital because of cheaper labor costs in the Third World and other factors. As the internationalization of the world market threatens the U.S. position as the Number One power, foreign investments become increasingly competitive with domestic ones.

The independence of U.S. capital from the health of the national economy is illustrated by the condition of U.S. current accounts, as discussed earlier. The U.S. current accounts are generally positive, while the U.S. balance of trade has often been negative in the last few years. The U.S. economy as a monolithic economic entity is having difficulty exporting as many goods and services as it imports (see Table 3.2, p. 40). U.S. firms are at the same time receiving large and increasing amounts of capital from foreign investments.[19] This makes the U.S. current accounts look good, but unless that capital is invested in U.S. production or consumed on U.S.-made goods, it does not produce employment for U.S. workers.

Of course, all returns on U.S. investments in foreign lands are not repatriated to the U.S. Much money is kept in tax shelters in small international banking centers such as Singapore and the Grand Cayman Islands where no taxes are paid. Similarly, international firms can shift costs and profits from one country to another in order to minimize their tax burden. Finally, U.S. laws reduce taxation on income that has already been taxed by another government.[20]

The freedom of capital to move internationally does not provide much in the way of domestic employment and tax revenue. If the U.S. stopped exporting all goods and services tomorrow, the income from overseas investments to U.S. corporations and financial institutions would continue to rise. U.S. corporations, like

British firms, are only nominally national. Their income is not dependent upon the health of the domestic economy. Their investment menu is considerably broader than the domestic economy in which they happen to reside.

The real British Disease infects the U.S. economy. It is fueled by a decline relative to the recent past in U.S. international trade position coupled with mobile domestic firms that are not averse to nor prevented from investing domestically produced capital (and credit) in foreign production. They may in fact compete with U.S. exports or produce for import into the U.S. economy. U.S. corporations as world corporations may be exporting unemployment to the United States.

There are two ways to deal with these phenomena. One is to control the investment process. The second is to lower domestic standards of living and labor costs in order to entice capital to stay home. Recapitalization embraces the latter policy option. Tax cuts to U.S. corporations and pressure on union wage demands are the main instruments. Although that pressure is presently indirect — high unemployment with reduced unemployment benefits, policy-induced recessions, the assault on the air controller union (PATCO), and linking inflation to wages — eventually we expect more direct wage controls may be attempted, if not successfully imposed.[21]

The regulation of international trade, so that trade fluctuations do not debilitate domestic employment and income, will become increasingly necessary. The New International Economic Order proposed by some Third World nations is one example of multi-nation attempts to regulate the flow of anarchic international trade.[22] More familiar to the U.S. are stop-gap measures to pressure Japan to limit its exports to the U.S. or at least to open up its markets to U.S. goods. International trade is destabilizing most countries. In the next few years many countries will find it necessary to impose trade barriers in order to protect their domestic economies. We believe (see Chapter 8) that the U.S. will need to find some negotiated path to a less anarchic place in the world marketplace.

Recapitalization policies aim to increase U.S. exports through surges in productivity. It is our conclusion that, to some extent, *international trade is the problem and not the solution* to U.S.

economic difficulties. In the next chapter we look at the productivity question and see why it is a more complex phenomenon than is assumed in recapitalization diagnoses and prescriptions.

Chapter 4
Productivity: producing confusion

All variants of recapitalization hinge on productivity. Money, particularly tax cuts, will oil the productivity hinge and stimulate movement. Like exports, productivity is a more complex phenomenon than the "accepted wisdom" of current political discussions recognizes. This chapter looks critically at the recapitalization discussions of productivity and inflation.

The myth of productivity decline

In the 1950s and 1960s growth was seen as the solvent of all economic and political ills; in the 1980s productivity is offered as a substitute for the failed god of growth. When growth was the cure-all it was seen as providing an all-win situation: as the economic pie expanded everyone would benefit with larger slices of goods and services while political struggles over the slicing would abate. Now that growth has been rendered malignant by fears of inflation, a new panacea has emerged – productivity. Only through great surges in productivity can non-malignant, that is, non-inflationary, growth be achieved.

Productivity is the new "cost-free game." Lower taxation will produce growth in investment which will result in growth in productivity. It will dazzle with its potential. Exports will increase with productivity increases; employment will rise as a result; inflation will be defeated as more output is generated with the same amount of labor input. We all, rich and poor alike, will be the beneficiaries of a new growth in productivity. Who could oppose

51

increasing productivity, especially after seeing the frightening statistics comparing U.S. productivity growth with that of competitor industrial nations? It has become both the darling and despair of economists and politicians. The media assail us almost daily with speculations as to the causes and cures of America's declining productivity. The cure to U.S. stagflation, we are assured by experts of all sorts, lies in the health, specifically the growth, of U.S. productivity.

Newsweek, in an article entitled "The U.S. Productivity Crisis," asks the poignant question, "why has productivity fallen so much faster in the United States than in other industrialized countries?"[1] This is a misrepresentation that has slipped onto the tongues of not merely journalists, but also politicians and social scientists. The decline in U.S. productivity is a myth.[2] U.S. productivity has been rising steadily since World War II. The recent furor has in fact been based upon *the decline in the rate of growth* of U.S. productivity, not the decline in productiveness of the U.S. worker.

U.S. productivity is a key measure for recapitalization proponents. The loose usage of the concept and its shaky measurement have been turned into a rather terrifying picture of industrial stagnation or even regression in the face of bold gains by foreign competitors. The failure of U.S. manufacturers to export successfully and the inundation of the U.S. market with foreign products are often portrayed as the direct result of this decline in productivity growth. At the same time we are told that productivity is rising slower than domestic consumption; that these consumption demands are inflationary.[3] Policy initiatives that endeavor to raise U.S. productivity at great social cost were blithely pushed by the Reagan Administration.

At first blush, the productivity data in Table 4.1 seem to support the anguish about their poor performance. Output per worker hour did grow much faster in the economies of the other developed nations than in the United States throughout the 1970s. As Table 4.1 shows, U.S. productivity growth was substantially slower than all other industrial countries except Great Britain. What does this table tell us about the ability of U.S. manufacturers to export their goods? Recapitalization ideology would interpret these data as the U.S. falling rapidly behind competitors in the race to produce commodities cheaply. The low cost of Japanese goods coupled with high-cost, low-productivity American production renders our manufacturers impotent. But the growth rate of productivity tells nothing of the sort. Table 4.2 reports a different story.

TABLE 4.1 *Index of productivity growth 1970–9 (1967 = 100)*

Country	1970	1973	1974	1975	1976	1977	1978	1979
United States	104.5	118.8	112.6	118.2	123.2	126.1	128.2	129.2
Canada	114.7	134.3	136.6	133.3	139.4	146.1	152.2	156.3
France	121.2	142.5	146.6	150.7	163.6	171.7	180.2	189.9
Germany, F.R.	116.1	136.6	145.0	151.3	160.3	169.0	175.3	183.8
Japan	146.5	181.2	181.7	174.6	188.7	199.2	215.7	230.5
United Kingdom	108.8	127.6	127.7	124.2	127.9	126.5	128.6	133.0

Source: *Statistical Abstract of the United States, 1980*, Table 1591, p. 913.

TABLE 4.2 *National productivity as percentage of U.S. productivity, 1950–79**

Country	1950	1960	1970	1979
United States	100	100	100	100
Canada	80	84	91	97
France	55	69	83	89
Germany, F.R.	52	84	94	98
Italy	27	38	48	48
Japan	18	28	57	66
United Kingdom	53	58	56	55

* Productivity is measured in terms of national per capita production. Because of lower U.S. labor force participation rates, the actual worker productivity as a percentage of U.S. productivity is lower than the Table suggests for all countries except Italy.

Source: *Statistical Abstract of the United States, 1980*, Table 1591, p. 913.

The actual level of productivity, not its rate of growth, determines competitive advantage. Absolute productivity remains higher in the U.S. than for any of its competitor nations. To quote Gus Tyler using statistics from the early 1970s: "If you use U.S. output per worker per hour as a standard by calling it 100, then next in line is Canada with 91.6; France with 84.7; West Germany with 79.1; Japan with 62.2; United Kingdom with 55.1; and Italy with 54.3."[4] The speed of these industrial countries' growth in productivity is at least in part a function of the low base from which they start. *The total level of productivity is more significant than productivity growth*, just as absolute exports are more significant than shares of world exports.

As Table 4.2 shows, U.S. productivity is higher than productivity in West Germany, France, and even Japan. It is not surprising that the U.S. has been able to export successfully. Both U.S. inability to export and to increase productivity are myths. They are both in large part a result of economists' typical obsession with shares of a market and percentage rates of growth and their ignoring of absolute changes.

Overselling productivity

Although the 'decline' in U.S. productivity seems less disturbing when viewed in this light, the mutterings of recapitalization proponents are not without merit. The growth rate of other nations' productivity is faster than that of the United States. Eventually, the productivity of these other nations may in fact match or even overtake that of the United States. Therefore, the nature of productivity, its importance for international trade, and the decline in the growth rate of U.S. productivity are still quite important and worthy of further analysis.

The formal definition of productivity is generally given in terms of output per worker hour. If worker A produces X widgets per hour, then we can say her productivity is X. Worker A's productivity goes up when she produces more than X widgets in an hour. It is a simple enough concept, but it begs the question: what meaning does it have?[5] The traditional answer is that the higher the productivity per worker, the lower the cost of production. If the U.S. economy, especially manufacturing, improved its level of productivity, then goods would be cheaper. Workers would be able to purchase more, manufacturers to export more, and inflation would be reduced as costs (and thus prices) went down. The formula is a simple one, and in a time of stagflation, it holds great and understandable attraction for business leaders and politicians anxious to pull the country out of its economic doldrums.

Productivity growth becomes the all-win game because it seems to hold the cure to all national (economic) ills. But, of course, the equation is incomplete. It is as if some economists, perhaps with a new Ph.D. dissertation in hand, produced models of productivity and failed to include the caveat that makes all economic models hold together – "all else being equal."

The growth of output per worker hour cheapens goods only if labor, material, and capital costs remain constant. Productivity holds hope as the all-win salvation of the economy only if nothing else changes. But economic processes are continually changing. Consequently, what productivity can deliver depends on relative labor, material, and capital costs, and exchange rates. Thus, examining the trading positions of the U.S. and its industrial competitors requires reflecting on more than simple productivity.

Labor costs
Unit labor cost is a better measure of export competitive advantage than productivity because it measures both productivity and labor cost. Unit labor cost centers on labor-based competitive advantage. For example, a worker working for $10.00/hour and producing 20 widgets/hour ($0.50/unit) has higher productivity than the $5/hour worker who produces only 15 widgets in that hour ($0.33/unit). The lower-paid worker, however, has the cheaper unit labor cost. Raising productivity through government tax cuts at high social cost does not tell us much about the eventual cost of the goods coming from high productivity industries.

Unit labor costs rose more slowly in the United States during the 1970s than they did in its industrialized competitors. Between 1970 and 1980 unit labor costs in the U.S. rose 56.7 per cent; in comparison, unit labor costs rose 106.1 per cent for France, 106.8 per cent for West Germany, and 79.2 per cent for Japan (all in U.S. dollars) during the same period. The U.S. is not falling behind other nations in the relation of wage costs to output.[6]

Labor productivity is an incomplete fragment of manufacturing cost. The American Productivity Center in Houston has attempted to devise a new index of productivity.[7] This index includes output per unit of labor and output per unit of capital. Eventually, they plan to include energy and material costs in their index of total-factor productivity to give a more inclusive statistic. Figure 4.1 charts the relationship between labor productivity and capital productivity since 1958. If anything, the data show that total factor productivity has grown more slowly than labor productivity in the U.S. The culprit is clearly output per unit of capital input: U.S.

capital investment has contributed *virtually nothing* to the total factor productivity of the U.S. economy since 1966. We will discuss the role of investment in productivity growth later in this chapter. As Figure 4.1 indicates, output per unit of labor is much higher than total productivity and even higher still than capital productivity. Significantly, the differences have widened in recent years.

The politics of productivity

Very real political dangers lurk behind the preoccupation with the growth rate of U.S. productivity. This orientation has all too often been interpreted to represent poor performances by American manufacturing workers. Currently, comparisons are made between U.S. and Japanese workers suggesting that the reliability of Japanese cars reflects superior Japanese workmanship. This analysis produces a simple-minded castigation of U.S. labor while little attention is paid to the key roles of investment as well as technology, management style, and the density of non-productive (management) workers on the payroll. As we will see in the next chapter, some of the productivity excellence of Japanese auto-makers can be attributed to superior management rather than to superior workers. Japanese management style transplanted to the U.S. has resulted in rates of worker productivity as high as those achieved in Japan.[8]

Simple-minded, propagandistic redefining of productivity into a mere reflection of the effort and industriousness of U.S. workers can be used to justify demands for lower consumption. If American workers are judged culpable for export weakness and industrial stagnation, this will legitimate political demands for lower government services and constrained wage demands by organized workers. This growing possibility is politically important. If the failures of capitalism are blamed on the workers while the successes are attributed to the owners and managers, workers will continue to pay for economic failure and corporations to collect in cases of success.

The simple equation which puts labor productivity at the center of the economy leads to political conclusions that justify the exploitation of workers and the curtailing of consumption. If labor productivity is the only acknowledged source of economic growth in the economy, then government policies will be aimed at increasing labor productivity with no attention paid to the important

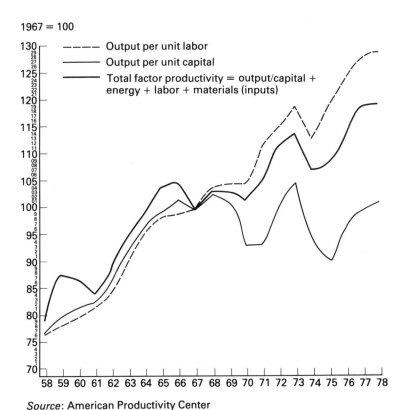

Figure 4.1 U.S. capital and labour productivity 1958–78

questions of total production, pricing, profits, and exchange rates.

In *The Zero-Sum Society*, Lester Thurow makes this mistake when he writes of productivity as if it were a thing with precise measurement. He says that closing a low-productivity plant raises productivity just as well as opening a new high-productivity plant.[9] This is absurd. Obviously, closing a low-productivity plant will raise the value of the labor productivity equation. But the productivity of the surviving firms has not increased. The national *average* has improved without gains in any individual firm. This result may be comforting, but it does not have an economic payoff unless one fastens on the dubious assumption that the capital and skilled labor of the closed plants aid production in the surviving plants. Otherwise, actual production will be lower in the economy. Profits and the standard of living will decline while the calculation of productivity rises.

Thurow's analysis leads to a policy of closing low-productivity plants (or regions? or workers?) simply to raise the national rate of productivity. Disinvestment must take place, Thurow writes, for productivity to increase. But the growth of productivity without the growth of real output does not advance standards of living. Shutdowns of plants, industries, or regions may raise the U.S. productivity growth rate, but essentially this is accomplished by modifying the wrong side of the equation. If labor productivity is not high enough, is the useful answer to fire workers, rather than increase the rate of production? Although neither Thurow nor other economists actually call for the firing of workers, implicit in the call for higher labor productivity is the belief that low-productivity plants must be closed and low-productivity industries and regions must be modernized. In this perspective, the route to higher productivity is not higher production, but relatively constant production with lower labor inputs through the intervention of high technology. The conversion of U.S. industry to high-productivity, high-technology (implicitly low-labor) production processes is to be accomplished through massive capital investment and less labor.

Productivity growth is not a panacea; it is a mixed blessing. In the absence of substantial economic expansion (or attractive alternatives to work) productivity surges lead to increased unemployment.[10]

A better diagnosis

Why has productivity growth slowed down?

A more complete understanding of the dynamics of U.S. productivity over the last decade is extremely important because of the centrality of this abused statistic in the recapitalization onslaught. The complicated answer includes four factors: the substitution of labor for capital; a shift in product mix in the economy; idle capacity resulting from anti-inflation policies; and the reluctance of management to invest in new production processes.

One reason productivity growth has slowed down is that many more workers are working. This is a curious formulation but it is worth analyzing. During the 1970s almost twenty million additional jobs were created; the labor force grew by about 24 per cent. The productivity of the U.S. economy (output per worker hour) grew 13 per cent. The result was a growth in total production of 41 per cent over the decade, second only to Japan. Slow productivity growth does not mean slow growth in production. An increasing proportion of the U.S. population is participating in the workforce; thus more goods are being produced.

Higher wages advance productivity. This happens because rising labor costs force employers to find more efficient ways to produce. One way to do this is by squeezing more work out of the workers. This method has obvious limitations. Management can coax and coerce only a finite amount of productivity out of workers. They can get much greater output per worker hour if they provide the worker with more efficient tools. Thus, the introduction of new productive technologies results from higher wages.

This analysis holds a partial explanation of the slump in the growth of U.S. productivity. Wages rose slower than inflation over the 1970s. In constant 1967 dollars, the average weekly earnings of a married worker with three dependents, working in the private sector actually *declined* by 2 per cent between 1970 and 1979. For similar workers in the manufacturing sector average weekly earnings grew by about 6 per cent over the 1970s while productivity in that sector grew by 19 per cent.[11] Many corporations preferred the relatively cheap labor of the 1970s over investment in new technologies, especially in uncertain economic times. As the baby boom children of the 1950s became the workers of the 1970s, employment surged. The highly competitive job market kept wages down and so removed one incentive for management to invest in productivity-enhancing technology.[12] Corporate performance is evaluated by return on investment. If workers are relatively cheaper than investment capital, managers will increase employment rather than invest in labor-saving but relatively costly technology.

Structural shifts in the makeup of economic activity, as discussed in Chapter 2, account for much of the slowdown in U.S. productivity growth. The shift in the product mix in the economy, according to Thurow, accounts for 40 per cent of the slowdown in productivity growth. The editors of *Monthly Review* put this figure at closer to 50 per cent.[13] Industries differ substantially in terms of productivity. Thus, as the computation of the output of the economy shifts, so will the growth rate of U.S. productivity. Low-productivity industries such as services, retail trade, and construction make up larger portions of total economic activity. Thurow points out that from 1948 through 1972 the shift in the U.S. economy was toward high-productivity industries. After 1972 low-productivity industries dominated the growth sectors. About half of the new labor hours in the economy created after 1972 were in services. Much of the rest went into mining, construction, and the utility industries. Utility productivity is low because of over-capacity as energy consumption moderated after 1973. Mining productivity actually declined over the 1970s as a result of health, safety, and environmental regulations and the increasing difficulty of locating oil and other minerals. The product mix in construction lowered productivity in that sector. Thus, a shift in demand rather than efficiency has lowered productivity growth. *The composition of GNP affects the productivity index.*

The slowdown in the rate of productivity growth is not unique to the United States. Japan and West Germany have not been immune from similar, if less extreme slowdowns during the 1970s.[14] The slowdown of the world economy encumbers productivity growth. Constrictive monetary and fiscal policies were adopted by all industrial countries in an attempt to stifle inflation. These policies slowed the growth of their productivity. Retarded economic growth, and hence demand, creates idle capacity in manufacturing sectors.[15] When activity slows down in a recession, especially in a steep recession, idle capacity increases faster than workers (especially office staff) are laid off. Often, as in the first three quarters of 1980 and again in late 1981 and early 1982, productivity statistics actually drop. Statistical productivity declines are the logical outgrowth of recapitalization monetary policy to combat inflation. Thurow attributes about 30 per cent of the American slowdown in productivity growth to idle capacity.

As we will discuss in Chapter 5, the data indicate that capital was at least as available in the 1970s as in the 1960s. They also show that U.S. business investment in manufacturing is growing at a slower rate than general business investment. If capital has been available but not invested in manufacturing industry, then it is possible that the responsibility for poor economic performance lies not simply with external factors but to some extent in the investment approach in the private sector.

American management was once the envy of the capitalist world. It produced more goods with less input than other countries. U.S. management became the benchmark, the ideal to be emulated. The French politician-editor Jacques Servan-Schreiber foretold the crushing of European firms by the superior management of American corporations.[16] Now, when U.S.-style capitalism seems to be in bad shape, management goals and methods are in need of re-evaluation.

Thus, we see that the slowdown in the growth rate of productivity results less from government incompetence and worker greed than from demographic shifts in employment, low wages, the slow growth basic to most anti-inflation policies, shifts in the composition of GNP (and perhaps government spending), and the myopic investment policies of big business. As such, the change in relative productivity is merely symptomatic of other ills in the economy. But hasn't low productivity led to inflation as wage gains outstripped increases in efficiency?

Productivity, wages, and inflation

The preceding discussion at least partially discredits the alarm about the comparative growth rates of labor productivity in the United States and other industrialized countries. Similarly, a case can be made for saying that tying slow productivity gains to inflation is the product of over-eager economic analysis. The proposed relationship between productivity and inflation is based

upon the claim that wages have been growing faster than productivity.[17] If we assume that capitalist firms will not accept some cut
in their rate of profit, this arrangement will drive up prices.

The facts contradict this analysis: real wages have lagged behind
productivity growth in the U.S. Average weekly real earnings (i.e.,
adjusted for the rise in consumer prices) of American industrial
workers grew by only 2 per cent between 1967 and 1979 – not a
two per cent average each year but only *a two percentage total
gain in more than ten years*. Productivity growth during the same
period in the industrial sector was over 19 per cent.[18] Obviously,
excessive worker demands are not pushing up prices. In any case,
it is hard to believe that savings in the cost of production resulting
from higher worker productivity would be translated immediately
into lower prices for manufactured goods.

Theoretically, increasing productivity decreases production costs,
leading to lower prices. More efficient production leading to lower
prices, it is reasoned, will lead to the controlling of inflation and
make U.S. goods cheaper abroad. We should not be quick to accept
this all-win game.

An important but neglected factor in the true productivity equation solution is who benefits from the fruits of higher productivity?
Will cost savings be passed along to the consumer or worker or
does the corporation absorb them? Consumers are unlikely to
benefit from productivity savings in situations of domestic
monopoly or oligopoly markets. Lower prices for export may
result, but again, this depends upon whether or not other nations'
oligopoly producers are passing along cost savings. The free market
that might translate productivity increases into lower prices seldom
exists.

Thus the all-win productivity analysis has meaning only in an
abstract, all else being equal, world which can ignore labor cost,
output per unit of capital, materials inputs, and oligopolistic
markets. That world does not exist.

The recapitalization analysis implies no oligopolistic influences
on prices. It is doubtful that those businesses which are relatively
insulated from market forces will simply pass along productivity
gains to consumers through lowering prices. The productivity route
to lower prices implies that other factors like pricing, the supply

and cost of money, and wage rates have little importance or can be continuously offset by increases in productivity. In the 1982 United Auto Workers (UAW) contract negotiations with Ford and General Motors, the UAW tried to link lower labor costs to lower car sticker prices. Ford agreed, while General Motors refused to pass their labor cost savings on to consumers. Recapitalist enthusiasts generally assume that rising costs cause rising prices ("cost-push inflation"). They downgrade the importance of market power in shaping the prices set by oligopolies.

Recapitalization proponents, especially some supporters of the reactionary variant, pay a great deal of attention to one direct cost factor. Federal budget deficits and protective environmental and health standards are seen as wildly inflationary. Budget deficits are judged guilty of driving up capital costs, and protective regulations are charged with arbitrarily adding costs to production. The effect of budgetary deficits on capital costs has been confounded by the Federal Reserve Bank's efforts to control the money supply through tight money, which leads to high interest rates. The perception in the early 1980s of the inflationary potential of a budget deficit drove the real interest rate (that is, adjusting for current inflation) very high. Tight money *and* deficit fears can produce discouragingly high interest rates. Regulation has become anathema to most business interests, which view environmental and health regulation protection as prohibitively expensive. They pay little or no attention to the benefits of such protection.

The inflation analysis presented by recapitalization is clearly a case of selective retention. Government disruption of markets through minimum wage standards, regulation, and government spending on social services is blamed for inflation while oligopolistic pricing and government spending on the military receive the benefit of inattention. Fortunately, the latter has lately received some public scrutiny.

Productivity gains will not limit inflation. This statement clashes with the accepted wisdom about the inflation-dampening powers of productivity. But not one historical example is ever introduced to support this contention. The opposite point can be made, that recapitalization approaches to productivity, even in non-supply-side versions, may have adverse effects. Increasing available capital will be at least mildly inflationary as spending increases. The more capital is converted into speculation, the more inflation. The more inflation, the more likely that corporate America will go for the quick and easy profit. And so the cycle will continue. Many recapitalists seem particularly blind to the many-faceted nature of inflation.

Tax cuts, deregulation, and free markets are a recipe for inflation in an age of oligopoly pricing, military boom, and speculative psychology.

Productivity and employment

The productivity argument assumes a high elasticity (expansion) of demand that would maintain employment. Lower prices, if they occur despite oligopoly pricing, may not lead to a gain in demand that would sufficiently compensate for the declining employment per unit of output resulting from productivity growth. While raising productivity will make it cheaper to produce cars or other manufactured goods, it will not necessarily increase demand for automobiles. If demand remains constant when productivity increases, the result will be higher profits per unit of output for the corporation in question and lower employment for its workers.[19] Employment will increase with increasing productivity only if national and international demand expands. But, if demand surges in an era of oligopoly pricing, inflation is likely to grow. *The market cannot cure inflation and provide employment.*

How likely is an increase in demand? Nationally, lower prices may be attractive, but the whole emphasis of the recapitalization strategy is on lowering personal consumption and thereby diverting capital to business (presumably for investment). If wages and transfer payments are stunted in the attempt to increase U.S. manufacturing productivity, then the needed increase in demand is not likely to occur in the U.S.

Internationally, the export strategy has less of this limitation. Curtailing U.S. consumption will only somewhat reduce demand overseas. Fears of inflation will do more. Fast domestic economic growth (triggered by increased consumption) will not be allowed by the U.S. or foreign governments because of the inflation threat. The attempt to cap prices forces governments to adopt slow-growth policies that dampen demand.

Part of the problem is that West Germany, Japan, Western

Europe, and the U.S. are experiencing similar problems – so no country can be the motor of change, the "locomotive" of expansion. The advanced capitalist economies are uniformly in a period of slow growth. International inflation limits the potential for world economic growth as governments pursue slow-growth, anti-inflation policies.[20]

Slow growth coupled with productivity gains means unemployment. Slow growth in demand for the new high-productivity goods generated by a recapitalized capitalism means limited job creation. As Chapter 2 pointed out, "jobless growth" is the prospect for the 1980s. Advancing productivity in a stagnating economy results in high unemployment rates. For some time conservative economists have been urging the acceptance of 5, 6, or even 7 per cent unemployment as "normal," the appropriate goal of "full employment policy." "Supply-side" economics originally hoped to avoid such trade-offs between productivity and unemployment by a rapid expansion of the economy which promoted productivity, output, and employment without inflation. The failure of this all-win conservatism presages continuing high unemployment rates as recapitalization thinking dominates economic policy.

We do not think that productivity-enhancing investment will happen in a straightforward manner. More likely, the money freed by tax cuts for the rich and for corporations will be used in a variety of ways. Some speculation will no doubt occur as well as non-productive takeovers of already existing firms. Some capital will be used to drum up increased demand through clever advertising and packaging of the same old products. And some corporations will use the capital to invest in productivity-enhancing technology only if business confidence in government policies and in the general near-term economic prospects of the U.S. economy is rather stable, then a substantial amount of productive investment may, in fact, occur.

Perhaps we are overly pessimistic. Cannot lowering taxes increase savings and profits, leading to higher investment and productivity with the result of more employment? The next chapter deals with recapitalism's analysis of investment.

Chapter 5
Investment panacea

In the recapitalization diagnosis, capital formation or investment is both the cause and the cure of the decline in the growth rate of productivity in the U.S. In this view the failure or inability of American manufacturers to invest in new productivity-enhancing technologies has caused current U.S. economic problems.

The proposed cure for the deindustrializing United States centers around the need to increase business investment. The growth of exports and productivity, it is argued, depends upon increased manufacturing investment by U.S. business. The evidence on the relation of investment to productivity does not support this contention. This chapter will not, however, contest the purported connection; rather, it will examine influences on investment, assumption of a shortage of investible funds, and the likely effects of reduced taxation on investment.

Wage demands, government taxation and regulation of business, and heightened capital costs have been identified by U.S. reindustrialization proponents as key factors discouraging needed business investment. Are these, in fact, the cause of U.S. economic problems? One way to answer this question is to look at competitor nations.

The conventional diagnoses of the cause of low rates of productivity growth in the U.S. do not hold up very well when they are applied to the economies of competitors such as West Germany. Those factors which purportedly held down productivity growth in the U.S. – government spending, high wage demands, and high oil costs – are all present and in exacerbated forms in West Germany. While the U.S. imports 50 per cent of its oil, inflating prices and consuming capital, Germany imports 95 per cent of its oil. Public spending involves about 42.8 per cent of German Gross Domestic Product, 10 per cent more than in the U.S.[1] And as we stated in the last chapter, German labor costs rose faster than U.S. labor costs in the 1970s. While West Germany has suffered these economic drags on productivity (at least according to the popular recapitalization analysis), its productivity rate grew at double the U.S. rate for the last twenty years.

The factors that are accused more recently of holding down investment do not fare much better in the diagnosis of productivity.

We have already seen that the earnings of the American worker have not approached the rate of growth of U.S. productivity. Between 1969 and 1979 the weekly earnings of all American workers actually declined by about 2 per cent, while productivity grew by about 1.5 per cent *per year*.[2] High wages are clearly not an explanation of the failure of U.S. industry to invest in productivity-enhancing processes. The tax cuts enacted in 1981 were, however, a direct response to this belief. Wages and taxes both limit corporations' ability to generate capital internally through retained earnings. The government, at that point, could not easily limit wages, so it did the next best thing and cut business taxes.

The recapitalization ideology, especially in its radical Reaganomics garb, castigates the government as evil while envisioning business as redemptive. This chapter looks at the two, first asking if government is as wicked as portrayed and then suggesting that business may be less holy than the accepted wisdom leads us to believe.

Wicked government?

Taxation and profits

The recapitalization diagnosis assigns taxation a major role in the sluggish growth of investment in new production processes. The argument is that the burden of government taxation cuts into profits and discourages firms from placing their capital in new productive investments.

The interrelationships of capital, investment, and taxation can be examined in a variety of ways. The higher the percentage of business profits taxed and the higher the government revenue derived from corporations, the less capital is available for business investment. On the other hand, the higher the rate of return on investments, and the greater the profitability of companies, the more money should be available for business investment.

Since profits precede taxes, it is best to examine first the profitability of firms over the last twenty years. From 1960 to 1979, total manufacturing sector profits as a percentage of total sales rose from 4.4 per cent to 4.9 per cent. More importantly, after-tax profits as a percentage of stockholders' equity rose from 9.2 per cent in 1960 to 13.9 per cent in 1980.[3] For the top 500 manufacturing corporations, return on sales after taxes grew from 4.7 per cent in 1970 to 5.4 per cent in 1979. Return on assets after taxes grew from 5.0 per cent in 1970 to 6.9 per cent in 1980. This improvement is particularly striking because the dollar value of sales for these corporations expanded by $981 billion or 311 per cent over this ten-year period.[4]

If we look at the rate of growth of the total economy (as measured by GNP), we find an even more striking pattern. Between 1970 and 1980 the Gross National Product of the United States grew by about 264 per cent. During the same period, corporate manufacturing profits grew by 304 per cent before taxes and 323 per cent after taxes.[5] Corporate profits were an increasing share of national income.

Clearly, the large firms that dominate the economy have not found self-generated capital impossible to come by!

Two conclusions follow from these data:

1 The value of profits increased enormously with this expanded sales volume, even after adjustment for inflation.
2 Major U.S. corporations have been able to garner as profits an increasing percentage of total sales income over the last twenty years. Thus, both absolute profits and profit rates grew for these corporations.

On the other hand, corporate taxes as a percentage of all federal tax revenue have declined since World War II, from 24 per cent of all federal tax revenue in 1960, to 17 per cent in 1970, to only 12 per cent in 1980.[6] While this decline can be largely explained by the expansion of social security taxation, a startling and largely ignored change occurred in corporate taxation:

the effective tax rate on corporations dropped from 47 per cent of their net income in 1960 to only a little more than half that tax rate in 1977.

Liberalized depreciation schedules and other federal tax breaks account for this reduction. Although the nominal rate of taxation on all corporate income above $50,000 was 48 per cent in 1969, the effective tax rate in that year on the 100 largest U.S. corporations was only 26.9 per cent. Mobil Oil, with an income of $4 billion, suffered an effective tax rate of only 7.4 per cent in federal income taxes. ITT paid at a 12.2 per cent rate on its income of $650 million. Seventeen giant corporations with incomes of over $2 billion paid no income tax at all in 1977.[7] The Reagan tax cuts of 1981 reduced the corporate tax bill still further, virtually eliminating the corporation income tax.

These statistics do not overturn the thesis of a capital-shortage-relative-to-investment-demand, but they do suggest that neither the profit rate nor the tax burden upon U.S. corporations devastated their ability to invest by limiting available capital.

Government spending

Table 5.1 shows that total government spending as a percentage of GNP fluctuated over the 1970s, although the government's share of the economy was higher than in the 1960s.

TABLE 5.1 *Total government spending (in $ billion) as a percentage of Gross National Product**

	1960	1965	1970	1975	1980	1981ᴾ
GNP	506.6	688.1	982.4	1549.2	2626.1	2922.2
Government spending	136.4	187.8	313.4	534.3	869.0	979.7
% GNP	27	27	32	35	33	33

* State, local, and federal spending.
ᴾ = preliminary.
Source: *Economic Report of the President*, January 1982, Table B-1, p. 233; Table B-75, p. 320.

Only a belief in the need for absolutely free markets validates criticisms of government spending *qua* government spending.

Efforts to reduce the impact of government spending upon private markets through limiting the size of the federal budget are at best premature. As Table 5.2 indicates, the size of federal budget outlays as a percentage of GNP shows minimal growth over the 1970s. When we disaggregate federal spending (omitting state and local governments included in Table 5.1) into some of its component parts (in Table 5.2), we find that not all areas of federal spending have been growing as fast as the overall economy.

TABLE 5.2 *Federal spending as a percentage of Gross National Product: selected categories ($ billion)*

	1960	1965	1970	1975	1980	1981ᴾ
GNP	506.6	688.1	982.4	1549.2	2627.4	2922.2
Federal spending	93.1	123.8	204.2	356.3	602.0	686.4
% GNP	18	18	20	23	22	23
Federal purchases	53.9	67.3	95.6	123.1	190.2	218.3
% GNP	11	10	10	8	7	7
Federal transfers	28.9	40.4	80.1	178.5	294.2	332.9
% GNP	6	6	8	12	11	11
Federal social security*	11.1	18.1	38.5	81.4	153.8	180.3
% GNP	2	3	4	5	7	6

* Social security payments including old age, disability, and health.
ᴾ = preliminary.
Source: *Economic Report of the President*, January 1982, Table B-1, p. 233; Table B-20, p. 259; Table B-75, p. 320.

Between 1960 and 1980 federal spending as a percentage of GNP grew 4 per cent. Over the same period social security payments alone, as a percentage of GNP, grew by 5 percentage points. Thus, transfer payments to the aged, the disabled, and the sick account for all of the growth in federal spending (relative to the growth of the entire economy) between 1960 and 1980. Government purchases, on the other hand, declined considerably as a percentage of overall economic activity.

Has federal spending contributed to economic stagnation? The popularity of the recapitalist/productivity diagnosis has obscured the possibility that the slowdown in government demand for goods (e.g., highway construction) might understimulate the manufacturing sector. Perhaps too little of GNP passes through the federal government? The U.S. government then may be less able to promote economic activity.

The use of aggregate economic figures of government spending may hide as much as it reveals. Direct government demand for goods, which declined as a percentage of GNP, might have a larger stimulative effect upon aggregate economic activity than do transfer payments, which have increased. The speculation that too little of GNP flows through the federal government for economic policy to be effective deserves empirical examination. Unfortunately, questions of this sort have been stifled by the ideological success of recapitalization.

Most government transfers are social security payments; much smaller are payments to retired federal employees and railway workers. Smaller still are welfare and veterans' payments. Does the expansion in social security payments as a percentage of overall economic activity affect particular parts of the economy? Do the aged spend their money differently than the rest of the population? We do know that the aged and the poor spend higher proportions of their income on the four most inflationary commodities – health care, housing, energy, and food. If they spend most of their income on food and fuel and little on consumer durables, then the shift in government responsibility from infrastructure to income maintenance over the last twenty years has been an implicit industrial policy that favors some sectors (food and energy) over others (construction, consumer durables).

If government spending is going to be the target of accusations that spending is disruptive to the economy, the spending patterns themselves must be examined.

Regulation

Analogous to the discussion of government tax burden upon business is the charge that government interferes with the "natural workings" of the free market. Regulation is a favorite whipping boy of many recapitalists. The argument is that regulation as well as government spending disrupts the natural equilibrium of the market.[8]

Government regulations have been indicted for adding to the cost of doing business, favoring some industries at the expense of others, and causing widespread mischief in otherwise effectively functioning free markets. Estimates of the total production cost of governmental regulation have run as high as $100 billion a year (in 1976). The majority of the $100 billion was attributed to the "social regulation" recently imposed upon the economy by a government eager to burden productive activity with the unproductive costs of environmental, worker, and consumer safety.

William K. Tabb criticizes the methodology that produced the $100 billion figure. That figure is extrapolated from very limited evidence. And only the costs of regulation are addressed. *Benefits receive no attention.* The benefits of social regulation range from a high estimate of $93.2 billion to a low estimate of $16.2 billion for only four categories of social regulation (air and water pollution, motor vehicle safety, and accident prevention). As Tabb concludes, "Considering the crude benefit studies which are available, the overall benefit-cost ratio for social legislation is substantially positive."[9] If we accept Tabb's conclusion, then it is reasonable to say that at least social regulation has a positive effect on total economic activity.

The problem is that the cost of regulation falls on the manufacturing sector, while benefits serve the general public. This nonsymmetrical incidence of costs and benefits conflicts with the reactionary and moderate recapitalist endeavor to shift production/investment costs from business to consumers and workers. When government forces business to produce more cleanly or safely, business bears the costs, citizens the benefits. When regulations are eased or abolished, business saves costs and workers, consumers, or localities bear the health and safety costs. A fundamental problem with American economic policy debates is that the different economic interests, burdens, and potentials of people are obscured by policy solutions that proffer a unified "national policy." Who wins, and who loses is obscured by the waving of the flag of "*the* national interest."

Capital crowding
A third recapitalization argument is that the cost of capital is pushed higher by government deficits. Governments are forced then to borrow money in the private capital markets. Interest rates increase and less capital is available to private concerns (what is called "capital crowding").[10] Despite the assurance with which this contention is voiced, the actual effect of government competition for capital on capital costs is undetermined. In fact, in an era of slow growth in which the Federal Reserve Bank followed the policy of keeping interest rates up, it is practically useless to differentiate between deficit spending and anti-inflation policy as the source of high capital costs.

The prime rate did rise from about 4.7 per cent through the early 1960s to around 8 per cent through most of the 1970s and up to 20 per cent in 1980. Surprisingly, the high cost of capital has not deterred U.S. corporations from going to capital markets. In fact, an increasing proportion of corporate capital needs over the 1970s has been financed by borrowing rather than from internal sources.

The crowding out of private investment by government deficits re-emerged to political glamour because of the very large deficits projected by the Reagan government. Those proposed deficits resulted from the massive tax cuts of Reaganomics coupled with intended increases in military spending. The fluctuations in stock prices on Wall Street made it clear that business men and women believed that large government deficits raised interest rates and limited available investment capital for private business. We are less sure of this assertion (even though it is the major business criticism of the Reaganomic version of recapitalization). The data of Table 5.3 are interesting in this respect: federal government debt *repayment* of past debt largely offset federal deficits. Government deficits do not seem to overwhelm capital markets.

The capital crowding hypothesis seems to assume that the money the federal government borrows is somehow removed from circulation in the economy. This is not so: it is put on deposit in banks or spent; thus the capital is still available for further lending. In addition, the government pays back past debt plus interest, offsetting its new capital claims with past capital services. The Reagan deficits, because of their historically unprecedented magnitude, may

TABLE 5.3 *Federal debt and debt payments ($ billion)*

	1972	1975	1978	1980	1981
Federal deficits	23.4	45.2	48.8	59.5	57.9
Federal debt payments	20.5	34.5	43.9	64.5	82.5

Source: *Economic Report of the President, 1982*, Table B-72, p. 317.

have had more deleterious effects. Our contention is simply that government debt, like business debt or consumer debt, is a normal part of economic activity, not a threatening aberration.

Wicked business?

Uneven investment

The question remains, however, of what has been the effect of all these purported disincentives to invest upon actual investment? The real questions that must be asked center around the actual process of deindustrialization in the U.S. How has business fulfilled its economic role as allocator of the collective savings of the American people? Has investment in the productive industrial sector of the economy actually declined? Are tax cuts necessary?

The astonishing story is that between 1960 and 1978 the average age of gross stocks of fixed non-residential business capital including manufacturing equipment and structures actually declined.[11] Contrary to popular belief and recapitalist propaganda, an *upgrading* of total productive capital occurred over this period as new technology was introduced.

Investment as a percentage of GNP was actually slightly higher in the 1970s than it had been in the 1960s. During the 1960s, the ratio of real investment to GNP was about 9.7; through the 1970s that ratio rose to 10.0.[12] The proportion of investment to total economic activity has not declined. If investment has not fallen, why does the U.S. need tax cuts to revitalize its economy?

The answer lies not in the rate of capital formation, nor in the amount of capital investment, but in the *structure* of capital investment. Money has not flowed evenly to all sectors of the economy. Total non-residential business capital investment (in constant 1972 dollars) rose 117 per cent for equipment and 85 per cent for structures between 1960 and 1978. Manufacturing capital during the same period rose, however, only 100 per cent for equipment and merely 24 per cent for structures.[13] Although private investment has certainly been substantial over the last twenty years, investment in materially productive industries lagged behind investment in other business ventures. The discussion of productivity growth in the last chapter indicates two reasons why manufacturing investment was not high – overcapacity and low labor costs. The structural change in the economy – the shift into services – discussed in Chapter 2 is consonant with this investment pattern.

Another way to examine investment in U.S. industry is to look at particular industries rather than aggregate figures. Over the 1970s primary production industries such as food, textiles, rubber and plastics, stone, clay and glass, and primary metal manufacturing experienced progressively smaller proportions of total capital expenditures. Gains were made in the share of capital expenditures by such diverse industries as transport equipment, fabricated metal products, paper and allied products, and lumber. The chemical, petroleum, and coal industries made the most prominent gains in capital expenditures.[14]

Available capital did not flow equally to all U.S. industries during the 1970s. Selective investment favored non-manufacturing industries over manufacturing. Within the manufacturing sector some industries such as chemicals and oil were favored and others such as primary metals and textiles were neglected. Structural changes in the economy produced declines in manufacturing investment relative to service investment and shifts in investment patterns within the manufacturing sector. Some manufacturing industries are being deindustrialized as capital flows to more profitable non-manufacturing industries or industries which promise quicker returns. At the same time, the service sector plays an increasingly important role in American economic activity.

Investment has been occurring. The disturbing phenomenon is that investment is taking place in industries which are not basic to export strength, nor have high or growing productivity profiles.

The older, familiar basic manufacturing industries such as steel, automobiles, and textiles are losing the profit beauty contest that attracts private capital. Although this pattern makes sense in terms of the interests of private enterprise, it often harms the economy as a whole. Imports climb and workers and communities are hurt by these developments. Corporations' decisions are uninfluenced by national investment and export–import needs. They are also free to abandon strategically important or large employing industries.

Profits and investment

Can a change in government behavior promote useful investment? Will higher post-tax incomes for the rich and for large corporations lead to an investment expansion and to the right kind of expansion?

The recapitalization solution centers on higher overall profits; but higher profits do not invariably lead to higher investments. For the latter occurs where the prospect of further profit is greater because of the additional investment. If demand is inelastic, lower costs and prices will not yield a higher profit volume. Or if a competitor threatens to take over the market, or a variety of other possibilities occur, then higher post-tax profits may not result in higher investment levels. As Rayner and Little argued in *Higgledy Piggledy Growth Again*, guesses about the future are more important than the experiences of the past in evaluations of companies.[15] The surprisingly low investment rates in manufacturing in the United States, despite rising profits in the mid-1970s, reflect uncertainty about the economy, the prospects of tax changes, and the political picture.[16]

Since the long-term aim of recapitalization is to increase productivity and improve the balance of trade by expanding investment in the industries involved in foreign trade – either by exporting or by warding off imports from abroad – the question is, will investment increase in the relevant industries or will higher post-tax corporate and personal incomes be deployed in less useful ways?

A large increase in income, savings, and after-tax profits might not lead to investment in international trade-related industries. In the absence of selective controls or "targeting" leading to or providing incentives for investments desirable from national economic needs, higher net incomes might have a negative effect. They can lead to greater luxury expenditures or speculation and financial maneuverings which do not deal with international economic difficulties. The reappearance of conglomerate takeovers and mergers in the United States after 1978 reveals that some corporations with high post-tax profits (particularly in the oil industry) were not investing in the expansion of their real physical capital but using these funds to buy control of other corporations. (We provide some data later in the chapter.) This approach not only leads to further concentration of control of corporate assets, but it does not increase productivity or total production.

In Britain in the early 1970s, higher post-tax incomes led to the infamous "property boom," in Prime Minister Heath's words, "the unacceptable face of capitalism" – a gross inflating of real estate prices with much less growth in physical investment rates. As the lower-taxes-to-increase-investment approach is linked with reduction in controls over business, increased post-tax income can go where it will, not necessarily where it would be economically useful.

Private expenditure and investment decisions are not necessarily going to follow the "rationality" prescribed by economists and recapitalization strategists. Reducing taxes, public social spending, and the protection of the environment, may free capital, but not inevitably for productive investment. Recapitalist policies risk increasing inequalities and worsening standards of living without a compensating restructuring or strengthening of the economy. Corporations allocate their investment capital on the basis of predicted profitability, not national long-term need. Only some of the funds made available by tax cuts will be invested. What is eventually used for domestic investment will most likely flow to the most profitable and secure areas of the economy, not to the weak or declining industries (or regions) that most need reindustrializing, or to export-oriented fields.

Non-productive investments
The availability of capital funds in no way guarantees that they will be invested in future productive capacity. Table 5.4 graphically depicts the change in the use of corporate capital over the last two decades. Capital available for investment in U.S. productive capacity is used increasingly in speculation. The bottom panel of Table 5.4 ("Increases in financial assets") includes all investment by U.S. non-financial corporations in other than productive assets – i.e., included are buying shares in other companies and the like rather than improving or extending productive capacity. The trend

TABLE 5.4 *The uses of available corporate capital, 1960–80 (non-farm, non-financial business) ($ billion)*

	1960	1965	1970	1975	1979	1980
Total available corporate capital	40.6	82.2	100.8	151.2	346.0	286.6
Capital expenditures	38.0	62.0	82.0	110.0	229.4	225.1
% of total	94	75	81	77	67	78
Increases in financial assets	2.7	20.2	18.8	41.2	116.6	61.5
% of total	6	25	19	33	33	22

Source: *Statistical Abstract of the United States, 1981*, Table 938, p. 551.

is disturbing: from 1960 to 1980 *financial speculation of all kinds grew from 6.4 per cent of all investment to well over a quarter.*

Table 5.4 reveals corporate America's great growth in available capital. This capital comes from many sources, including short- and long-term borrowing, the stock market, retained earnings, and increased depreciation allowances. In fact, available capital has been growing much faster than investment in fixed assets. Between 1960 and 1979 available corporate capital grew by 740 per cent; during the same period, capital expenditures – investment – grew by only 509 per cent. Particularly interesting in Table 5.4 is the enormous rise in available capital between 1975 and 1979. This evidence does not show a financial *inability* to invest in U.S. productivity but a *refusal* to invest.

A Conference Board time series estimates the adequacy of the capital facilities of the top one thousand corporations (almost all of which are in the manufacturing sector) for current demand. They concluded that through the late 1960s about 30 per cent of the top one thousand corporations had inadequate access to capital: only a few per cent had more than adequate capital facilities. In the late 1970s they judged that inadequate facilities had dropped to 20 per cent of the top one thousand. Between 1975 and 1977 capital-rich firms became increasingly numerous. Clearly, *capital is available.*[17]

Speculation increasingly absorbs capital that could be invested in U.S. productive capacity. This speculative use of capital is most clearly seen in the conglomerate movement of the late 1960s and early 1970s and again more recently. Corporate takeovers entail the expenditure of capital on already existing facilities rather than expansion of the productive ability of the national economy. Both G. William Miller and Paul Volcker in their roles as heads of the U.S. Federal Reserve System have warned that the purchasing of corporations in order to strengthen and diversify portfolios destroys investment capital.

In 1981 corporate mergers occurred at the highest level in seven years. The number of merger announcements totaled 2,395, up from 1,889 the year before. The dollar value of those purchases soared to a record $82.6 billion. The 1981 merger record of $82.6 billion was nearly double the $44.3 billion spent in 1980 on purchasing other companies' assets. Larger companies were investing their capital in larger acquisitions.[18] Since gross private domestic investment in 1981 was about $215 billion, speculation on already existing corporate assets accounted for over 38 per cent of all investment.[19]

The apparently low-risk, quick-payoff benefits of buying up already profitable (undervalued or cash-rich) firms may make great sense to corporate upper management and accountants looking to expand short-term profit rates and assets of a corporation. (At least the returns look very good in prospect, though not always in retrospect.) But such takeovers accomplish little positive for the national economy. They divert capital from investment in new industrial structures or equipment that would have created new jobs and generated taxes.

Another form of speculation burgeoned in the U.S. in the 1970s: individual and corporate investment in commodities. The opening of a commodity market by the New York Stock Exchange and the 1980 debacle in the silver markets illustrate this attempt by U.S. investors to find short-term profits rather than risk long-term capital ventures.

Tables 5.5 and 5.6 illustrate clearly the speculative nature of the U.S. investment process in the 1970s. The commodity markets absorbed a great deal of capital as nervous investors tried for quick profits in a volatile financial situation. Although the volume of stock or commodity trading and the absolute levels of domestic investment are not intrinsically connected, Table 5.6 provides a

TABLE 5.5 *Market value, all sales of stocks and commodities, all exchanges, U.S. 1960–80 ($ billion)*

	1960	1965	1970	1975	1976	1977	1978	1979	1980
Stock	47	93	136	167	203	198	269	323	522
Commodity futures	42	86	145	571	821	1243	2122	N.A.	N.A.

Source: *Statistical Abstract of the United States, 1981*, Table 872, p. 523.
Statistical Abstract of the United States, 1979, Table 899, p. 545.

sense of the growth of speculative investment in the United States. In particular, the volume of commodity futures speculation was 103 per cent of gross private domestic investment in 1970 (almost twice what it was in 1960) and grew to an astonishing 603 per cent of private domestic investment in 1978. The investment process in the United States is characterized by a short-term search for profits.

TABLE 5.6 *Total stock and commodity futures volume as percentages of gross private domestic investment, 1960–80*

	1960	1965	1970	1975	1976	1977	1978	1979	1980
Stock	59	79	93	82	80	61	71	76	64
Commodity futures	55	77	103	299	338	410	603	N.A.	N.A.

Source: calculated from Table 5.5 and *Statistical Abstract of the United States, 1981*, Table 700, p. 421.

Table 5.5 highlights the divergence of stock and commodity market activity over the 1970s. Prior to 1973 the two markets were quite similar in the growth in the volume of capital passing through them. The tremendous rise in commodity trading in 1975 reflects the speculative desire for quick financial payoffs characteristic of available but volatile commodities. Investment in corporate stocks, on the other hand, demands a certain amount of patience and faith in both the economy and the management of individual corporations. Obviously, both stock and commodity investments involve a degree of risk. The difference is that stock investment is a bet on future corporate production and profitability while commodity investment implies an assumption of or desire for short-ages and inflated prices. Both can become self-fulfilling prophecies as corporate capital is augmented by investment or commodities are inflated by a speculative spiral. The amount of capital passing through U.S. commodity markets is a reflection of corporate and institutional investment with an unusually short-term and inflationary profile.

Managerial incompetence

Managerial incompetence produces another set of barriers to investment. We do not mean incompetence in the sense that corporate managers are individually incompetent, but that the managerial system is often unsympathetic and even antagonistic to long-range investment plans, as Abernathy and Hayes have charged.[20] The role of management, especially top corporate management, is not very well understood. While sociologists have studied the interlocks between managements of different corporations and the interlocks between corporations and the state,[21] they have less knowledge about management structure and what might be called management culture.[22] Three management-related processes are effective barriers to recapitalizing investment, at least in the short run. They are structure, style, and individualism.

The sociological literature characterizes the role of management as basically dual. The first function of management within the corporate structure is to extract profits from the workforce, preferably the greatest (optimal) amount of profits but minimally a base amount. The second function is one of control. It is management's job to see to it that management, not individual workers, controls the production process. Harry Braverman made this observation in *Labor and Monopoly Capital*. Other social scientists have since expanded his analysis.[23] These two functions are mutually reinforcing; corporations need control in order to insure profits.

Although we agree with this basic formulation, we also recognize that it is possible for the control imperative to become counterproductive. Worker alienation may rise in the face of an inhumane workplace. Productivity may drop or stagnate, regardless of investment, because of the high density of managers who are there to insure a level of control which is potentially unworkable. Too much management may limit productivity simply by multiplying the number of non-productive workers on the corporate payroll. The return on investment in control may be substantially smaller than most U.S. management realizes.

Preliminary work by David Gordon on this question indicates

that the density of non-productive (management and clerical) workers in the economy plus stagnating wages is the best single predictor of the slowdown in U.S. productivity rates. U.S. management's political quest for control has reduced some of its capacity to realize the prime economic goal of profits.[24]

Theoretically, this outcome could be very damaging to much of micro-economic and organizational theory. What if the private capitalist firm, even while questing after profits, failed to maximize (or optimize) profits, not because of market barriers, but because management structure was more centered on control or equated control with profits when that relation is not such a simple one? The rational pursuit of defined interests would be in disrepute.

While Gordon's work is at a fairly high level of methodological abstraction, a more convincing argument for the dysfunctionality of current management emphasis on control comes from the major U.S. corporations themselves. American Telephone and Telegraph and General Motors along with many other lesser giants are beginning to change supervisory and worker domains. They experiment with Japanese-style management techniques that emphasize cooperation and joint decision-making between workers and management. Other corporations such as IBM, that have long stressed a cooperative management style, are currently receiving increased attention from the rest of the business world. The fact that corporate America (e.g., Motorola) proudly advertises its quality work circles and other approaches to management is a tacit admission that the control emphasis of U.S. management may be counterproductive. Whether or not the Japan Inc. humane management model will spread and endure or wither as a new publicity fad rises to prominence is an open question.[25]

In terms of recapitalization, the control orientation characteristic of U.S. management may contribute to the decline in productivity and exports that untargeted recapitalization policies hope to remedy. Poor, non-productive, or alienating management structure may block efforts to enhance U.S. competitiveness. Both the theory of corporate rationality and the goals of recapitalization are threatened by U.S. management behavior. This threat is especially striking in light of our earlier discussion of the threat of corporate concentration on U.S. social structure. The management decisions

and style of the largest enterprises may have far-reaching consequences for the very structure of U.S. social and economic life.[26]
Not only can management structure be counterproductive but
individual rationality or personal style can diverge from long-term
corporate rationality. The Hayes–Abernathy analysis contends that
corporate management styles contributed substantially to the
current troubles besetting the U.S. economy.[27] Their appraisal
supports our identification of an increasing tendency to invest
capital in low-risk, short-term ventures rather than in the creation
of new productive capacity. They comment that U.S. managers
increasingly act like bankers interested only in return on investment
and getting their money back. This path is often accomplished
through buying other companies or managing investment portfolios rather than selling products to customers. When attention is
given to developing new products, play-it-safe ventures in imitative
product lines rather than investment in new product lines are
increasingly the rule. Here we see managers protecting individual
careers at the cost of long-term productiveness of their corporation
and of the economy in general.[28]

Abernathy and Hayes attribute this shift to an increasing dominance of top corporate positions by people with financial rather
than production or sales backgrounds. It is more likely, we would
argue, that corporate management is being held accountable for
profits on a short-term basis. The importance of large institutional
holdings of stocks (mainly by banks and insurance companies)
resulted in Wall Street managers stressing "results" as they turned
over their portfolios to demonstrate gains to their institutional
bosses. In turn, corporate managers are made vulnerable. A dip in
profits or even growth rate while the corporation invests its capital
in long-term ventures such as new plants, technologies, or products
is not attractive if corporate management is going to be evaluated
and fired according to short-term performance.

Table 5.7 illustrates this process. An increasing percentage of
corporate profits has been distributed as dividends over the last
twenty years. Available capital is being paid out to institutional
and private investors rather than reinvested in the firm's long-range
interest.

Abernathy and Hayes's explanation highlights a shift in the
criterion for management rationality. As corporate upper manage-

TABLE 5.7 *Corporate profits and dividends*

Years	Profits ($ billion)	Dividends	Dividends as % of profits
1960–4	151.3	73.4	46
1965–9	230.1	103.1	45
1970–4	205	129.3	63
1975–9	355.4	211.4	59

Source: Economic Report of the President, 1982, Table B-12, p. 246.

ment becomes increasingly dominated by people with financial backgrounds, the centrality of production in the corporate organization decreases. Our explanation, which we see as complementary rather than contrary to that of Abernathy and Hayes, is that corporate management is increasingly expected by inflation-jittery investors to show short-term high profits. Whether the explanation lies in managerial background or outside pressure, managers' quest for short-term profits may damage the long-term health of their firm or the economy.

American management was once the envy of the capitalist world. U.S. corporations produced more goods with less input than did those of other countries. U.S. management was the benchmark, the ideal to be striven for. Now, when U.S.-style capitalism seems to be in bad shape, these 'ideal' managers are in need of re-evaluation.

At a qualitative level, the recent popular memoirs of John De Lorean, *On a Clear Day You Can See General Motors*, are striking in that the book gives outsiders a look at how corporate decisions are made in the uppermost reaches of what was then the largest manufacturing firm in the United States.[29] These memoirs, although admittedly from a single and rather dissatisfied source, who had once held a top position in the GM hierarchy, paint a startling picture of the interplay of personal links and enmities, blind loyalty, and stubborn traditionalism within GM. De Lorean points out that for a quarter of a century (1949 to mid-1970s) the automobile industry introduced not a single noteworthy innovation. "In the place of productive innovation, the automobile industry went on a two-decade marketing binge." He provides four reasons why a more product-conscious management style could not dominate GM:

1 innovation and decisions were organizationally centralized in topmost management;
2 corporate politics were the key to success for individual managers within GM, not innovation or forward-looking plans;
3 short-term profits were expected from managers at all levels;
4 investment was discouraged, as was adding cost to cars by extra inspection for quality or safety.

De Lorean declares that GM upper management "spent little time looking at the big picture, instead occupying themselves with minuscule matters ... that should have been considered and disposed in the divisions much further down the corporate management line." The control functions that we discussed earlier in this chapter combined with short-term profit requirements to overwhelm the capability of GM to innovate or plan for the future. De Lorean paints a picture of layer upon layer of management forwarding all but the simplest decisions to the top of GM. The corporate brass had total control but practically no time or inclination to plan for the long-term future of GM.

De Lorean's analysis is particularly interesting not simply because he shows the non-rationality of GM as a corporation and GM management as individuals, but also because GM over that period was the most profitable capitalist firm in the United States, if not the world. How can we reconcile tales of managerial incompetence and myopic planning with excellent profitability? Our interpretation is that in an expanding market GM's extremely large size – its sheer economic power – coupled with no threat of aggressive competition from its oligopolistic partners, Ford and Chrysler, freed it of the need to please customers. With the relatively short reign of the average chief executive officer, GM did not concern itself much with the future, concentrating instead on immediate profitability.

We would not want to generalize this one example to all of corporate America, but many corporate giants depend upon their economic power within sheltered markets. The quality of decision-making may be as non-rational in many large corporations as it seems to have been at GM without outsiders becoming informed or corporate profits falling.[30] Of course, the GM story does not end with a profitable but unresponsive giant, for this giant is struggling today to hold on to its historical market share in the face of technologically superior and fuel-saving Japanese and European cars.

Monopoly or oligopoly power in national markets is always tenuous in the long run, especially now with aggressive international competition to overcome routinized or uninnovative policies. Within a nation giant firms may expand beyond their usual markets to compete in new products. This is happening today in the U.S. where IBM is branching out into telecommunications, a historic monopoly of ATT. Protected and monopolized markets may give the impression of corporate rationality and stability where in fact little exists. The GM case seems to be an example of short-sighted management's running for a long time a very profitable corporation. Monopoly or oligopoly power is a fragile protection over the long-run for poor management structure, style, and cronyism. Institutional monopoly or oligopoly private corporate power is a dangerous and undemocratic base from which to decide the fate of the collective savings of the American people.

In general, a corporation's actions follow the rational needs of its management, not the other way around. Of course, the goals of both management and corporation can coincide but there is no guarantee under present arrangements for such a happy mutuality. Non-rational or mixed rationality in corporate behavior may be at least partially obscured. Other factors such as market power, effective advertising, or aggressive political activity (recapitalization) shield a corporation from the consequences of bad management. The importance of giant concentrated capital in U.S. economic life makes leaving decisions to self-seeking corporate management a doubtful route to improved national economic performance.

The non-rational market
The preceding discussion argued that corporations are not always acting either in their long-range self-interest or even in terms of maximum profitability in the middle-term. The best that can be said for corporate America is that there seems presently to be a tendency to maximize short-term profits at the expense of long-term productiveness and stability. Recapitalization, especially in its reactionary Reaganomic form, is a political attempt by large

corporations to have both their short-term profits while hoping for long-term productivity growth. As a national policy, recapitalization is an attempt to inject long-term rationality into the market.

The critical reader might object to this characterization as overly facile, failing to understand the role of the market. That reader might go on to point out that GM failed to prosper precisely because of management inattention to the long-term. Japanese automakers, with help from OPEC-inspired price rises, re-introduced competition in the American market and forced GM to invest in new facilities, production processes, and innovation. GM asserts, however, that it needs government-led recapitalization policies such as tax cuts to boost investment, lower interest rates, regulatory restraint to enhance competitiveness, and governmental pressure to reduce imports if it is to compete with Japan. Political instruments, not the magic of market rationality, are relied on by major American corporations. This is not surprising because the market has never been the mechanism of adjustment that capitalist ideology ascribes to it. Rather, since the American Revolution, the U.S. government has played a major role in the development of U.S. industry.

Recapitalization focuses on profits and the market as the road to national economic improvement. But the quest to maximize profits is an undependable ally in the struggle to improve the long-term economic fortunes of the U.S. If investment is left to the market, it will tend to follow the god of immediate profit, not of national need. Key industries will be underfunded as not offering high short-run profits. They will remain as uncompetitive in the international market as they are now. The goal of private profit often conflicts with collective or rational economic goals of enhanced productiveness and strong exports as called for by recapitalization. As Marx pointed out so long ago, capitalism produces an economics based on exchange value, not use value. Today "use value" has a broad national meaning, not only that particular to individual consumers. It implies long-term economic development. By this enlarged criterion, the market and recapitalization are likely to fail.

If capitalists envision greater profits in speculation or services, automobiles and steel can be expected to be sacrificed. Many interests compete for the investment funds freed by recapitalization-inspired tax cuts. We predict that investment will be based on short-term *private exchange values* for economic decision-makers, not on *national use values* that would counter the internationalization of the market and deindustrialization of the U.S. The interests of specific corporations and their particular managements will dominate the allocation of capital and the development of industries. Long-term national benefits depend heavily on the invisible hand of the market working its magic of uniting individual and national, short-run and long-run, interests. That is asking a great deal of a highly imperfect market.

The threat of inflation particularly undermines market magic. As long as corporations fear that long-term prospects are unpredictable, if money is untrustworthy because of inflation, then play-it-safe or high-flying short-term ventures will predominate. Real estate and art treasures, as well as other firms, seem safer, more rewarding investments in an inflationary era than the construction of new plants and the creation of new jobs. Market logic forces corporate investors to make investments which oppose the recapitalization goals of increased productivity and exports. The next section explores this issue further.

Investment lures
Overseas investment by multinational corporations competes with investment in U.S. manufacturing assets. Foreign capital expenditures by U.S. multinational corporations in 1980 totaled 41 per cent of the value of all capital investment in the United States in that year. U.S. total assets abroad in 1980 were worth $513 billion.[31] United States corporation tax laws, which allow the deduction of taxes paid overseas from taxes on corporate income, encourage multinationals to invest abroad rather than at home. Again, the availability of capital does not insure that it will be invested in enhancing the productivity of U.S. manufacturing. On the contrary, the logic of the market encourages foreign manufacture rather than the export of U.S.-based commodities because of lowered shipping costs, tariff restrictions on imports, and U.S. tax laws.[32]

Non-manufacturing, non-mining industries, particularly the fast-growing service sectors of the economy, may receive much of the freed investment capital that recapitalization promises. As the

1980s begin, U.S. Steel not only has fewer employees than McDonald's but it also has substantial investments in hotels and amusement parks. Investments in the service sectors are not necessarily bad. They provide jobs and there seems to be ample demand for the services. But they will not promote U.S. industrial exports nor solve the problems of a deindustrializing nation. There is no reason to believe that capital freed for general untargeted business investment will not continue to flow to the service sectors.[33]

If and when capital is invested in U.S. manufacturing as a result of the recapitalization strategy, there is no guarantee that it will lead to a revitalization of the economy. In 1980 the return on investment (stockholders' equity) for *Fortune 500* corporations analyzed collectively by industry, ranged from a 19.5 per cent return for the tobacco industry to only 7.6 per cent for automobile producers.[34] Although attractive investments, cigarettes are not as important for the quality and quantity of American economic life as less profitable but necessary industries such as steel or automobiles.

The deindustrialization of the United States can best be understood not simply in terms of failure to invest in U.S. manufacturers but in the tendency of investors to put their money in those industries where the rate of return is highest. In 1979 the basic infrastructure industries of metal manufacturing, glass, concrete, abrasives and gypsum, motor vehicles, and textiles all returned 15.7 per cent or less on stockholders' equity. The pattern of corporate investment over the 1970s not surprisingly parallels the profitability of corporate capital in that period. In such industries as chemicals and petroleum, investments rose by over 125 per cent between 1970 and 1976. Investments in textiles and primary metals rose only 34 per cent and 52 per cent respectively while those in motor vehicles actually declined over that period by 1 per cent.[35]

The freedom of private business to invest its capital wherever it can find the best rate of return is probably the real cause of the economic decline of some key industries in the U.S. The increased availability of capital for investment by U.S. corporations will in no way ensure survival for and may even exacerbate the plight of declining industries and regions. Banks and corporations, like Citibank of New York and U.S. Steel, have no special allegiance to steel or to any city in the U.S. They exist to make money, not steel, nor to create jobs or taxes. Of course, when they invest in manufacturing of some sort, it can be in steel and it will produce some jobs and some taxes, but that is not why they invest.

In short, across-the-board increases in post-tax personal and corporate income do not assure commensurate rises in physical investment, and certainly not in international trade-related fields. Nor do they ensure that other obstacles to increasing exports or diminishing imports will be overcome. It is a blunderbuss approach which, at best, disperses large benefits to a privileged group in order to make much smaller investment gains in appropriate industries.

American corporations and financial institutions have failed to perform their social and economic function of allocating capital in an economically and socially desirable manner. Money has flowed away from crucial but less profitable industries such as automobiles, railroads, and steel, and into more profitable but less crucial service and non-durable manufacturing industries and speculation. To the individual capitalist, now most often not an individual at all but a corporation, acting in his, her, or its short-term self-interest, these investments were perhaps appropriate.

For the long-term growth and stability of the national economy of the U.S., such investments are far from rational. Recapitalizing capitalism, giving increased control over available capital to those institutions and individuals who have in the 1970s failed to do their jobs as capitalists, will prove a grave mistake. The productive capacity of a national economy is, in a very real sense, the collective wealth of the people of that nation. Taking some of the disposable income of the American people and giving that money to the corporations in the form of tax breaks may prove to be little more than a redistribution of income from the poor to the rich. Speculative and destructive investment may occur. Short-range planning, inflationary panic psychology, and slow-growth policies may make the recapitalization of capitalism little more than a well-orchestrated rip-off.

This chapter has characterized corporate behavior on the individual managerial, organizational, and market levels as non-rational or at least mixed-rational in both action and consequence, especially when national economic needs enter the evaluation. On all levels the private giant corporation is not the super-rational, always effective decision-making, profit-making machine that is its characterization in the social science literature and recapitalization prescriptions. The goals and rationality of corporations are private goals and rationality that do not necessarily add up to the collective national goal of expanded investment, productivity, and exports embodied in recapitalization (or any other national goal, for that matter).

In their present form, recapitalization efforts to restore the United States to international competitiveness are doomed to failure. The super-rational, efficient market of economic and conservative rhetoric does not exist. The efficacy of the corporations that dominate the U.S. economy is problematic, as is their likely contribution to U.S. exports efforts. The rational model of corporate behavior is not a useful predictor of the economic effects of recapitalization because neither corporate goals nor efficacy can be assumed nor predicted.

Tax cuts for the well-to-do and corporations are the current political solution to the relative decline of the United States's position in the world economy. Even liberals and neo-liberals have supported drastic reductions in corporate taxes in order to increase profits and promote investment. Productivity is lagging; the potential answer is to spur investment. Figures on how much West Germany and Japan invest relative to their Gross National Product are offered to show how U.S. investment rates lag. These statistical contentions support the political argument that many must suffer through reductions in social programs so that the few can prosper and invest in everyone's future.

All U.S. industrial policies should be concerned with which industries expand. Targeting is essential; otherwise, increased after-tax profits and incomes, savings, and even investments can have little effect on productivity, exports, and the containment of imports. The issue is *what kind of economic expansion?* Merely to advocate an investment-led expansion rather than a consumption-led one is inadequate. The long-term development of the U.S. requires increasing exports and lessening imports; at least, that is what is necessary if current economic structures are to continue.[36] That long-term development depends on investment in manufacturing, and probably not all of manufacturing.

Thus, a concern with investment leads to the issues of targeting and decision-making. Which industries are to be encouraged to expand and modernize? This question is central to any effective industrial policy. The next chapter discusses trends in employment and wage levels and recapitalization's likely effects on them.

Chapter 6
Can recapitalization
provide the jobs?

We have already seen that the current wisdom which guides presidents, beguiles the media, and threatens to cow the indigent into submission is by and large wrong.

The recapitalization diagnosis is badly flawed. In fact, it is a misleading and dangerous misrepresentation of the U.S. social and economic structure.

No simple formulae can lay the blame for American economic performance upon government or labor. Productivity is not nearly so important as the level and cost of production. Exports are not stagnating, although the U.S. does import a lot of oil and international competition is increasing. Investment has not declined, although it is going into unrewarding areas of the economy. Although unemployment has been at historic highs, employment, on the other hand, has grown much faster than ever before in our nation's civilian history.

The diagnosis that supports and legitimizes those social and economic initiatives, which we have dubbed the "recapitalization of capitalism," is little more than ideology masked by bad theory interpreting the wrong statistics incorrectly. But what of it? Good practice may flow from bad theory and vice versa. Consequently, the recapitalization prescriptions for reindustrialization must be carefully examined, not dismissed. In this chapter, we examine the likely employment and redistributive effects of recapitalization. In particular, we investigate the employment potential of that new genie, high-technology industries.

What are the likely developments in the 1980s – even with recapitalization efforts? Workers and consumers will experience continued inflation of housing costs, the production of few jobs (if any) in manufacturing, while the low-paid service sector will provide an increasing share of available jobs. The older cities of the Northeast and Midwest, areas of urban poverty and aging factories, will be characterized by a general stagnation of jobs and tax base, perhaps accompanied by more of the urban renewal-led expansion of downtown corporate control functions.[1] This scenario of the 1980s is basically that of the 1970s — only more so: much of the freed capital will be used for inflationary speculative investments; capital investment in manufacturing (if and when it occurs) will take place in low-wage and low-tax areas such as the Southwest and overseas, draining jobs and capital from older regions; the control functions of older cities may increase, driving up real estate prices and providing a few good jobs (e.g., for lawyers, accountants, and executives) leading to local gentrification; and the service sector, particularly services for the downtown business elites, may grow, providing mostly low-paid, dead-end employment.

Untargeted recapitalization policies will encourage states and cities to compete for investment and jobs. Urban enterprise zones, already proposed by many states and favored by Reagan and company, may be the form this competition takes in the older industrial cities and states. Urban residents will suffer further erosion of their standard of living due to cutbacks in city services as budgets are pared to compete with low-service, low-tax cities in the South and West.

Economic policies of upward income redistribution and market freedom are, however, inherently unstable. They do not address the structural shifts in the economy, including the dangers of international trade, the relative decline in manufacturing and rise in services, or the fiscal crisis of older urban centers. It is unlikely that this tax-based bribe of the wealthy will endure long as a political stabilizer because it burdens many without producing compensating benefits such as a rise in manufacturing exports (and employment) or economic stability. It is possible that the present form of recapitalization may work, but only if capitalists start acting like capitalists, rather than speculators; if they invest in potentially productive businesses rather than attempting to make money out of money. More likely, present recapitalization policies will fail and be replaced by more targeted policies (which we discuss in Chapter 8).

Employment

The service sector

It is obvious at this point that manufacturing and the other materially productive industries, although generally profitable, will not be creating many jobs. In the 1970s, as the United States was introduced to a new economic phenomenon, stagflation – simultaneous stagnation or recession coupled with high inflation – employment actually soared.

While the rise in unemployment was quite large over the 1970s, the rise in labor force participation of 22 million people and of total employment of 19 million is equally important (see Table 6.1). As Emma Rothchild has pointed out, close to 13 million new jobs were created from 1973 to 1979, a period of severe economic difficulties.[2] The growth of employment was largely in three sectors of the economy: services, wholesale and retail trade, and state and local government. Between 1969 and 1979 these three sectors provided 14.6 million new jobs, accounting for 77 per cent of total employment growth over the period. Manufacturing, mining, and construction contributed only 2.2 million or 11 per cent of new jobs over the decade. The manufacturing sector accounted for only 800,000 additional jobs. During the same period, federal

TABLE 6.1 *Growth in U.S. population, employment, unemployment, 1959–79 (by thousands)*

	1959	1969	% change 1959–69	1979	% change 1969–79
Total population	177,800	202,700	13.5	220,600	8.3
Total civilian labor force	68,369	80,734	18.1	102,908	27.5
Employed	64,630	77,902	20.5	96,945	24.4
Unemployed	3,740	2,832	−24.3	5,963	110.6

Source: *Employment and Training Report of the President, 1980*, Table A-1, p. 217; and *Statistical Abstract of the United States, 1980*, Table 2, p. 6.

government employment actually declined slightly.[3] Thus, growth areas of the economy are in the service sector and in state and local government. Neither industry nor big government is presently expanding.

We want to make two more points in terms of the growth of services in the economy. The first relates to the types of employment provided; the second to the types of businesses that are growing.

Some analysts, such as Daniel Bell, have characterized the growth of services as the hallmark of a post-industrial, high-skilled, knowledge-based society.[4] In fact, however, those expanding sectors provide relatively low-level employment. As we discussed in Chapter 2, two shifts have profoundly affected U.S. employment. The entrance of millions of baby-boom generation children – now adults – and ex-housewives into the labor force kept wages down. The expanding non-government service sector has always been a low-wage, labor intensive sector. The boom years of the 1970s were no exception.

The new jobs in the service industries differ from the jobs in production that they replace. First and most important, these new jobs are lower-wage jobs. In 1979, weekly earnings in the service sector were only 80 per cent of national average weekly earnings and only 65 per cent of manufacturing wages. Retail trade, which provided most of the new trade jobs in the 1970s, paid only 63 per cent of average weekly earnings and only 52 per cent of manufacturing wages.[5] The weekly wages in these sectors are low for two reasons: low hourly earnings, often close to the minimum wage, and short hours.

The service sector generally provides employment for women and young people.[6] Not surprisingly, many of these jobs, as presently constituted, are dead-end positions with little or no room for advancement. In addition, there is little or no union protection in the expanding service sectors (except in some state and local governments). The American economy depends upon the expanding service sector to provide employment for the surplus labor force of women and young black male adults. That employment is low-wage, dead-end, and unprotected.

The rise in jobs in the service sector was an important and necessary occurrence, but a mixed blessing! Without this expansion, unemployment would have been astronomically high and human suffering and perhaps unrest intolerably high. In a sense the supply of low-wage labor created a demand. The resulting new jobs are unsatisfactory, providing inadequate income, stability, or opportunity.

The economy is becoming dichotomized between a narrowing good job sector and an expanding marginal job sector. The U.S. is increasingly characterized by a dual labor market with separate labor forces and very different income prospects. Much of the rise in two-career families is due to declining wage prospects of male employees which force both wives and husbands to work in order to earn a sufficient income.[7]

Small business
When we switch from an examination of employment to an examination of employers, a striking pattern emerges. Almost all jobs created in the 1970s were created by small businesses. In one sense, this is not surprising. Big business is concentrated in the materially productive industries, not in the expanding service fields. In another sense, however, this has profound implications for the creation of jobs. David Birch found in his study of 5.6 million U.S. business establishments accounting for 80 per cent of private sector employment, that about two-thirds of the increase in new net jobs between 1969 and 1976 were generated by businesses with twenty or fewer employees![8] In addition, firms less than four years of age generated 80 per cent of new jobs in the economy. The service and trade sectors introduced many more new jobs than the industrial sectors. Half of new jobs were due to the "births" of new firms and half were produced by independent businessmen and women. Birch argues:

> A pattern begins to emerge in all of this. The job-generating firm tends to be small. It tends to be dynamic (or unstable, depending on your viewpoint) – the kind of firm that banks feel very uncomfortable about. It tends to be young. In short, the firms that can and do generate the most jobs are the ones that are the most difficult to reach through conventional policy initiatives (*The Job Generation Process*, p. 17).

To expand Birch's policy implication: recapitalization policies that attempt to strengthen industrial America are aimed at large companies, those least likely to create jobs. The low-wage, unstable, small-business service sectors are generating the jobs in the United States as the 1980s begin. Policies designed to recapitalize and reindustrialize the manufacturing or industrial sectors must be examined in terms of their ability to provide increased employment, preferably of good jobs.[9]

High technology

The recapitalization strategy exacts costs. Services, especially government services, will decline as capital is funneled into industrial renovation. But, over the long run, the contention is, the growth of highly productive industries will emerge and provide more employment and higher incomes. High-technology industries are singled out as among the "winner industries." They are not only profitable, but provide the technology for reindustrializing American industry. Gains in productivity in particular are dependent upon new technology, new machines, and processes that increase production per worker. Such industries as computers, microelectronics, and instruments have been forecast as the growth industries of the near future.

Microelectronics in particular, and computers in general, are seen by some analysts as tools with which to overcome the slowdown in productivity growth that practically all industrial countries have encountered. The U.S., it is claimed, leads the world in high-technology production processes. As demand expands for high-technology processes in all industries, U.S. exports will expand apace. The reindustrialization of the United States, at least the logic of recapitalization argues, demands to a greater or lesser extent the growth of high-technology industries and processes.

What concerns us here is the capacity of high-technology industries to generate jobs. We suspect that relatively few jobs will be generated by high-tech firms. As technology is introduced and productivity increases, fewer workers are needed to make the same amount of goods. Thus, for high-technology industries to expand, employment demand for their products must expand faster than productivity growth. Since the growing high-technology industries are heralded as the employers of the future, we decided to study the employment effects of high-tech in recent years.

Defining high technology

The first task is to decide which industries to include or exclude. We discovered that defining high-technology industries in terms of an inner logic is a difficult task. The phrase "high-technology" is not only a possible categorization of industries or technologies; it is also political advertising hype for U.S. industry.[10] High technology as a gleaming phrase is not dissimilar to the familiar advertising tags of "new" or "new-improved." As technologies became suspect in an increasingly environmentally conscious age and as traditional manufacturing industries declined, U.S. technology (and industry) needed re-legitimating. Suddenly, in the 1970s, political rhetoric and economic analysis pointed to two kinds of technology: plain, old, dirty *technology*, and new, improved, clean *high technology*. Great political importance has been attached to productivity as a panacea and to high technology as its wellspring.[11] Industries lucky enough to be identified as high-technology are likely to be the main beneficiaries of reindustrialization policies targeted at productivity and exports.[12]

We are not interested so much in the reality or integrity of any single definition of high technology. Rather, this discussion can be seen as an attempt at political forecasting. Some combination of industries may benefit in the near future from government policies targeted at the slogan of high technology. We look at a number of combinations and try to assay their employment potential.

We have located three different definitions of high-tech and corresponding industry lists. The first (the "Sci-Tech" definition) characterizes as high-tech those industries with high levels (13.7 per cent or more) of scientists, engineers, and technicians in the labor force. The second definition of high-tech concentrates on industries with an above average intensity (9.6 per cent of investment) of research and development ("R & D" definition). The last list uses a combination of high proportion of scientists and technicians with a highly skilled labor force. This list we call the "Mass." definition because it originated in the Massachusetts Division of Employment Security and has no formal definition. We do not defend any of these definitions; we too find them peculiar.

But they are what is used to delineate high-tech industries. Table 6.2 presents the three lists of industries that derive from these definitions.[13]

These three lists of high-technology industries encompass twenty-five industries; only eight qualify under all three definitions. The nebulous quality of the high-tech concept makes the choice of various definitions, of course, political decisions (see Table 6.2).

TABLE 6.2 *Twenty-five high-technology industries classified by three definitions*

Def.	SIC*	Name
@‡	281	Industrial chemicals
@‡	282	Plastics
@‡$	283	Drugs
‡	287	Agricultural chemicals
$	348 (19)	Ordnance**
@‡	351	Engines and turbines
@‡$	357	Office and computing machines
@ $	361	Electrical distribution equipment
@ $	362	Electrical industrial apparatus
$	363	Household appliances
$	364	Electric lighting and wiring equipment
‡$	365	Radio and TV equipment
@‡$	366	Communications equipment
@‡$	367	Electronic components
$	369	Miscellaneous electrical equipment, supplies
@‡	372	Aircraft and parts
@ $	376	Space vehicles and guided missiles***
$	379	Miscellaneous transport equipment
@‡$	381	Engineering and scientific instruments
@‡$	382	Measuring and control instruments
@‡$	383	Optical instruments
‡$	384	Medical instruments
‡$	385	Ophthalmic goods
@‡$	386	Photographic equipment and supplies
‡$	387	Watches, clocks

@ Mass. definition.
‡ R & D definition.
$ Sci-Tech definition.
* For source of definitions see notes to Table 6.3.   SIC, or standard industrial codes, are used in various Commerce Department statistics to identify industries by product.
** The SIC code for ordnance was changed from 19 to 348 in 1972.
*** Data not available prior to 1977.

The recent growth of high-technology industries provides a means for predicting their future growth. Table 6.3 compares the number of jobs created between 1969 and 1979 in the various lists of high-technology industries with the employment experience in the manufacturing sector, the private sector, and the overall economy.

TABLE 6.3 *Employment levels in high-technology industries (various definitions), manufacturing, and the private sector, U.S. 1969–79 (thousands)*

	1979	1974	1969	1969–79 absolute change	% change 1969–79	% change 1974–79
9-industries	2132.8	1623.2	1688.8	443.9	26.3	28.6
R & D def.	3622.8	3269.3	3467.9	154.9	4.5	10.2
Sci-Tech def.	3645.9	3288.5	3574.3	71.6	2.0	9.5
Mass. def.	3492.0	3325.4	3322.8	169.2	5.1	5.0
24-industries	4694.1	4596.0	4834.0	−139.9	−2.9	2.1
All manufacturing	20972	20016	20121	851	4.2	4.8
All private	73870	64050	57914	15956	27.6	15.3
All employment	89482	78334	70141	19341	27.6	14.2

* The three definitions of high-tech include a total of twenty-five industries; for one of them (SIC 376) data are not available prior to 1977. Thus, "24-industries" is the largest sample of high-tech industries. "9-industries" is made up of the eight industries that overlapped on all three definitions, plus SIC 385, which was combined with SIC 383 in the 1969 and 1974 data sets.
Source: *Employment and Earnings*, March 1980, vol. 27, 3, pp. 58–70; March 1975, vol. 21, 9, pp. 52–64; March 1970, vol. 16, 9, pp. 44–58.

Employment increases
Strikingly few of the total number of new jobs in the 1970s were created by the three sets of high-technology industries. Job generation ranges from a low of 71,600 for the Sci-Tech definition with a growth of employment of only 2 per cent, to a high of 169,000 jobs with a 5.1 per cent growth for the Mass. definition. Compared to the 19 million jobs and growth of 27.6 per cent in employment in the economy as a whole during the 1970s, high technology does not seem like a promising job generator. Taken together, the three definitions suggest that in terms of employment, the high-technology industries produced jobs at about the same slow rate as

manufacturing in general. The process of job generation by high-tech firms is, however, more complex.

The *all-inclusive* (the twenty-four industries named in the three lists of Table 6.2) and the *all-exclusive* (the nine industries on all three lists) definitions of high-technology industries, show a much more variable employment picture.

The all-inclusive definition experienced a *net loss* of about 140 thousand jobs in the 1970s. (The three-digit Standard Industrial Classification or SIC code that we use to define industry is widely used.) A tremendous drop in employment in a few industries produced this contraction. Industrial chemicals (SIC 281) declined by 142.9 thousand jobs, ordnance (SIC 19 in 1969, which was changed to SIC 348 by 1979) decreased by 267 thousand jobs, and aircraft and parts (SIC 372) lost 200 thousand jobs over the ten-year period. In addition, plastics (SIC 282), electrical distribution equipment (SIC 361), household appliances (SIC 363), radio and TV (SIC 365), engineering and scientific instruments (SIC 363), and watches and clocks (SIC 387), all reduced employment in that period. The employment gains in the other fifteen industries did not offset the losses in these nine. Explanations for this net loss include the decline in war purchases (SIC 348 and 372, ordnance and aircraft) by the U.S. government after Viet Nam. For the others, some combination of loss of demand to foreign competition (e.g., SIC 365, consumer electronics) and productivity-related displacement of workers (e.g., SIC 281, industrial chemicals) led to a decline in employment.

Defining high-technology industries as only those nine industries which fulfil all three definitions suggests a much rosier employment potential. These nine industries grew by 443.9 thousand jobs. Although this is a small proportion of total employment growth (2 per cent) over the ten-year period, the growth rate of these nine was similar to that of the economy in general and much higher than that for manufacturing as a whole. This finding should be understood in terms of the variability of manufacturing employment. While a limited set of industries grew quickly (9-industries definition), the broad pattern (24-industries definition) of high-tech employment growth was stagnation and decline. As some sectors of manufacturing such as office and computing machines (SIC 351) and communications equipment (SIC 366) add employees, others such as chemicals (SIC 281) and ordnance (SIC 348) contract. This pattern holds for the glamour industries that have recently been called high technology as well as for manufacturing overall. High-tech employment growth is at least partially tied to military spending.

Much of the growth that did occur in high-tech employment has been concentrated in the most recent years (post 1974). In the late 1970s there was acceleration in the high-tech job creation by all except the "Mass." definition. High-tech employment has been growing but is only now catching up with the high levels of the Viet Nam period. Certainly, the inflated military budgets of the 1980s will fund it further.

Output and jobs

The growth in demand for high-tech goods has far outstripped the growth of high-tech employment (see Table 6.4). In the 1970s, the output of (value added) high-tech goods using the most restricted and favorable definition ("9-industries") grew by 144 per cent while employment expanded 26 per cent over the same period. Conversely, using the most inclusive definition ("24-industries") value added grew slowly by 99 per cent and employment actually declined. High-tech was no more nor less efficient in producing employment from increased demand than were manufacturing

TABLE 6.4 *Growth in value added and employment in high-technology industries (various definitions) and manufacturing sector*

	1967–77 % growth value added	1969–79 % growth employment*
9-industries	144	26
R & D def.	97	5
Sci-Tech def.	132	2
Mass. def.	88	5
24-industries	99	−3
All manufacturing	123	4

* Value added data are not presently available for all industries in the various high-tech definitions after 1977. The 1966–77 and 1969–79 data for value added and employment should be treated as a rough comparison.
Source: computed from *Statistical Abstract of the United States, 1980*, Table 145, pp. 814–19, and Table 6.3 above, p. 101.

industries in general. For the entire manufacturing sector, a 30 per cent growth in demand produced a 1 per cent growth in employment. High-tech, in the "24-industries" and "Sci-Tech" definitions, did substantially worse than manufacturing in general in producing increased employment. The other two definitions ("R & D" and "Mass.") fared slightly better than manufacturing as a whole in converting demand into jobs. The "9-industries" definition of high-tech produced relatively large growth in employment with growing demand.

Of the more than 19 million jobs added to the U.S. economy between 1969 and 1979, less than 3 per cent (440,000 jobs) are attributable to employment expansion in high-tech fields (using the fastest growing "9-industries" definition). Even going from the 1974 trough in high-tech employment to 1979 these industries still furnished less than 5 per cent (510,000 jobs) of the growth of total employment.

The conversion of economic growth into employment growth is not a direct process. Intervening factors such as productivity changes, original employment and demand levels, and perceived future prospects will determine the level and rate of new jobs created by the high-technology industries. The question of which industries or constellations of industries are favored by general economic conditions or specific economic policies has important employment effects. More jobs will be created if high-tech industries such as those in the "9-industries" definition are favored than if a more global "24-industries" grouping is the target of economic incentives. Of course, which industries are favored by U.S. economic policy is a political outcome dependent on industry lobbying. In the U.S. it is more likely that an all-inclusive rather than relatively exclusive definition of high-tech will be favored by lawmakers.

A spokesperson for high-tech industries, such as the Massachusetts High-Tech Council, might argue that much high-tech employment is generated indirectly. Software companies, keypunchers, people who work on computers or word processors, and many other employment slots are created by high-technology outside of the high-tech industries. There is some truth in the suggestion that new employment, particularly software employment, has been generated by high technology. Computer programming and systems analysis are growth occupations spawned by the advent of computers. The expansion is at best partial because those programmers often replace bookkeepers and accountants. Increased secretarial efficiency through the use of word processors reduces the need for secretaries. Certainly, robots on the assembly line and "intelligent" cash registers reduce both the skill and number of required workers. The general point is that the loss of positions more than offsets the gains in the new types of employment.[14] Individual employers selectively reduce their labor force by using "high-tech" equipment.

The limitations of high-tech employment are not only quantitative; they also appear in its composition. High-tech firms employ proportionally fewer production workers and minorities than do manufacturing and the private sector (see Table 6.5). These groups suffer high unemployment rates and have the greatest difficulty in securing satisfying employment. Growth in high-tech employment, if it does occur, will not necessarily help those groups that need help the most.

TABLE 6.5 *Production workers, women, and minorities in high-technology industries (9-industries def.), in manufacturing sector, and in total employment (%)*

	Production workers*	Women**	Minorities**
High-tech	50	36	8
Manufacturing	72	31	11
Total U.S. employment	82	41	11

* Data for 1979.
** Data for 1978.
Source: *Employment and Earnings*, March 1980, Table B-2, pp. 58–66; January 1979, Table 30, pp. 179–80.

The preponderance of women in high-tech industries is not the result of affirmative action in the hiring of female engineers and computer programmers. Rather, the production workers who comprise half of high-tech industrial employment are typically women. These positions are, as Robert Howard has pointed out, characterized by "low-wage, dead-end jobs, unskilled, tedious work, and exposure to some of the most dangerous occupational health hazards in all of American industry."[15]

High-tech industry employment is no more (or even less) attractive to production workers than other manufacturing industries. In addition to low wages and hazardous work, employment is not stable. As the low percentage of production workers in Table 6.5 indicates, these industries are among the most automated in the U.S. economy. We can expect further loss of production jobs as these industries use their own products and engineering talent to further limit their work forces. For this reason the potentially deskilled, low-wage production jobs that do furnish some employment in high-tech firms will probably not grow as quickly as U.S. industries as a whole or move overseas to cheaper labor areas. Of course, the boom–bust cycle of military spending exacerbates this long-range instability.

Job location

Table 6.6, on the regional distribution of high-tech employment (again using the most restricted definition, now down to seven industries: see footnote* to Table 6.6), shows that the older industrial areas with their high unemployment rates actually lost high-tech jobs between 1972 and 1976, the latest year for state level

TABLE 6.6 *High-technology employment by region (7-industries def.), 1972–77*
(thousands)

Region**	1977	1972	Absolute change	% change
New England	166.3	136.9	30.6	21.4
Older industrial	447.1	459.7	−12.7	−2.8
South	99.3	78.4	20.9	26.6
West	351.6	261.6	90.0	34.4
U.S.***	1590	1396	194	13.9

* This definition of high technology included SIC codes 283, 357, 366, 367, 382, 383, 386. SIC 381 was omitted because employment was so low in surveyed states that it was not included in the Census's regional Tables.
** A sample of states was taken for each region, which included all states that had high-technology industries among their top five manufacturing industries plus a few large states with substantial employment. New England includes Massachusetts, Connecticut, and New Hampshire; the older industrial region includes Michigan, New Jersey, Indiana, Illinois, and New York. The southern region includes Georgia, W. Virginia, N. Carolina, Florida, Tennessee, and Alabama. The western region includes Arkansas, Louisiana, Texas, Arizona, California, and Washington.
*** Data for U.S. are not a sample; they cover the whole country.
Source: U.S. *Census of Manufacture*, 1977.

data. Two things are immediately apparent from the Table. The first is that much high-tech employment is in the older industrial states. The second is that as high-tech employment expanded across the entire U.S., the older industrial states suffered a net loss. If the pattern of regional employment growth between 1972 and 1977 continues, significant high-tech-generated employment benefits will not occur in the older industrial states. Competition with the union-free, low-wage, low-tax South and West will be difficult for older industrial areas with their expensive urban infrastructure, high wages, and large poor populations.

The New England region demonstrates that a once declining region can compete for manufacturing jobs. Massachusetts has improved the "business climate" for high-technology firms by limiting property and business taxes as well as spending a good deal of money on advertising to attract firms. Massachusetts was in a favorable position to attract these firms because it already had a reputation as a high-tech state as well as offering a highly skilled labor force and an attractive place to live. It is now becoming apparent in Massachusetts, however, that the high-tech boom is limited by slow growth in demand and competition from other regions of the U.S. and abroad. Of course, schools, roads, and other state services suffer as government funds are diverted to improve the "business climate."

The general point is that high-tech firms, like other manufacturing firms, are fleeing the high-cost older industrial states in search of cheaper production costs. Clearly, high-technology industries will not produce many jobs for the regions of the U.S. that most need jobs.

The regional distribution of high-technology growth highlights the limited usefulness of industrial expansion in these industries. High-tech growth has taken place in areas of low wages and low unionization. The regions of the country that are plagued by high unemployment and local government fiscal problems are not likely to benefit from the minimal employment (and taxation) expansion of high-tech industries. A military-led boom in high-tech production and employment will not evenly benefit the different regions of the U.S.[16]

The job creation prospects of the high-technology sector are not bright. Those jobs that are created will be unevenly distributed across the U.S. and, except for the white-collar professional positions, will generally be of poor quality. The political decision to favor high-technology, high-productivity, high-export industries is only beginning to be discussed. Those industries which benefit from targeted economic incentives may grow and provide increased employment. Unfortunately, that employment is unlikely to be substantial or to benefit those regions of workers in greatest need of a job boost.

In the 1970s employment in the United States had been increasingly segmented between a contracting primary or good job sector and an expanding secondary or bad job sector. The recent new jobs have appeared in trade, finance, and services; by and large, they are low-paying, low-security, dead-end positions. Although high-technology industries expanded in production and profitability, they contributed little to employment growth.

Our fear is that recapitalization policies will produce very limited growth in employment even if the high-tech, high-productivity, export-oriented goals are achieved. But we do not believe that those economic goals will be easily accomplished. It is more likely that capital freed by government will be invested in a rather unstructured search for profits. If the future extends the past, much of recapitalization investment will move into the already expanding service sector and produce employment there – albeit of dubious quality.

Upward redistribution and recapitalization

The dominant economic ideology of America is shifting from stressing consumption and growth to promoting austerity and growth. In the old ideology growth bred consumption which bred more growth. The more and faster the economy grew, the richer everyone would become. Now we are told that consumption stops growth or at least slows it to the point where it no longer makes us richer, because consumption erodes savings and reduces business investment.

The recapitalization analysis becomes suspect when viewed in those terms of consumption vs. investment capital, and taxes and wages vs. profits. The recapitalist form of reindustrialization depends, at least in the short-term, on redistribution, i.e., negative redistribution aggravating inequalities. The degree of inequality in American society will be exacerbated as income and services to the poor and near-poor are constrained and higher profits and lower taxes for the corporate elite are legislated.

Although the outlines of the recapitalization ideology became clear with Ronald Reagan, recapitalization as a political movement is older than Ronald Reagan's presidency and will outlive his peculiar political amalgam of policies. In fact, the recapitalization approach has filtered into federal policies and business-wage bargaining since the mid-1970s.

The recapitalization policy prescriptions, begun in the Carter Administration but vastly sped up under Reagan, consist mainly of a redistribution of national income upwards, expanding inequalities, threatening the poor, the old, and the near-old, as well as working people who find their bargaining position weakened in an atmosphere of economic crisis orchestrated to legitimate draconian policies.

The ideology of recapitalization policies differentiates it from other attempts to deal with economic difficulties. Recapitalization policies, not only the reactionary variant, *deliberately* set out to increase inequalities. Explicit in the tax cuts to spur personal savings and investment is the goal of increasing the income of the rich, who hopefully will save or invest rather than consume their extra income. Corporate tax reductions will immediately benefit the already comfortable shareholders, particularly if great surges in investment do not absorb the funds released by the tax cuts. The economic ideology of recapitalization is productivity; the social ideology is the widening of inequalities.

Recapitalization legitimates and accentuates the tendency in recent years toward inegalitarianism and the lowering of income for those already less well-off.[17]

Many, if not most Americans experienced a decline in their real incomes over the last few years of the 1970s. Payments to those dependent upon government transfers did not keep up with inflation as government spending was increasingly attacked as inflationary. For the average production worker the situation was little better. Real incomes lagged as the government under Carter pursued slow-growth, pro-business economic policies.

Table 6.7 indicates that spendable real weekly earnings rose slowly for both the average worker and the worker with a family of four between 1960 and 1977. Between 1977 and 1980 sizable decreases of about 10 per cent in real income occurred across the board, even for relatively highly paid workers in the manufacturing sector of the economy.

TABLE 6.7 *Average weekly earnings in constant (1967) dollars*

Sector	1960	1965	1970	1975	1978	1979	Jan.–May 1980
All private non-agricultural							
Average worker							
Gross	91.0	101.0	103.0	101.5	104.3	101.0	95.2
Spendable	74.0	83.9	82.7	82.2	84.7	81.8	76.8
Family of four							
Spendable	82.3	91.7	90.2	90.4	92.5	89.5	84.0
Manufacturing							
Average worker							
Gross	101.2	113.8	114.6	118.4	127.6	123.5	112.4
Spendable	81.8	94.3	99.6	94.1	101.1	97.6	91.6
Family of four							
Spendable	90.3	102.4	99.4	103.2	110.0	106.6	100.1

Source: *Statistical Abstract of the United States, 1980*, Table 700, p. 422.

Further, Table 6.7 gives us some insight into the redistributive effects of recent economic policies, the forerunners of deeper recapitalization efforts. Although slow growth and high inflation plagued the late 1970s, Gross National Product continued to grow in real terms, albeit slowly. The average real income of American workers declined. What is particularly striking about this Table is the lack of growth in income of the average worker since *1960*. While the GNP doubled in real terms over that period and per capita GNP grew by 61 per cent, average earnings stagnated. Even the highly unionized manufacturing sector worker only increased her or his spendable income by 10 per cent in this twenty-year period. While labor's earnings were stagnant between 1965 and 1977, they are no longer. In more recent years they have declined. Real losses in earning power even for manufacturing workers have been occurring.

Family income did not decline (not shown in Table 6.7) because more and more American families became two- or three-income families. What is striking about family income is that in real terms family income was the same in 1980 as in 1970 even though the labor force participation rate of married women grew from 40.8 per cent in 1970 to 49.4 per cent in 1980.[18]

For people dependent upon the federal and state governments for income the situation was just as bad. Social security payments in constant dollars have declined since 1977. Aid to Families with Dependent Children payments also declined over the 1970s. Table 6.8 compares the growth in public aid payments in the late 1970s with the growth in the Consumer Price Index. Government payments for social security and for the poor did not keep up with the inflation rate, although social security payments did outpace real wages.

TABLE 6.8 *Average monthly transfer payments ($), percentage change from the previous year, and the Consumer Price Index, 1974–9*

	1974	1975	1976	1977	1978	1979	
Social security	$	$	$	$	$	$	
Aged	91	91	94	97	100	123	
Disabled	142	141	146	150	155	182	
AFDC	216	229	242	250	256	271	
Percentage change from previous year							*Total change 1974–9*
Social security							
Aged	–	0	3	3	3	23	35
Disabled	–	−0.7	4	3	3	17	28
AFDC	–	6	6	3	2	6	25
Consumer Price Index	–	9.1	5.8	6.5	7.7	11.3	47

Source: *Statistical Abstract of the United States, 1980*, Table 570, p. 345; Table 794, p. 478.

In the late 1970s the calls for consumer austerity began in earnest and attacks upon government spending intensified. An ideological shift to the political right occurred, scapegoating organized labor and the poor and championing the free enterprise system. The poor, the aged, and the average worker were already experiencing declining standards of living as their earning power was eroded by inflation and social service cuts and new jobs became increasingly low paid. The far-reaching recapitalization policies of the early 1980s will exacerbate the already declining fortunes of the average American as government transfer payments and private consumption are curtailed to stimulate investment in U.S. industry. Reactionary recapitalization has a strange attitude towards targeting: lower taxes to promote investment are untargeted while some already low-income groups are sharply targeted for even lower incomes.

The burden of changing the U.S. economy is being placed upon the most vulnerable populations, who will be slow and unlikely gainers from those changes.[19]

Dim prospects

In a pure reactionary Reaganite form, the recapitalization prescription will prove to be unworkable. On the economic level, it cannot work because of the basic contradiction between controlling inflation and increasing investment at the same time.[20] The U.S. presently has excesses of productive capacity and labor (high unemployment). Investment in new business ventures is conditional upon demand. If business does not foresee new demand, then the logical use for the capital freed to reindustrialize the United States is to buy up already existing firms, close down low-productivity plants, and replace them with high-productivity plants (which increases both profits and unemployment) and/or imitative marketing strategies (new versions of old products). Curtailing wage demands by labor, cutting government transfer payments and services, and pursuing anti-inflationary monetary policies tend to limit demand.

Thus, recapitalization will lead to increased profits for those big businesses that can count on relatively constant demand or have the market power to raise prices to cover sales losses, the loss of services and possibly wages by the poor and working classes, and a generally stagnant economy. An exception to the stagnation will probably be found in those sectors of the economy where demand will probably grow irrespective of consumer spending. High-technology industries, those industries which produce the tools that increase productivity for big business, will expand, creating a relatively few high-skilled jobs. It is doubtful, however, that the high-technology sector will create more jobs within the sector than its tools eliminate in manufacturing in general.

High-export sectors such as aerospace are relatively low employment industries. As we indicated in Chapter 3, export industries employed proportionally fewer workers for the quantity and value of goods produced than did U.S. manufacturing in general. Similarly, the high-technology sectors of the economy employ relatively few people because of their already high productivity. Increasing productivity in these sectors, which to a large extent overlap, will not create jobs.

If new jobs are not going to be created and business is to receive a larger share of the national pie, where will that capital go? To date, most of the recapitalization–reindustrialization–revitalization discussion and legislation has centered on taking money from certain groups (the poor, students, the old, the unemployed, through cuts in government spending) and delivering that money to business, particularly big business. Within America's largest corporations at least four groups struggle over the distribution of the corporations' resources: workers, management, lenders, and owners. Wages and salaries, investment, and dividends are competing possible uses of the corporate windfall that recapitalization promises. We have already discussed investment at length and our conclusion is that at best investment is conditional upon other factors such as inflation and perceived future demand. The struggle over wages and dividends has largely been ignored by recapitalization analysts, probably because the struggle is already ongoing and the forces representing the shareowners are winning.

Our analysis in Chapter 5 demonstrated the tendency of manufacturing firms to pay an increased proportion of profits as dividends to stockholders. The current tendency toward higher interest rates will tend to distribute a greater proportion of corporate income to those large institutional investors (banks, insurance companies, money market funds) that provide capital to corporate America. Finally, the prospect of increased labor income, either absolutely or proportionally, is dim. The labor market effect of recapitalization, particularly cuts in social services ("the social safety net"), is to undercut worker bargaining power *vis-à-vis* management. Piven and Cloward interpret the Reagan attack on social welfare programs as a "new class war" to undermine the bargaining power of labor.[21] Certainly the decline of the unionized manufacturing sector signals a limiting of union influence (at least in the short run) over wages as well as over national political activity. The present prospects for the distribution of national income in the case of economic recovery seem to point toward increased inequalities, as the rich and their corporations profit, while the majority of working Americans learn to survive with less.[22]

The reindustrialization strategies will not have a beneficial effect upon employment or inflation. They will worsen inequalities between groups within society, as minorities and women suffer in a job market increasingly split between a few high-paid, high-technology employment opportunities and a growing low-paid, low-skill service sector. They will also exacerbate the problems of the aging U.S. industrial belt running from the New England area to the Midwest. U.S. corporations with increased capital for investment will continue to put that capital in the Southwest or overseas where labor costs are cheaper. The reactionary and moderate supporters of recapitalization favor the lifting of the very few controls society has over the investment process, freeing corporate capital to follow the god of profits. First and foremost in the pursuit of that god is the need to keep labor costs (and union organization) as low as possible.

For certain areas such as Detroit, the state of Maine, and St. Louis, a permanent or semi-permanent depression can be expected as money moves out and people stay. The high Detroit unemployment rate of the early 1980s is likely to continue or worsen. Even if the auto industry rebounds, the new plants will be located outside the industrial Northeast and Midwest. Further, the new or retooled plants are increasingly capital- rather than labor-intensive. On Chrysler's new K-car assembly lines, welding, once done entirely by human workers, is now 99 per cent the task of robots. Even with expanded output the growth in auto employment will be low and may even decrease.

Recapitalization policies will be disastrous, even if they momentarily benefit from a defense-led industrial boom. Unemployment will rise, incomes will fall, the economy will, at best, grow slowly and big-business will do very well. What is good for GM (or

Exxon or ITT) is not necessarily good for America. The threat of increasing inequalities between regions, races, and the sexes will exacerbate as business freedom and wealth benefit.

These policies will not be pursued with impunity. Resistance may arise; compromises will be made, especially if the economy falters. Opposition will force some movement away from the worst offenses of the reactionary recapitalization that was initiated by Reagan in the early 1980s and may produce a call for progressive alternatives to recapitalization, in all of its forms. We deal with this theme in the next section.

Part Two

Moving beyond Reaganism and liberalism

Chapter 7
Old beginnings: contradictions and tensions in bureaucratic liberalism

The answer to the reactionary recapitalization onslaught of Reaganomics is not a return to liberalism or an outing with neo-liberalism. The recapitalization experience should lead liberals and progressives to rethink what they seek and how to get it. A re-evaluation and redirecting of liberal and progressive policies and programs is desperately needed. Restoration of past ideas and programs to their former seats of glory and levels of funding should not be the objective. For the U.S. has changed very drastically since 1964, and liberal programs encounter major tensions and resistances. Consequently, a moderate, less expensive welfare state and more pro-investment neo-liberalism à la Senators Paul Tsongas (Mass.) or Gary Hart (Colorado) is inadequate. Nor is it a sufficient response to advocate a modified welfare liberalism (à la Secretary of Labor under Carter, Ray Marshall, and the AFL-CIO) which maintains the welfare state and adds to anti-inflation policy both price-wage controls and some investment targeting.[1]

At best, current liberal approaches are essentially policies largely geared to the next elections. Certainly that is a necessary orientation, but it must be infused with new thinking and approaches, not just modifications of the past. The Democratic economic policy announced in June of 1982 was a clear example of neo-liberal recapitalization. It endorsed the need to recapitalize but did not abandon the welfare state. A jobs program to rebuild U.S. infrastructure financed by a cap on the third year of the Reagan tax cut was the modified welfare state proposal of the Democrats. Although clearly more caring than reactionary recapitalization, the Democrats have not come to grips with the changed U.S. political economy of the post-post-World War II period. Caring recapitalization is only somewhat more likely to deal with U.S. economic problems than the heartless recapitalization of Ronald Reagan.

Some do not accept this orientation because they view the Reagan election as a result of the Carter failure. If Jimmy Carter had been a more effective president and candidate, this interpretation runs, an out-of-the-mainstream extremist like Ronald Reagan would not have been elected. This explanation is not only reassuring to liberals, but has much to support it, as political scientist Douglas Hibbs of Harvard University has shown in his analysis of factors influencing voting in the 1980 election.[2] Public opinion data indicate that a majority favor liberal welfare state policies. In 1982 the opposition to the drastic Reaganite cuts in social programs lends further backing to this view. According to this interpretation, Carter lost because the economy and his presidency were in bad shape, not because the welfare state had been repudiated.

This view presents several difficulties even if one rejects the now common themes that liberalism is in disarray or eroding or that radical baggage is too heavy for a conservative time. The Carter Administration itself embraced "moderate recapitalization" and rejected many liberal platforms.[3] Concern with productivity and the lagging economic supremacy of the U.S. led to its proposals for "revitalization" or "reindustrialization." On a lesser scale, Carter's Administration paralleled Reagan's tax reductions on corporations, though the Carter program would not have been so flagrantly inegalitarian as Reagan's. As we pointed out in Chapter 1, Reaganism and Carterism are variants of recapitalization.

We accept the contention that Reagan's success was largely a reflection of Carter's failure as a candidate and leader. This means that Democrats, maybe even liberal Democrats, may soon regain political control. Liberal or moderate recapitalization policies will appeal to an electorate bludgeoned by the coldness of reactionary recapitalization. But liberal or neo-liberal Democrats who accept the tenets of recapitalization ideology or prefer to return to the days of bureaucratic liberalism will be no more successful in dealing with the problems of the day. The "accepted wisdom" is wrong because it ignores the "great transformations" that render past policies inadequate.

Major changes in the structure of the American economy have produced new, important issues so that reinstalling liberal policies will not be effective. This issue was the theme of Chapter 2.

Throughout this book we have demonstrated that the "accepted wisdom" of recapitalization is seriously flawed. Returning to pre-recapitalization liberal policies will be no less flawed. For the U.S. is no longer the economic and military colossus that could dominate the world with its foreign policy and industrial exports. U.S. international power, while still great, is no longer overwhelming.

The decline of U.S. power in the world political economy has been accompanied internally by the growth of major corporations' independent structural power. Investment and production decisions by the largest corporations presently hold the key to the economic health of the United States. Through their concentrated decision-making power these corporations chart the course of future prosperity or decline. In addition to the inherently undemocratic nature of private corporate power, the U.S. must now come to grips with the reality that big business is not a benign, rational godfather that will protect the U.S. economy. Rather, U.S. multinational firms play nation against nation in order to make the best business deal, domestic conglomerates gobble up available U.S. investment capital in order to diversify their portfolios, and speculation rises as clever capitalists eschew the task of production and job generation in favor of "playing" the various markets.

Private investment decisions benefiting the corporation making them are often disastrous for the U.S. citizenry. Speculation and international production mean that fewer U.S. jobs, taxes, and exports are generated by U.S. corporations. The new destructive reality of corporate investment behavior joins the old realities of oligopolistic inflation, business power in politics, and over-controlled workplaces. These dangers suggest that *business* rather than government power needs curtailing.

Industrial shifts that are intimately linked to corporate investment decisions are producing new forms of employment. The service industries, characterized in many of their segments by low-paying, low-productivity, unprotected, and marginalized employment, provide the growth occupations of the 1980s. High technology holds little hope of providing many jobs. Jobless growth may be the social disaster of the 1980s.

The loss of world dominance, the destabilizing web of international trade, irrational corporate power, and an economy that produces inadequate employment (both quantitatively and qualitatively) are the new realities of U.S. economic and social life. The bureaucratic liberalism of the New Deal and Great Society, with its reliance on regulation, tax policy, and transfers is better equipped to cope with this "great transformation" than reactionary recapitalization with its decimation of the transfer and tax system and its religious commitment to private corporate profits and decision-making. But it is not well enough equipped to offer effective economic and social redevelopment. While the old liberal goals of a caring, just society are still worthy and certainly worth struggling for, the liberal policies of welfare Keynesianism are not adequate means to those goals.

Even if Reaganism is largely repudiated, the changes made and signified by Reaganite recapitalization are profound. *The U.S. cannot simply go back to Carter's 1976 or 1978, much less to Johnson's 1964.* It is now a different country politically, economically, and morally, requiring new ideas and processes.

In the next section, we discuss the social changes affecting U.S. political life. The following section on bureaucratic liberalism analyzes some difficulties in liberal/welfare state policies in light of the transformations that are occurring.

The limited roles of taxes and transfers

The changes and strains that we have noted make it difficult to propose restoring New Deal/Great Society liberalism. New approaches, new thinking, new images of a better society are necessary; for the very basis of the post-war consensus which permitted an activist government has been severely weakened.

American-style liberalism was based on economic growth, taxation, and transfers (e.g., Social Security, Aid to Families with Dependent Children, unemployment insurance, veterans' benefits, social services, Medicaid, Medicare, food stamps). National governmental measures followed Keynesian lines in their emphasis on monetary and fiscal policies to produce growth with minimal interference in the economic market. Growth would swell tax revenues. Taxes would be on a progressive basis, and the post-tax distribution of income would be more egalitarian than the pre-tax. A slice of these swollen government receipts would be spent on transfer or social programs to provide a level of security to all citizens. Both cash and non-cash transfers would concentrate on low-income people, further reducing inequalities and encouraging a more caring society.

Large federal, state, and local organizations developed to regulate activities and to dispense services. Lacking direct control over crucial processes of decision-making, government relied on procedures, regulations, and guidelines to achieve its aims. Government employment, especially at state and local levels, increased mightily.

"Bureaucracy" has become an epithet aimed at governmental agencies largely because of the irritation with red tape, "outside" control (i.e., power seemed to rest in the governmental funders and the bureaucratic employees rather than in the localities and neighborhoods which received funds or services), and overly detailed, hard-to-follow regulations. "Bureaucratic liberalism" is not too severe a judgment of the approach.[4]

Many trends and pressures oppose this form of liberalism, making its restoration in a pure or modified (neo-liberal) form unlikely and undesirable. The danger of inflation has made high, fairly continuous growth like that of the 1960s unlikely. Supply-side economics' hope of blending cost-free high growth with low inflation has failed. It was always an unlikely conjurer's trick. For an economic expansion kindles fear of price rises, leading to policy efforts to retard growth. Low, discontinuous growth is likely to be the hallmark of the 1980s as combating inflationary tendencies remains the primary target. Consequently, the important growth basis of liberalism is undermined. Nor, as discussed in Chapters 2 and 6, is the kind of growth that the U.S. will experience likely to generate much employment.

Taxation as a liberal strategy is also in long-run and short-run difficulties. As a long-run redistributive approach, it has largely failed. In the U.S. and in many other countries, the pre-tax and post-tax distributions of income are little different. (Indeed, in France a study showed greater post-tax than pre-tax inequalities!) A redistributive tax structure is difficult to enact and more difficult to maintain.[5]

More important, perhaps, is that taxes are resented as "the taking away of hard-earned income by the government." Since the generation of enough tax revenues to make a pronounced difference in the share of national income going to the minority at the bottom would require increasing the taxes of the many, as well as the few who are the very rich, it will be difficult to have a strong tax system.

The Reagan Administration has made changes in the tax structure that will have short-run and perhaps longer-term effects. The deep reductions of the 1981 Reagan tax package mean that it will require enormous political will and/or high economic growth to raise governmental revenues swiftly. In particular, the indexing of tax rates (so that individuals are not moved into higher tax brackets as their money but not their real income increases), will be difficult to repeal and will dampen governmental revenues. The tax basis for expanded public expenditures and improved redistribution, if not closed off, is severely narrowed. As neo-conservative Irving Kristol noted: "The conservative deficit ... resulting from [tax] cuts ... has put the welfare state in a moderately tight straitjacket for the rest of this decade at least."[6]

On the spending side, social policies, the cash and service programs, are attacked from the right, left, and center. Dissatisfaction with them often takes the form of a misguided attack on their staffs – as though they had untrammeled decision-making power. Whatever the truth may be, their costs and financing are indicted; they are charged with creating dependency and invading personal liberties; they are regarded as ineffective, wasteful, abused, or pernicious; they are said to destroy rather than build communities and a sense of community. Attitudes toward the welfare state are deeply ambivalent. Opinion data consistently make the point that Americans are generally eager for those particular benefits coming to them personally. But they also make it clear that the welfare state is not well loved among most Americans.[7] In short, social policies are not attractive to many. Welfare recipients much prefer a job to receiving welfare. Many others regard welfare as "handouts" to the unneedy, ungrateful, or undeserving.[8]

The transfer system will increasingly benefit the non-poor as the social security system grows in size absolutely and relatively, and benefits become more closely related to wages received during one's working life than they have been. (Social security benefits for the aged retired were fixed to replace more of the income of low-income wage-earners than of high-income wage-earners; that policy is being eroded.) Perhaps more important is that the clamor against transfers is great and the non-social security, means-tested transfers specifically aimed at low-income populations (e.g., AFDC) are likely to continue in disfavor.

In short, taxation and transfer have not, even under favorable growth conditions, produced much greater equality, though certainly inequalities would have grown without them. "Tax revolts" and "welfare backlash" now have a disturbing reality that further limits the usefulness of tax- and transfer-based policies. Economically, taxation in the capitalist state seeks to avoid adversely affecting the processes of profit and investment. Politically, an adequate transfer system can cause negative reactions, leading to its contraction – adequacy of benefits may lead to loss of political support. In general, letting the economic market do its work and then trying to offset the ensuing poverties and inequalities is a very limited strategy.

Taxation and transfers do have major positive roles in modern societies. But they cannot be relied upon to do as much of the task of humanizing and equalizing American society as liberalism has assigned to them.

Keynesian macro-economic policy versus industrial policy

Recapitalization and bureaucratic liberalism share an implicit Keynesian model of the U.S. economy. In this macro-economic model, economic aggregates (e.g., total national investment, savings, or GNP) point to the dynamics of the economy, and government economic policies are designed to affect these aggregates. This model assumes that the behavior of these aggregates accurately mirrors the ongoing daily functioning of the households, businesses, governments, and other institutions whose actions and interactions make up the economy. The institutions and disaggregated functioning of the economy are ignored. Macro- or Keynesian economic policy rarely concerns itself with the actual, detailed workings of the economy. This approach has always been flawed; now it is unworkable.

Keynesian policy and theory gave the appearance of coherence between 1950 and 1973 because the economy was growing under the umbrella of U.S. world dominance. The macro-economy has since disintegrated into various disorganized and even antagonistic micro-economies.

The recapitalization push will have varied economic repercussions on different sectors of the economy, leading to some investment in favored sectors and stagnation elsewhere. The macro-economic policies of Kennedy, Johnson, Carter, and Reagan were industrial policies – with specific (generally unknown) effects that differed by industrial sector and social class. Kennedy and Johnson, the beneficiaries of growth, did not politically need to separate out the differing costs and benefits because they were largely different rates of growth. More recent presidents are held accountable for the sectoral and class costs and benefits of economic policy because these effects are more apparent and damaging in an era of low or no growth. The micro-economic, targeted approach of industrial policy will become politically necessary as the essential reification that macro-policy implies is destroyed by the individual and corporate reality of uneven development.

Political mood

A simple return to liberal growth and welfare state policies is further complicated by changes in political mood and understanding in the United States. An important value shift has occurred. It began before Reagan but Reaganism strengthened it. The center of American politics and values has shifted to the right even though the ferocity and blatant unfairness of Reagan policies slowed the slide. A most striking and significant example of this shift is that, for the first time in many generations, politicians and prominent academics openly proclaim the doctrine of inequality. Some argue that it is the natural order of human nature. They see moving against inequality as requiring continual coercion. Greater equality, in their view, requires a more authoritarian social order.[9] Others say that it is too difficult to accomplish. Many contend that this society "cannot afford" greater equality: the rich and corporations must have more in order to save and invest; social programs not only require destructive taxation but maintain wage rates so that the U.S. economy cannot effectively compete in the world scene. The spread of such attitudes and beliefs undercuts the funding of social programs and retards the development of a positive consensus in American society.

That greater equality is hard to achieve, unsettling, and economically dangerous is an old argument. What is now said for the first time in several generations is that inequality is a good thing in itself. While some formulations and defenses are laughable, the important note is that the espousal of inequality has intellectual and moral respectability today. That was not the case only a few years ago. American beliefs in fairness and humaneness have been important props for the American welfare state of taxation and transfers. These beliefs are difficult to maintain when there is little chance of reciprocity, of gaining at another time from aid or generosity to those in less fortunate circumstances now. If a people accept the notion that "life is unfair" and that they have no interest in or possibility of doing something about that unfairness, the moral or normative basis of the welfare state erodes. Its economic basis collapsed earlier with the advent of low and unsteady growth.

Finally, the turn from liberalism has deprived policy of a theory of the American society and state. American liberalism largely accepted the once-popular political science dogma of a pluralist society, made up of a great variety of competing groups which enrolled people on the basis of a specific interest. Each of us was then represented in one concern or another by these interest groups. Parties competed for the support of interest groups; the secure democracy of America rested in the two parties' non-ideological, coalitional form which blunted the threat of extremist politics. A basic consensus on the desirability of growth and the welfare state was said to be triumphant and durable. Problems were increasingly technical rather than ideological issues, as President Kennedy declared in his 1962 speech at Yale University. Since no interest group dominated, democracy consisted of the choices offered by competition among interest groups. Representative democracy flourished,prevented authoritarianism, and offered the possibility that one might lose on a particular interest for a period but that one's position might be favored later or that the loss would be offset by a gain on another.

This textbook version of American democracy was hardy despite its obvious lack of relevance for the American case. The Reagan blitzkrieg of 1981 underlines the importance of media manipulation and heavy political spending, the lack of effective political counter-weights, and the domination of a particular ideology – rather than the smooth, responsive working of a pluralist political process. While Democrats did contest the unfairness of the Reagan tax cuts and the hardships of his reduction in social programs, their basic argument was the failure of his economic program "to work."

Most left analysts have fared no better. An indication of the left theoretical void is that many who were sharp critics of social programs suddenly moved to support them against the Reaganite onslaught. The change in position is defensible. What is lacking is a clearly thought out explanation of the switch and a re-evaluation of why they were in error in their former position. Self-criticism is absent on the left in regard to their analysis of the welfare state.

The absence of a "good" theory indicates the changed circumstances of the U.S. and of its liberals and progressives. The world is more unsettled than they thought. New ways of thinking are needed. In the final two chapters we recommend departures from recapitalist and liberal orthodoxies.

Chapter 8
Progressive departures

Difficulties, tensions, and contradictions should not be occasions for despair. They are likely to be the spur to creativity: they certainly need to be if liberals and progressives are to carry more weight in this country. The danger in the post-Reagan period is of falling back to past practices or of moving forward with attractively packaged gimmicks, the meretricious appeal of the newly minted.

There is no easy solution to the compounded economic problems and conflicts produced by the transformations of the U.S. political economy – the instability of international trade, the irrationality and undemocratic nature of corporate power, and the threat of jobless growth. To solve these problems while preserving liberal/progressive commitments to equality and fairness in a conservative political era is a difficult task. Panaceas are easy to produce, and tend to follow one another as reality and elections discredit their authors.

Progressive departures from the unworkable or limited paths of recapitalization and bureaucratic liberalism require breaking through the boundaries of accepted economic thought and present political outlooks. The restorationist non-solutions of Reaganomics and neo-liberalism cannot work.

A new inning will follow for liberal/progressive politics. As Reaganomics strikes out in the harsh light of economic reality and popular struggle, other business-biased panaceas will come to bat. Liberals and progressives must be ready to contest them and offer more effective, fair alternatives.

In this chapter we seek to stir fresh thinking by offering challenging lines of development. These arguments present untried alterna-

129

tives, but they should be part of a debate about new ways of improving the American economy and society. Liberals and progressives should not be stuck in old ways and ideas. We hope to stimulate debate about a substitute for Great Society liberalism with its bureaucratic welfare state and obsession with growth rates. A more democratic–egalitarian vision is suggested in the context of new approaches to dealing with old issues of growth and employment and new issues of planning and work relations.

Macro–micro

The economic policies that America needs will be complex. Unfortunately, the current discussion has hit upon "industrial policy" as a panacea-like solution to America's ills. Industrial policy, whatever it means and whatever variants develop, cannot be enough.

The present industrial policy outlook arises in reaction to the Keynesian growth policy of the postwar period, which has been indicted for focusing exclusively on macro (economy as a whole) issues of regulating demand and ignoring the micro (firm and industry) issues of improving productivity and organization. The charge is largely inaccurate since the deliberate growth policies linked with the American version of Keynesianism have been devoted to reducing taxes on business to stimulate investment (the capital goods sector), generally through accelerated depreciation allowances. Chapter 5 reported the great effort devoted to this purpose: the percentage of profits going to taxes had been declining even before the gigantic business tax cuts of 1981.

The current call for industrial policy seeks more than tax reductions as governmental aid to business; it demands not only deregulation but capital funds as well. That help may be necessary and even desirable, especially where assistance is linked to *quid pro quos* – a specification of what aided firms are expected to do in terms of investment, employment, and prices.

The possibilities of industrial policy should not obscure its dependence on successful macro policies. An economy caught in recession or stagflation will not be able to generate demand or stimulate innovation. Industrial policies to improve the prospects of particular industries will encounter difficulties in a stagnating economy. Inflationary pressure will reduce chances of sales abroad. Industrial policy cannot provide an escape from questions of demand, interest rates, exchange rates, and inflation. Micro policies cannot be effective without a supportive set of macro policies.

Macro policies are in trouble. The instruments of monetary (money supply, rates of interest) and fiscal (budget deficits, changes in taxation) policy have no certain consequences today. The financial community invents money, circumventing efforts to regulate – and even to measure – the supply of money and credit. Accounting procedures and capital mobility reshape the intent of tax policies. The traditional macro instruments are too blunt and manipulable to affect positively the growth of the economy or the maintaining of stable prices. Nor does general stimulation of the economy assure that major industries will be saved or developed.

New orientations to macro policy are needed today which recognize the necessity of affecting the nature and the content, as well as the rate of growth, of GNP and which accept the possibility of wage–price–profit controls. But, as we discuss later in this chapter, the terms of those controls are a crucial social and political issue.

The macro-micro mix is more complicated than either a macro or a micro industrial policy approach. Technological developments, such as the majic of high-tech industries, which underlie much of the industrial policy outlook, cannot alone solve America's problems.

International trade

The espousal of free trade has become the hallmark of a sophisticated, knowledgeable understanding of economics. The absence of tariffs, quotas, and other barriers to the free and easy movement of goods and capital across national borders is considered the essence of efficiency, productivity, and the wise allocation of resources. Protectionism runs the danger of high prices, sheltering inefficient industries and firms, the misallocation of resources, and retaliation by nations harmed by the trade barriers.

The argument for free trade is certainly substantial. But unrestrained commerce and finance exact heavy costs for many countries. The difficulties of one nation compound the problems of others. For example, high interest rates in the United States in the early 1980s attracted funds from West Germany, making it difficult to stabilize the mark and forcing higher interest rates (and prices) there in order to encourage capital to stay at home where it might be invested productively. Devaluing the dollar, as the Carter Administration permitted to happen in its early days, may promote exports but makes imports more expensive, increasing inflationary pressures. A visible danger is that Japan's exports threaten major industries in several capitalist countries besides the U.S.

The question that should emerge from its burial place is whether the U.S. and other countries can effectively run their domestic economies with the astonishingly high level of imports and exports and free capital movement which now prevail. (Chapter 3 offers data on this trade expansion.) In the U.S. there is an emerging contradiction between domestic economic health, which requires raising employment and consumption, and the need for high-investment, high-productivity, high-technology export growth. The issue is not mainly the safeguarding of threatened industries like auto and steel, which is the usual way that protectionism emerges as an issue. The broader, more significant, more enduring issue than this "piecemeal protectionism" is the worldwide instability that is produced by enormous international trade and capital movements. Can the U.S. (or any other nation) solve its economic problems if it is so deeply pressured by international economic questions?

The Organization for Economic Cooperation and Development (OECD) nations, including the U.S., are pressuring Japan to lower its exports. The demand is not only for fewer exports of a particular kind but for Japan to decrease its overall level of exports. This is a modified protectionism, centering on the total level of imports and exports, rather than on the protection of a particular industry. If one examines what the nations in the European Common Market do rather than what they say, creeping, segmented protectionism is an important part of their collective policy, particularly in agriculture. Free trade is the slogan; protectionism is everywhere the practice.

It is now time to raise the heretical question of whether the plight of many countries can be lightened without a general reduction in the flow of goods and capital across national borders. It has been raised in Britain. "The Alternative Economic Policy" that has been suggested by the Cambridge Economic Policy Group contends that Britain must break with international trade orthodoxy.[1] Britain can only recover economically if it limits imports and capital outflow for some period. The plan has two drawbacks. One is that a nation like Britain with an enormous need for imports in its productive processes and a similar need to export will have great difficulties in regulating its international trade. The other is that the policy is a go-it-alone strategy for Britain without the concurrence of its trading partners.

An effort to reduce the level of international commerce and finance must be based on an international concord. It should not be Britain or the U.S. alone trying to work out an individualistic policy. It is now in the interest of many countries to design a common policy of reducing the instabilities produced by a heavy reliance on trade and the easy movement of capital.

Obviously, it will not be easy to work out such a policy of managed trade. But large trade and capital movements exact heavy prices in instability and in thwarting economic policies. The U.S. needs to rebuild its domestic markets and not aspire to the unattainable goal of restoring itself to world dominance.

A protectionist policy should be accompanied by a *dynamic development* policy obligating protected industries to improve their product and price attractiveness over a limited time period. The German economist Friedrich List advocated protectionism for "infant industries" and nations in the early nineteenth century, and influenced U.S. trade policy at that time. Today the need in the U.S. is to protect "redeveloping" and new industries. The older industries should not have an indefinite protectionist defense. They have to learn to measure up.

A little heresy about foreign trade may stir up some new ways of proceeding. Despite the growth in American exports, most American firms do not participate in international trade. They may be harmed by imports. The heavy emphasis on free trade and free mobility of capital primarily benefits the *Fortune 1000* and large banks. The longer-term national economic interest of the United States does not necessarily coincide with the interests of Big Business and Big Money. (A similar situation exists in other countries.) If medium and small businesses move to protect their own economic interests, profound changes could occur in America's international economic policies.

Economically, small and medium businesses and most U.S. workers would be better off with stable, if not limited, international trade. There is a large *potential* political constituency in the United States for such trade limitations. That constituency will remain only a potential one, as long as the expansion of exports is discussed as the no-option policy. Many Third World nations suffer mightily from unrestrained trade fluctuations. They are pressing for trade restrictions and orderly markets through the New International Economic Order. It should be possible to manage trade so that Third World countries that are industrializing do not suffer.

It is time to ask serious questions about who benefits and who does not from unrestrained international currency, investment, and trade flows.

Job-centered growth

The difficulties of the tax-transfer policy model and the prospect of jobless growth accentuate the need for a new approach. Rather than concentrating on overall growth, especially in investment or business profits, the need is for a policy of job-centered growth.

Employment is the central social policy. A high-employment situation would contract the need for many transfers, especially if more jobs were "decent," offering adequate levels of pay and protection, reducing feelings of stigma, and building the important possibility of reciprocity and interdependence that we discuss at the end of this chapter.

The job-centered approach is especially necessary if the United States moves or falls into a lessened role in world exports. It will encourage the development of domestic markets. The June 1982 Democratic Party platform proposals for government job creation in the infrastructure are necessary, but do not go far enough. As Reagan's elimination of the public component of the job training program demonstrated, government-created jobs can be cut back in a new political moment. It would be better to concentrate on permanent job creation, now largely in the private sector, than on temporary job slots in the public sector. The latter have a cyclical role, but they do not deal with the long-term shortfall in the number of jobs.

The concept of "targeting" is inadequate to convey what is involved since it is now employed by economists to refer exclusively to tax incentives and benefits for investment. Job-centered growth requires more than influencing investment and more than relying on tax incentives.

An employment-focused policy seeks to foster demand for the goods and services offered by industries and firms that are likely to provide employment for many, not for a few highly skilled workers. Consequently, it is not oriented only or even primarily to high capital-intensive industries like high-tech firms with their low employment potential, especially for persons of low skill. *What is produced and how* are the central questions in employment-centered growth. This orientation brings to the fore the issues of which needs are to be met and what kinds of demand should be fostered. The content and quality of GNP, not only its overall rate of growth, are now policy issues. That is what industrial policy should be about, not bailing out one or another distressed firm or promoting a low-employment, high-technology company.

Government can use its taxing, buying, lending, and regulating instruments to encourage the expansion of industries which will add workers. Those instruments are in place and in use although rarely acknowledged. For example, military spending – sought as a way of restoring American world hegemony – does not generate as much employment as some civilian spending options.[2] Further, high military spending *à la* Reagan competes with civilian spending, limiting the capital and skilled labor available for public and private socially useful production of goods and services. It is now unmistakably a question of guns or margarine. Military spending in search of lost American dominance is an adverse use of government power to influence production, consumption, and employment. Other, more benign uses of the federal budget can be envisioned (e.g., the Boston Peace Budget) which would aid industries with high employment potentials.

These ongoing activities of government are, as Barry Bluestone has declared, the "de facto industrial policies" of the U.S. government.[3] How they are used, not whether they should be used, is the question. The choice is whether to promote capital investment in already high capital fields or to foster more employment directly. *Which investment, which jobs,* not only the overall rate of investment or growth, is the issue. A job-centered policy is much broader than that involved in the proposal of a full employment guarantee, backed by the government as "employer of last resort." Job-centered development recognizes and redirects the wide range of governmental activity that affects employment. It does not rely on a general call for "full employment" to be fulfilled by high general economic growth or a fallback position that the government serve as employer if all else fails. Job-centered growth focuses on specific targeted policies which would make a difference in employment.

"Cost effectiveness" has become a key, if frequently spurious, measure of the desirability of government programs, trying to match costs to benefits. A better measure is needed – *job effectiveness*: how many and what kinds of jobs are produced by competing types of governmental activities.

Employment is a key issue, but the quality and equality of that employment is also central. Otherwise, American society will be marked by a decreasing percentage of the population in well-paid protected jobs and the great bulk of workers crowded into low-paying and unprotected sectors. That segmentation would not be conducive to a consensual rather than an oppressive road to productivity and employment.[4] The need is to increase the number of jobs and improve their content at the same time. Although this seems like a tall order, it is the appropriate order. Increasing the growth of GNP or corporate profits in the hope that the quality and quantity of employment will automatically increase is naive.

An employment-centered policy does not necessarily mean supporting labor-intensive, low-paying service industries. Nor does it mean that investment should not be spurred, for some low-capital industries might increase employment if they were enabled to increase or improve their physical capacities. A better *balance* between further investment in already high-capital sectors and low-capital sectors is what is needed. The recapitalist stress on building manufacturing industry, especially high-tech, should not overwhelm the need for improving jobs and capital investment in the service industries. These sectors seem to be the "natural" growth areas of the economy. Their improvement as employment locales is important.

U.S. roads, mass transport, and housing are also in poor shape, the result of years of government and, of course, private neglect. The rebuilding of U.S. roads and mass transport, as well as the insulation and renovation of old housing stock and the creation of new housing stock, are necessary and inevitable areas for future investment. Many jobs could be created through serious government investment in these areas, providing skills for the unskilled and energy efficiency for a nation sorely lacking in both.

A job-focused strategy would promote smaller enterprises rather than the big-business conglomerates which waste capital, promote the centralization of power, and frequently are less productive than smaller firms. Big businesses are the current targets of federal economic policy in the belief that they are the wellspring of prosperity. Since they provide few new jobs, are dangerously irresponsible in their use of U.S. investment capital, and, due to the 1981 tax cuts, will no longer be providing much in the way of federal revenues, the belief that they bring prosperity should die quickly. Small businesses, on the other hand, are providing most new employment and have the versatility to work within the framework suggested by the alternatives we will discuss later in this chapter.

An employment-centered policy will, of course, have to be concerned with regional issues – the geographical location of the employment growth. As government policies become tailored to employment, rather than profits, it will become apparent that the key mechanism is no longer incentives to produce or invest, but incentives to employ in the locales where the unemployed reside.

An employment-centered policy is also likely to be less inflationary than a policy narrowly oriented to physical investment in heavy capital-using industries. The heavy-goods investment policy is likely to encounter supply bottlenecks and oligopolistic price fixing (by both the capital goods-producing industries and the industries using the heavy capital goods). The result would then be rising prices.[5]

An employment-centered growth with quality jobs must be directly promoted. It will not be an incidental by-product of the investment expansion that has been the hallmark of American growth policies. These policies not only formed the center of liberal and neo-liberal macro policies but were basic to Reaganomics. If the employment of low-skilled people – who are disproportionately minorities and female heads of households – is a high concern, as it should be, a directed employment policy will be crucial.

Towards a new GNP

New ways of thinking and profound changes in the economy require new measurements. Economists have degraded John Maynard Keynes's concern with economic expansion during a depression into an obsession with the growth rate. Keynes knew the importance of what is produced and consumed and the dangers of wanting more and more; he understood that well-being is not locked into goods. The modern economist disdains the content of what is produced and how, and with what positive and negative effects, focusing only on the total monetary value (Gross National Product) corrected for price changes, and what the percentage gain (or loss) is from the preceding year. This narrow lens is astigmatic for two reasons. First, the very calculation of GNP contains deep faults. Second, and more importantly, the total production represented by GNP tells us nothing about the composition or distribution of product.

The major difficulty is that only what goes through the market and has a price is counted as part of GNP. This approach leaves out non-marketed goods like household services while counting as useful growth practices such as medical double billing or repairs resulting from car accidents. Further, it assumes that goods and services with the same price make an equal contribution to economic well-being. It ignores "externalities," the destruction of the environment, and pollution caused by the production of that output.

Technical difficulties abound and distort the understanding of economic behavior. This confusion is particularly true of the measure of "productivity" as outlined in note 5, p. 191. Well-known is the unreliability of measures of improvement in the efficiency of services. Quality gains in service fields are largely unmeasured and productivity is seen as increasing more slowly than it actually is. But even in the "hard" manufacturing fields, productivity measures are unreliable though widely used. The calculation of productivity is not based on a single relation of physical output to physical inputs of capital and labor. Rather, output is in dollar terms, then converted for estimated changes in prices, and divided by reports of labor hours. A lot of slippage from physical outputs and inputs occurs in this complicated process. This is not a very sturdy measure on which to base our understanding of the economy.

Without new ways of measuring well-being, we will be severely limited in our understanding of economic structure and events. Mindless concentration on short-run changes in the American economy will continue to cloud long-run concerns. New modes of thinking about the economy are desperately needed. Otherwise, it will be difficult to move in new ways. How and what we measure shapes how we think. If we measured the employment and income distribution consequences of various policy alternatives, debate would quickly shift from aggregate GNP growth to *whose growth*? Statistics themselves are now part of the economic process, as the misguided debate around productivity demonstrates. As Thorstein Veblen said many decades ago, "A habit of thought is a habit of action." Creative, realistic, and phenomenological interpretations and measuring of economic processes and outcomes are vitally needed.

Direction without bureaucracy

The difficulties of the American economy call for more central direction: a widened role for government in curbing speculation, channeling investment funds to particular industries, improving the basic infrastructure of the economy, reducing inflationary tendencies, and protecting vulnerable populations. "What is good for General Motors" may not only *not* be good for the U.S.A., but it may require extensive governmental action (e.g., tariffs, tax cuts) to achieve what GM considers best for itself.

An employment-focused policy requires more governmental involvement in the economy than does a narrow emphasis on tax inducements for general capital investment. The job-centered approach avowedly is more selective than a macro economic policy whose targeting is limited to favoring capital goods investment. For example, how public transportation is developed and constructed, rather than an exclusive concern with the amount of transportation activity, would be an important issue.

The current code word for economic direction is "targeting." The type of targeting is the political issue; for example, should tax cuts go to all firms which invest at home or should the effort be to get export-oriented firms to invest? In the Reaganite tax program of 1981 "targeting" had low importance, and corporations and well-to-do households received sizable tax cuts regardless of what they did with them. "Targeting" is a mild form of the economic guidance necessary to improve the American economy.

At the same time that the need for central direction is great, many Americans want "less government," "less regulation," "less bureaucracy." The disasters of Soviet-type command planning have certainly strengthened the dislike of bureaucratic/political centralization. Dislike of bureaucracies is at a high pitch, leading to opposition to many liberal-progressive actions.

But direction of the economy and control or, at least, influence over investment processes is desperately needed. Without it speculation will abound, capital will flow abroad, growth will be uneven, lopsided, and of limited value. Sooner or later, economic guidelines or controls will emerge as part of the means to rescue stalled economies and to pursue social objectives. The risk inherent in avoiding new regulation or planning is that things may get so bad that strong state direction would be imposed in a crisis atmosphere and would lead to repression.

Can detailed intervention be avoided in favor of general direction? Compounding this issue is the situation that a strong public social sector is also essential if the vulnerable are not to suffer. The problem is how to pursue targeting or planning without over-direction, bureaucracy, inflexibility, dangerous limitations on liberty, and the over-centralization of authority.

This charge is not unmeetable although difficult to achieve. The social science literature on organizations has unfortunately concentrated on the emergence of encrusted red tape and failed bureaucracies, not on their avoidance. The popular management books offer largely psychological, that is, non-structural, ways to reduce bureaucratic strains, frequently in a manipulative way. A progressive, humanistic, and democratic literature on bureaucracy and organization is only slowly emerging. A non-bureaucratic approach to liberal and progressive goals could gain considerable support.

Despite the lack of a useful theoretical literature, programs are emerging that avoid the pitfalls associated with the epithet "bureaucratic." The experience with many instruments and agencies is positive. Direction requires reshaping many ongoing activities rather than starting from scratch. For example, the Community Reinvestment Act of 1977 offers an approach that comes close to meeting the design of direction without bureaucracy. It requires banks to invest some of the funds deposited from an area in that neighborhood. This provision limits the draining of capital funds from, say, the declining Northeast to the Southwest, from the United States to other countries, or from slum areas, desperately needing finance, to favored localities. Banks are not required to make specific types of loans, although that might be a valuable step. Rather, the minimal, expected volume of loans in the depositing area is indicated. Thus, the goal is achieved of making capital available to the locality from which the deposits are made without saddling the banks with highly detailed, specific requirements about loans. The banks still make those daily decisions.[6]

The principle is attractive, and some groups led by Gail Cincotta of the National People's Union are influencing the national advisory body of insurance companies to adapt and adopt it. The aim is to lead to greater capital availability in the neighborhoods which pay insurance premiums. A Minnesota community organization tried to influence banks receiving Tax-Savers deposits to follow the same practice of investing some of the funds in the depositors' localities. It is studying the possibilities of getting the large financial agents of Individual Retirement Accounts (IRA) to follow the same practice in the varied portfolios that they offer depositors.

Competitive opportunities may make such local investments less attractive – although national legislation requiring all financial institutions to provide some capital to the localities from which their beneficiaries come would reduce this tendency. But the approach is attractive even if it encounters difficulties. For it provides direction without imposing detailed controls and creating a bureaucracy.

A similar, more familiar policy approach relies on *incentives* rather than on coercion or penalties. The effectiveness of incentives, inducements, or rewards for corporations (or unions) to behave in desired ways has been exaggerated. But incentives can be a useful instrument. Decision-making is still left to the independent organization; government policy attempts to tip the balance in favor of a given act. The issue is: can detailed intervention be avoided in favor of general direction? For example, accelerated depreciation of physical investment decreases taxes, thereby providing an inducement to invest, without detailed requirements. Swedish employment expert Gösta Rehn has suggested providing special grants to businesses which increase their employment at particular points.[7] Neither proposal requires investment, for firms may decide that their projects do not warrant further investment. The Urban Development Action Grant (UDAG) of the Carter Administration or Reagan's "urban enterprise zones" are inducements to establish employment-making enterprises in low-income areas. While such proposals are usually over-sold, they contain interesting leads.

The tax-based incomes policy (TIP) proposal would lower taxation on corporations that do not exceed wage–price guidelines rather than impose controls on wages and prices. The proposal is derived from European experiences in connecting the tax system to the wage system. In the American adaptation, the stress is on the behavior of individual corporations; in European countries it has been on the behavior of the central organizations of corporations and unions. In return for accepting moderate wage increases, personal income taxes are reduced or transfer payments to low-income families increased. Again, the issue is how to reconcile direction with the minimizing of the bureaucratic role. In the current U.S. debate, TIP could be used to penalize as well as to reward. Taxes could be raised for corporations that exceed price guidelines. In this approach good behavior is considered the norm and bad behavior punished, the opposite of present economic incentive policies.

In the next sections we discuss some policy departures which should be debated. We do not present a systematic platform but touch on a diverse set of important issues.

'Planning' as politics

The issues of inflation, the threatened failures of firms, and faulty economic growth have led many liberals and union leaders to call for a more interventionist government. Despite objections to active government, the grave and continuing difficulties of the economy are likely to force the federal government to undertake some planning even if that name is not applied to the activity. The U.S. economy is much less publicly directed than other capitalist economies. Planning will emerge sooner or later as a device to meet inflation dangers through wage or price controls or to provide better use of capital funds. In the mild form, capital funds would be made available to some ailing firms; in the stronger planning form, a wider and deeper field for governmental allocation of capital could emerge. The discussions of industrial policy are often confusing because they do not distinguish between these very different degrees of governmental action.

One argument for planning is that inflation will continue as long as wages rise. But workers cannot be expected to give up wage increases if prices and profits are increasing. The possibility of mutually adjusting wages, profits, and prices requires a national agreement in which labor and corporations (read "management") face each other and make an arrangement. Joint, voluntary agreement is more likely to secure compliance than are guidelines or more strict wage–price controls solely promulgated by a national administration. As Felix Rohatyn declared: "sacrifice has to be negotiated and not legislated."[8]

Similarly, some liberals and many neo-liberals, including Rohatyn, have been calling for the revival in some form of the Reconstruction Finance Corporation (RFC) established by President Hoover in 1932, greatly expanded by President Roosevelt, and discontinued by World War II. The modern RFC would lend funds to businesses in distress. The liberal intention is that the unions would be represented on the board in order to secure their cooperation. The Rohatyn approach would be to isolate the RFC from "politics" and rely on experts to make "rational" decisions.[9]

In a broader and politically more attractive perspective, a planning apparatus to influence production and investments is called for by some liberals and progressives. The objective is much wider governmental decisions about promoting or inducing investment in particular industries and facilitating exports. This planning mode has aspects similar to the other two in that many of the proposals about the structure of the investment board would have a tripartite form involving business, unions, and government. The following remarks about the corporatist-type model apply to this expanded planning board, for we reject the notion that an "independent" board of experts can and should be above politics. For the very form of accepted economics is value-ridden, although its practitioners consider themselves non-ideological.[10]

For some, "corporatist" or "corporatism" is a term of derision and fear, for they think in terms of fascist-style corporatism *à la* Mussolini's Italy, in which labor interests are submerged in government- or business-dictated bodies that regulate activities. Civil liberties are curtailed by an authoritarian government. Business leaders object to the fetters of an expanded and more detailed government role in economic activity.

Those liberals and neo-liberals who think in terms of a Scandinavian-type corporatism, in which an economically and politically strong labor movement has a dominant role in tripartite actions towards a "social contract," have a much more favorable outlook. Indeed, some worker-oriented American supporters of greater governmental intervention in the economy foresee the increased visibility of decision-making as a way of politicizing economic issues and increasing the strength of liberal-labor forces in the economic-political scene.

For some liberals and many progressives, corporatist-like ventures are dangerous, fostering possibilities of "incorporation," in which labor and politically dissident groups are coopted into the public bodies with little real influence in them. The effect is to win acceptability for policies which harm many. This view leads to deep distrust of tripartite bodies and other corporate-type measures.

But many if not most progressives, liberals, and neo-liberals embrace some form of planning as necessary if economic difficulties are to be resolved and broad social objectives accomplished. At times, planning takes on the aura of a panacea, supplanting the more popular magic of productivity.

An extreme "free enterprise" administration like that of Reagan's is unlikely to proffer corporatism in the form of tripartite boards, but a Democrat or even a moderate Republican administration might pursue it if economic conditions were very distressful and policies difficult to carry out. We believe that recurring and deepening problems of stagflation and structural strains and shifts in the economy will sooner or later lead to a level of economic-political difficulties that will strengthen previous labor, liberal, and neo-liberal calls for "planning." Under those circumstances, clear-cut rejection of involvement in planning may not be easy.

The issue then for liberals and progressives will be under what conditions would wage–price controls and/or allocation of capital not submerge the needs of workers, the poor, and others into a "transcending national interest" that somehow benefits mainly corporations, especially the larger ones? There is no simple "national economic interest" that equally benefits all: *who pays, who decides, and who loses is crucial.* There is no "technical fix" which can achieve *the* national interest and transcend politics.

A simple implementation of current ideas and practices about planning is insufficient and dangerous. They are exclusively couched in terms of disturbing economic issues and ignore the politics of a planning operation. To outline what is desirable in terms of price controls (e.g., concentrate on the largest corporations) or the allocation of capital (pick "winners" or support some important "losers") is inadequate. For such an approach refuses to recognize conflicting interests and ignores the continuing changes in economic terrain requiring adaptation and modification of policies.

The *form and practice* of economic guidance agencies is crucial. Greater labor–public participation in economic policy bodies may become a crucial path to influence economic decisions in a pro-labor way.[11] In the American context, that does not seem the most likely result of involvement, especially if the labor movement does not grow in strength and move to the left in attitudes. Consequently, the grounds of participation and the mode of behavior in a planning body are very important.

The representatives of labor and the public in the planning unit should not conceive of themselves as independent individuals but should strive to mobilize interest groups to which they are responsible. In the workings of the planning organization, they should regard themselves as in a *contest*, offering and fighting for better programs, willing to go outside the board to mobilize support for their policies.[12] Instead of permitting the planning agency to be utilized as a muting board, it should be a sounding board, calling people to battle for important policies. The actions of the panel should be viewed as political issues, not as technical questions best kept out of the public domain.

From the beginning, local and regional planning, not only national planning, should be encouraged. Planning can be a method for expanding democratic processes by bringing the electorate and their interest groups into the economic decision-making process. Presently the U.S., while democratic in formal political organization, is quite undemocratic in economic organization.[13] The power of management and private capital to invest and organize production as they will is largely unchallenged. The progressive approach to planning is to increase those challenges. In the words of Carnoy and Shearer, what we must press for is *increased economic democracy* at all levels of economic organization and government.

Groups should be formed to monitor and press the national and local boards even if one's nominal friends and coalitional partners sit on the board. Planning boards should be used as a way of organizing people for disagreement and action. The tendency of planning to become technocratic and to defuse situations has to be recognized and consciously fought against – at the very start. Counter-policies and counter-mobilization will be necessary if planning is not to divide and conquer, sliding into acquiescence in limited or distorted policies.[14]

Planning is not automatically in the interests of the majority of the population. In the present ideological context, planning will most likely follow recapitalization lines, serving to promote and insure business profitability. Desirable social and economic objectives have to be fought for. The act of planning neither assumes nor assures their primacy.

Work relations

New Deal/Great Society liberalism had little to do with the nature of work relations. AFL-CIO unionism also largely left control of the work process and decision-making to management. The New Deal affected the wage level by establishing a minimum wage and overtime pay requirements and by promoting unionism. In the 1960s, occupational safety and health became a national issue, affecting shopfloor activities. But liberalism's main impact on work relations was through the early promotion of unions in the National Labor Relations Act of 1935. In general, the price of collective bargaining was little union involvement in the shopfloor processes of production and in the basic corporate decisions about investment and employment. Seniority ruled the order of promotion and disemployment; supplementary benefits aided some union workers who were laid off. But basic corporate and shopfloor decisions were beyond the purview of unions and government. In the light of our discussion of corporate irrationality, this hands-off orientation should be changed.

Four issues are undermining that hands-off policy. One is the concern about improving worker attitudes and enhancing productivity in order to make U.S. products cheaper and more competitive in the world market. Some firms are attempting to emulate the Japanese model of work circles with some worker participation in shopfloor decisions. A second is that the economic plight which is leading some firms to look for public subsidies and loans (e.g., Chrysler) has opened the door to worker representation on the board of directors. A third is that corporations are demanding that their unionized workers provide "givebacks": they should forgo now traditional benefits and practices won in collective bargaining in order to reduce labor costs. In return unions are negotiating for decision-making rights. For example, the UAW recently demanded that Ford, in return for givebacks and wage freezes, pass all productivity gains on to consumers rather than absorb them as profits.[15] Finally, plants that may be shut down by their corporate owners because of inadequate demand, or a shift to less costly factories owned by the company, or to gain tax and other benefits from a closedown, are candidates for change into a new economic form – the worker- or community-owned cooperative.

A crucial element in the planning orientation should be the promotion of cooperative forms and government participation in corporate boards. Rather than only providing support for private enterprises in difficulty, or occasionally nationalizing a distressed but vital industry or corporation, new forms of worker- and community-owned and managed enterprises should be encouraged.

Coping with America's economic ills does not depend on maintaining forms of corporate life which have contributed to these ailments. The aim is not to "save capitalism" as it has been sadly experienced in recent years. The economic unit of late capitalist America should increasingly be regarded as open to modification and innovation, not fixed in a big-business, conglomerate corporate form.

The producer cooperative form of enterprise should be encouraged as one way to modify the character of property in the United States, for it can lead to more democratic–egalitarian possibilities for workers and communities. The older left notion of nationalization of firms and enterprises has had mixed results internationally (e.g., French nationalization has done better than British) and a decidedly bad name in the U.S. It should be complemented by a mix of worker- and community-owned enterprises, and employee, union, and governmental participation on corporate boards.

Undoubtedly, some industries may have to be nationalized if they are to develop usefully, if national economic needs and plans rather than private business objectives are to be realized. Since the U.S. has a very limited history of nationalized firms and industries it will take time to learn how to conduct nationalized firms and industries in efficient ways. David Gordon has suggested that one firm in each major concentrated industry be nationalized so that the government can force competition into the market.[16] The oil and banking industries, in particular, are promising targets for eventual nationalization because of their central role in both investment (recall that the oil companies in 1981 realized about 25 per cent of all corporate profits) and inflation. Government control of these industries would provide the economic leverage necessary for effective investment and inflation policy.

Two important processes are involved in these varied concerns. One deals with the control of production, investment decisions, and employment; the other with the organization of the work process itself. Neither the work circle and allied attempts to improve morale and productivity, nor the attempt to borrow public money, nor giveback demands, are used to enlarge workers' control over the decision-making policies and shopfloor practices of corporations. Governmental and union contributions to the enhancement of productivity, the diminishment of labor costs, and the availability of capital, should be coupled with sharing in the power to affect decisions of the aided corporation.

Governmental policies could promote such developments. The Employee Stock Ownership Plan (ESOP) now provides tax inducements to corporations to offer stock ownership to their workers. It could be extended to reward giving greater power and control to employees. The European Communities (the Common Market) have promulgated a directive requiring employee representation in corporate boards. The U.S. lags far behind the capitalist countries of Western Europe in efforts to democratize the large corporation by increasing worker and union influence over investment decisions and shopfloor practices.

Changes in the mode of property and decision-making do not ensure changes in the character of daily work in an enterprise. Many, if not most, cooperatives have not changed work relations and the division of labor. The division of labor that prevails in firms and among occupations is not solely the result of rational processes which assure efficiency. It is also the result of tradition, old and new demand-and-supply conditions and expectations, managerial fears, political jousting, status differences, and happenstance. A restructuring of the division of labor is desirable. It can both increase employment by reducing bottlenecks of skilled workers and enhance the quality of work for more people.

The chief benefit of changing the division of labor may be the promotion of greater equality in American society. It is difficult to gain acceptance for narrowed income differentials when people's labor differs widely in terms of contribution and effort. To secure greater equality in resources (income and wealth), a goal of many liberals and most progressives, requires greater equality in tasks. Again, the tax and subsidy/transfer systems could be used to induce changes in task distribution.

To increase the number of decent jobs – defined by the quality of the work situation as well as by wages – requires changing work relations and benefits. One way to encourage such changes is to increase across-the-board public benefits, such as medical coverage which is available to all, not just to those who work for particular firms.[17] A public benefit program reduces inequalities among jobs.

Taxation and revenues

The recapitalist changes in personal and corporate taxation will require deep shifts in thinking about taxation, shifts which have been in the making for a long time. The so-called "tax revolts", exemplified by Proposition 13 in California and Proposition 2½ in Massachusetts, revealed widespread irritation and discontent about taxation even if some who voted for them regret the service reductions that followed. Both the level and forms of taxation are under attack. Direct, visible taxes like federal, state, and city personal income taxes, state and local property taxes, and the federal social security taxes are those that incur the greatest resentment. As was pointed out in the previous chapter, liberals' reliance on taxation as an instrument for social betterment has been undermined.

If taxation is to generate revenues for social as well as for other programs, less direct or "invisible" taxes and user taxes will have to become more important. Invisible taxes are usually sales taxes, whether called by that name or, in more complicated variations, termed "value-added tax," in which each stage of sale in the production and marketing of a product is taxed and the cost of the tax is added to the price paid in that stage. Sales taxes have a regressive bias, but that could be overcome, at least partially, by having higher taxes on luxury items and no taxes on basic consumption items like food, which constitute a high percentage of the expenditures of lower-income households. If a tax credit – available in cash to those who pay no or low taxes – were provided to offset the burden of sales taxes, then the tax might have some degree of progressiveness. In addition, the social security tax, which hits lower-income wage earners hardest, could be reduced for all workers, or the tax rate lowered for those earning, say, only 150 per cent of the minimum wage. Contributions from general revenues could make up this loss. Since general revenue taxation is more progressive than the social security tax, the overall tax structure might improve.

A national sales tax could be used to reduce or eliminate state and local sales taxes. The federal government would return some of the taxes collected in that area to state and local jurisdictions which eliminated sales taxes. One benefit would be to reduce competition among states in taxation.

A user tax has the benefit of linking beneficiaries directly to costs. Instead of spreading the costs of a governmental activity over all taxpayers (potential beneficiaries), user taxes concentrate more of the costs on actual beneficiaries. Major problems are that non-users may become eventual beneficiaries, direct or indirect; the taxes on the relatively small number of actual users may be very high if the revenue is to be large enough to make a difference in covering the cost of the facility; the calculation of an appropriate charge is no easy matter; and the people who should be attracted to use a service or facility may be discouraged from doing so. Still, in some activities, user costs could be utilized. Interestingly, this was the main source of new tax revenue for the deficit-ridden Reagan budget in 1982.

Reaganism has profoundly reduced the progressiveness of a tax system that was not very progressive to begin with. While the effort to achieve more progressivism in the tax structure should not be abandoned, the hope for at least the next years can only be that it generate revenues for social purposes without too much disturbance. That is a severely limited objective, especially for New Deal/ Great Society liberals who saw taxation as a tranquil and effective way of changing society. But even that lesser objective will not be an easy one to achieve and maintain. Fresh thinking about taxation is necessary. That thinking must consider the psychology of taxation – how people respond to different tax forms – and not only its economics.

The tax system is not well loved, and probably never will be. The raising of revenue by the state for social (non-business) purposes is always a problem. Alternative revenue sources do exist. The military budget is potentially a source of much revenue within the existing pie of federal funds. To spend less on guns and other instruments of destruction requires the U.S. to give up its quest for world dominance and find a meaningful halt to the arms race with the Soviet Union. Nationalized industries could also be a source of state revenue. The profits of legal monopolies such as the various utilities would fund many public works projects. Most effective for reducing the need to raise federal (or state and local) revenues would be a policy orientation – changing the content of GNP to stress job-centered growth – that prevents poverty and distress rather than bandaging it.

A participatory social sector

The shift from the Great Society and the welfare state requires rethinking the social sector – cash and non-cash (service) programs, recreational activities, and other (once) governmentally-supported activities. Merely restoring Reaganite cuts in existing welfare state programs is not what is needed. Profound change in social programs is important. The general principle is to avoid dependence and promote independence and autonomy, what is now thought of as "empowerment." The basic idea is to shift decision-making and day-to-day operations out of the top-down bureaucratic setting towards a more participatory form. Those who use the service should play a major role in controlling and running it. The form should move from a bureaucratic and professional to a community enterprise. Those who benefit, do; those who do, benefit.

This orientation is a drastic departure from the way the welfare state and social programs have operated. In the now-traditional centralized social policy model, funds and decisions have been concentrated in the hands of governmental employees who are not accountable to the neighborhood in whose benefit they presumably operate.

It is a model which has produced great irritation, promoting today's anti-bureaucratic, anti-government, anti-politician ethos. The participation/empowerment orientation is responsive to American values and desires in ways foreign to the bureaucratic welfare state. For one of the great, continuing strengths and delights (as well as constraints) of American life is localism. The popular theme of empowerment enables neighborhoods and communities to determine organizational structures and to carry through the activities and programs that affect them. Models of service organization and delivery which emphasize local decision-making and democracy, the realization of the positive American ideas of community and liberty – well expressed by Harry Boyte[18] and others – should largely displace "Big State" welfare state/socialist models of centralized direction and heavy bureaucratic control. Enhancing freedom and autonomy are important American themes which progressives and liberals have underemphasized in recent years.

Programs within a policy should vary considerably from area to area as local groups devise activities which they feel would benefit them. The locus of power should shift from the outsider politician, bureaucrat, or professional to the local community. Professionals should be in the service of the community or their governing body rather than independently operating an agency.

A great variety of ongoing activities illustrates the possibilities of the empowerment model. Self-help activities by people once regarded as necessarily reliant on professional aid have become important for many with medical, physical, or emotional difficulties. They work out ways of helping one another.[19]

In many localities, groups emerge to prevent negative things from happening in their neighborhoods, whether crime or the loss of important facilities. Some consumer groups and community organizations have established daycare and other facilities needed in their neighborhoods. The New York Public Interest Research Group (NYPIRG) has formed energy coops to reduce fuel bills. Thus, there is a burgeoning of "for" groups as well as "agin" efforts, only trying to prevent bad things from occurring.

These and other activities are "spontaneous" in that they are not instigated by a governmental agency, although legislative requirements for community involvement in decisions can be important. Goverment money can be provided in ways which promote initiative and local decision-making rather than restricting or narrowly channeling them. For example, the Canadian youth employment program provided summer stipends to youth who convinced a locality that they would perform a useful service for the community. While national governmental funding was involved, the locality and the youth made the decision and shaped the activity.

Localism and empowerment are vital themes for a new progressivism. They shift the center of political, social, and economic life from the national bureaucracy to the community. But one should not be naive about them. There is a conservative empowerment as well as a progressive empowerment.

Unfortunately, the desire to empower people is often coupled with the notion of fewer governmental resources. "Reprivatization" and empowerment have become associated for many with the idea of lessened resources. The Reaganite shift of programs to states was not accompanied by requirements about the scope, character, and maintenance of programs. This is "conservative empowerment." It is "the transfer of pseudo-power" for without resources not much can be achieved. To empower people should not be mainly a policy of less resources but one of more choice in the ways that resources can be used.

The need for substantial governmental and some professional aid is not ignored in "progressive empowerment." Some important activities like medical care frequently cannot be supported or managed by neighborhood groups alone. Outside effort may be necessary to stimulate some needed activity in a locality. Empowerment through self-help can degenerate into a condition of exile – from resources, from technical aid, or from stimulation. In the absence of externally imposed constraints, a community-based organization can decay into inaction or become authoritarian, corrupt, or a field for feuding.

Further, localism can foster inequalities. Without efforts to reduce differences among regions and localities, inequalities are likely to grow. The point is clear, disturbing, and part of the "new federalism." The usual order of things is to maintain or widen inequalities. Communities with a substantial tax base can provide resources and services unattainable in poorer districts. If inequalities among localities are to be reduced, national action is usually necessary. This need operates against the principle of local direction and autonomy. Inequalities are unlikely to be reduced without pressure or intervention in the operations and decision-making of localities. Inequality-reduction requires a larger perspective and pressure than exists at local levels. The principles of greater equality and local autonomy are often in conflict but not irremediably.

National guidelines are necessary to prevent ethnic and social stratification and segregation, to promote equitable use of facilities, to guard against abuses, etc. But these are essentially monitoring roles rather than centralized construction and control of services. Governments will have to learn how to monitor service delivery without overloading localities with rules and regulations. National standards are also needed for environmental, tax, and labor costs so that communities do not need to compete with each other for corporate leavings.

Awareness of these issues should not inhibit the movement away from centralized, outside, bureaucratic social programs. For if old-style structures prevail, then we would have – as often occurred in programs in the 1960s and 1970s – "the pseudo-transfer of power," as localities had little autonomy. A blend is needed of outside direction-setting through national guidelines as well as a much more dominant neighborhood, self-help implementation. The social sector has been severely unbalanced in the other direction. It should swing to greater local empowerment.

Beyond liberalism

The basis of compassion

A major difficulty of welfare state programs is that they lacked a rationale for their development. They expanded mightily, but public understanding of them did not grow with that enlarging of scope and expense. People were not aware of their own benefits from transfer programs or from tax expenditures. The concept of a "social wage" deriving from governmental benefits rather than from wage and salary income did not emerge in this country as it did elsewhere.

If social programs are to gain support, they need a basis in values, feelings, or self-interest. This is particularly true for programs in aid of the worst-off sections of the population. The middle classes, the non-poor, lack consistent motivation for supporting social programs for the needy.

Concern about the poor and disadvantaged and the reduction of inequalities may be motivated by fear, reciprocity, moral codes, or love.

Sometimes changes occur because turmoil or its perceived threat disturb a society, making it difficult for the rulers and establishments to play their accustomed roles or carry through their usual practices. Then they may make "concessions," institute "reforms," accommodate the new pressures, lessen their own fears by "coopting" or "incorporating" the clamoring outsiders. Or, of course, they may seek to repress the unruly – or, more likely, combine cooptation of some leaders with repression of the more militant. While turmoil is important in forcing attention to issues of inequality and poverty, it is difficult to sustain and can be isolated and squashed by adept elites.

Fear, then, has its problems as a mode of improving the plight of those at the bottom. Since turmoil is difficult to continue for long, the erosion of gains is frequent as establishments learn how to handle the situation. But without some fear on the part of elites, little is done for the disadvantaged.

Reciprocity occurs where action for a disadvantaged people might yield political or economic returns. Ethnic groups may vote for those officials and legislators who act to benefit them. Johnson's Great Society was in part a way of keeping black votes in the Democratic column.

Votes are important for reciprocity. If low-income citizens did vote – as many do not – they could have an impact on elections and politicians. As the number of non-poor citizens grows, however, disadvantaged voters might lose impact, except when a swing vote is important. But if they usually vote in the Democratic Party, then they may have significance in Democratic primaries more than in elections, unless the size of their actual vote drastically increases or decreases. The political problem of the low-income population is, however, that they do not vote.

Reciprocity can take an economic form as well. The two periods of active pursuit of some of the needs of low-income populations were the New Deal of the 1930s and the Great Society of the 1960s. In the former situation, spending money on the poor was intended to stimulate the depressed economy. The situation of the 1960s was different. The Johnson tax cut to heat up the economy threatened to generate high tax revenues which could brake the economy if unspent (the so-called "fiscal lag"). Spending on the poor was a way of getting revenue out of the Treasury Department and maintaining growth rates. In both periods, spending on the poor and national economic policy coincided. The latter was a main, though not sole, pressure for the "reform" programs.

The economic basis of reciprocity is weak at this time. Stimulating the economy through public social spending is not in the cards when the fear of inflation and the desire for tax cuts to stimulate investment are high. With tax increases difficult to sustain and an economic gain from public transfers missing, the tax–transfer route is jeopardized.

Moral codes also seem in the 1980s to be a weak reed for support of public programs and low-income populations. The emphasis on savings and investment by the well-to-do is legitimating inequalities and disregard for the poor. The economy requires inequalities, the argument goes, in order to encourage those who are well-off to save. Providing income to the poor will not increase savings.

Some are cynical about moral codes and feel that only fear or reciprocity can induce attention to the disadvantaged and the ordinary citizen. But moral issues do affect how people react to events, as in the famous case of Sheriff Bull Connor's use of dogs against those seeking to vote in Birmingham, Alabama. No human being, the feeling was, should be treated as prey for animals. The groundswell of opinion opposing Reaganite policies in 1982 was partly fueled by feelings about the unfairness of the tax cuts and the harm to the needy resulting from social program reductions.

The broader issue is that profound changes from within a society require new ways of thinking about that society, a new normative outlook, if those changes are to be initiated and to survive without coercion. In a period when a self-proclaimed moral majority has embraced conservative economic programs while pronouncing in disturbing ways on basic issues of personal and community relations, liberals and progressives need new perspectives, explanations, arguments, philosophies, and values.

The "moral majorities"
New cleavages in American society overlie and interact with older ones of religion, race, and ethnicity. Style-of-life and value differences are acute, as exemplified by the contrast between the "Moral Majority" outlook and liberal-humanist philosophies, let alone the "counter-cultural" way of living. The United States has never been a homogenous country, but its cultural splits are at least as severe and immediate as they have ever been.

Cultural difference is not limited to a few and assigned to a geographically separate Bohemia in a big city. Value disagreements are hard to ignore or escape. These differences affect the willingness to support transfer payments to those in need. Repressive and reactive tendencies grow under such conditions.

The splits are about the most intimate personal roles – the family, the role of women, the controls over youth. It is one thing to hate Communists, blacks, Catholics, rednecks, or Jews without knowing them and to think of them as remote threats, not part of one's immediate environment. It is quite another issue when the availability of abortions is seen as encouraging your children and those of your friends to engage in sex or, in a conflicting viewpoint, to regard limitations on sexual behavior and abortion as not only threatening one's own choices but as condemning one's values and expressiveness.

Economic difficulties and contentious policy debates criss-cross the style-of-life tensions. Racism and sexism are often hidden issues in the struggles. Who should get jobs – men, women, blacks, whites, the younger, or the older? There is anxiety about black women on AFDC; angry black youth; interracial mating; uppity white women. Sex, age, power, jobs, money, independence, and authority are all centrally involved in the creation and implementation of social policies.

Such divisions are difficult to reconcile; compromise is not easily negotiable. For example, promoting daycare to aid families where women must earn to sustain the household might be viewed as enticing other women to work who would not if daycare were unavailable. Although public opinion data on many issues show that a liberal cosmopolitan outlook seems to have more adherents than the conservative traditional orientation, at least some strands of the traditional outlook capture considerable support. Few do not have concern about some of the issues affecting family and youth that the traditionalists contend are their exclusive domain. Since public attitudes shape what policies are enacted and how programs operate the debates about values are of great significance.

The split is not only deep and difficult to compromise in terms of ideology but is also complicated in the arena of political strength. The Moral Majority's organization and intensity offsets its lack in numbers. In addition, the economic ideology of the New Right makes it one of the prime beneficiaries of corporate political donations. The competing claims to values and morality are passionately felt on all sides of issues. Not pluralism, but attack and divisiveness characterize the moral-ideological scene. Nor is it clear what might heal this split. While economic gains and war smooth many disagreements in U.S. society, they are unlikely to heal this fracturing of values. These two balms of internal quarrels are likely to have perverse effects today: military action can produce anti-war activists and economic growth can deepen inequalities and make them evident and disturbing. What could lead to accommodation between the two views or the withering of one of these strongly-held normative life-experience outlooks is not apparent.

Current difficulties accentuate these splits in several ways. The shortage of jobs and social funds exacerbates the competing interests of the young and the old. Should social security taxes increase to protect pension recipients? Should older workers be encouraged to leave the labor force to open jobs for younger workers? The Reaganite revival of the concept of the "undeserving poor," who manufacture their own problems, accentuates division and prejudices along racial lines. Relatively few of those who will be regarded as the acceptably "truly needy" are likely to be from the black poor. Conflicts over desegregation and affirmative action are likely to polarize further American society and weaken the position of minorities and women. At the same time, the pressure to contract social programs (raising eligibility requirements and lowering levels of benefits) will worsen the conditions of many relative to the mainstream of society.

Although Moral Majority-type ideas were fostered only mildly in the beginning days of the Reagan Administration and were resisted by moderates, liberals, neo-liberals, and progressives fearful of their long-term repressive effects, they may gain prominence if the economy falters or overseas military adventures misfire. With weak moral arguments for liberalist and humanist approaches, Moral Majority thinking may have a strong impact – especially if political trade-offs are negotiated between economic conservatives and social conservatives. The moral majorities may trade electoral support for repressive social legislation.

The promotion of savings by large tax incentives (e.g., Individual Retirement Accounts; Tax-Savers), the removal of inheritance taxation on all but the largest estates, and the Reagan tax cuts for business and the rich, will widen inequalities. In an environment of inflation, instability, and speculation, one's economic well-being is uncertain and unpredictable. Some will do very well; others will fall far behind. Cleavages among the aged will become pronounced as some succeed and others fail in their financial maneuvering, while most Americans are unable to afford speculation. As fewer and fewer young people can afford to own a home, divisions between renters and owners may grow in many communities.

Class conflicts may become more apparent in the production as well as in the consumption realm that we have just been talking about. "The new class war," as seen by Frances Fox Piven and Richard Cloward in their book of that title, is an effort to contract not only "the social wage" of governmental benefits like social security and unemployment insurance, but also the wages and fringe benefits that workers receive from their employers. The pressure of the Reagan and other recapitalist administrations to keep down real wages on a permanent basis may engender disturbing disputes.

Sharing and caring

To deal with the large-scale changes and difficulties occurring in the American economy requires a consensual sharing of burden, gains, and power. *Who loses, who gains, who makes the decisions?* In the absence of agreement on these issues, in a situation where many believe that the core American value of fairness is violated, policies will be difficult to implement. But the need for sharing goes further than its role as an instrument in implementation. It raises the question of the aims of American society and the possibilities of converting people to seeking a fairer and more democratic society.

A fairer and more local society builds on important values of community, caring, and autonomy. It requires a deep sense of bonds and commitments to one another and to larger values. New Deal/Great Society liberalism became a largely economically-centered set of policies with continuing but dwindling attention to the less successful. There was and is inadequate understanding that economic issues are not only political but also social and philosophical questions. *A kindling of moral sentiment is necessary to make a society, especially a more caring one, work.* In the absence of moral ties, unproductive and undemocratic conflict within and between communities is likely. A cleaved society which has suffered "defeat" as the U.S. has in its dethroning from its dominating role in the world, needs new values, hopes, and ambitions; otherwise, it will thrash about and disturb the world as it refuses to accept the inevitability of its loss of supremacy. Liberalism as well as Reaganomics has failed to provide this value mooring. A more communitarian and humanitarian outlook is needed.

Social values which do not restrict personal liberties and punish outsiders and marginals cannot be ordered from a political or philosophical menu. They develop from experience and understanding. The Reagan Administration may have provided the appropriate experiences. Its emphasis on inequality, heartlessness about the needy, neglect of the impact of its policies on the many, concern for those reveling in luxury and ostentation, the embracing of greed as motivator – may contribute to revulsion, especially if the economy sputters and many are harmed. Then, caring values may spread.

But events and feelings could go in the other direction. Increasing inequality, harshness, and greed may lead people to feel increasingly competitive with others, to act on the basis of envy and self-aggrandizement rather than compassion, with the results of greater nastiness and greed.

A positive, strong social movement deeply involving people in a caring life and action, and clarifying the significance of that design for living, is necessary if the selfish, materialistic mode of American life is to be avoided. The diverse social movements and concerns (anti-war mobilizations, citizen action organizations, minorities' and women's actions, environmental groupings) have attracted many people to politics, broadly conceived. While they have many humanistic interests in common, they have only nascent unifying political themes and meager philosophical or value connecting threads. Action and philosophy, coalition and diversity, are what is needed to lead a more economically effective and socially desirable America. Our final chapter develops this outlook.

The struggle for a progressive coalition should also involve stronger groups working with weaker groups because the former feel a responsibility to aid the weaker.

The base of a more just society rests in treating individuals and communities with dignity and respect for their individual attributes.

Each then is accorded equal respect, which can be manifested in very different treatments. Individuality requires recognizing differences and responding to them; equal respect for all, as philosopher Ronald Dworkin has concluded, can be manifested in differential rather than standardized treatment.[20] That is the ultimate goal — that we can embrace one another while accepting our differing qualities and needs.

The problems of the American economy cannot be resolved without an ideology which supports the changes undertaken. The "this-way-only" approach — that there is no alternative — does not appeal to basic values but to a deceptive interpretation of inevitability. The deep conflicts of American society require an outlook based on a renewal of American values of fairness, compassion, and neighborliness.

The politics of creativity

The recapitalization challenge should lead liberals and progressives to rethink the character, processes, and sustaining forces of a more fair, caring, and economically effective society. The economic and political travails of liberalism have weakened its always fallible basis. Now is the time to move beyond restoring bureaucratic liberalism to pursuing and developing new forms and goals of a better society. Without a strong movement involving many in developing and experiencing humanistic as well as economic goals, the harm of Reaganism and recapitalization cannot be undone. The struggle is not only about economic policies but about the values and tone of American society. The restoration of liberal economics and the welfare state is an inadequate response both to Reaganite recapitalization and to the deep changes occurring in American society. A new sense and direction for an economically and socially healthy America are needed.

To raise the issue of alternatives to liberalism as well as to recapitalism is not to imply that liberal programs have no current usefulness or that they have not played an important role in improving American society. Rather, it is to assert the importance of pushing beyond the received liberal practices of the New Deal and Great Society. These emerged in a different era than the 1980s promise. The circumstances of today require fresh approaches to exceedingly more complicated circumstances than existed in the 1930s or 1960s when liberalism flourished.

One reason for this is the likely disastrous aftermath of Reaganite recapitalization – high unemployment, greater inequalities, ineffective economic policies, less tax revenues, reductions in social programs, a decreased federal role, more segregation and discrimination, high military spending commitments, foreign relations in great and dangerous tension. But even without the muddling experience of Reaganism, there has been need for an approach that builds beyond the bureaucratic liberalism of the past and creates different possibilities for the future.

New circumstances require new ways of being and acting. Considerable creativity is occurring in pockets and segments of American society. Certainly, local citizen action movements and the anti-hierarchical emphasis of sections of the women's movement are very positive developments. Little positive is occurring, however, at national levels. The capacity for creativity is still great among liberals, progressives, and ordinary citizens without a political or ideological affiliation. The major tasks are to encourage that creativity – to rethink and to reconstruct ways of doing things – and to connect it with social movements and electoral strategies. One way to encourage creativity is to reject the "accepted wisdom" of recapitalization, even in its more palatable neo-liberal and liberal forms of industrial policy.

The struggle against recapitalization will not be advanced by a narrow defense of liberal programs and ideology as they have been experienced; it should be a fight for new or additional ways of effectively and compassionately dealing with the problems of American society. To go beyond Reaganism and recapitalization requires going beyond liberalism and industrial policy.

Chapter 9
Breaking political boundaries

Is it possible to break beyond recapitalization and liberalism? That possibility certainly exists: not only do the times demand more than either can deliver, but the signs of the makings of an unusual politics are appearing.

We hesitate to proclaim another "new politics." For every few years the American public is treated to an analysis which exclaims that a "new politics" has emerged – whether in the form of "television politics," "the permanent campaign," "the dealignment of political forces," or the awakening of the "middle American" "silent majority." But important developments are occurring. A variety of single-interest and community movements which previously shunned electoral politics now contend that they want to play an electoral role. The willingness to work with other movements and more conventional politicians is growing. The Democratic Party appears more attractive as Reaganite recapitalization has scared many groups into wanting to be more effective at the national political level in redirecting policy away from harming the poor, accepting high unemployment rates, throwing money at the military and business, and making war more likely. A jobs-oriented, pro-social programs, cut-military-expenditures agenda is appearing.

A strong progressive politics is gaining the two dimensions it requires: a coalition of diverse forces and a cutting through of the pro-market haze that chokes American politics. The two developments are obviously connected. They involve moving simultaneously toward an electoral, coalitional politics and a movement politics. We discuss first coalitional prospects.

164

Toward coalition

"Coalition" is in the wind again as it was in the 1930s and in 1964. Four reasons discussed below account for this awakened concern: broadened awareness, fear, weakness, and opportunity.

The so-called single-interest and community organizations are becoming *aware* that their goals require the refashioning of national economic patterns. Their span of interest and concern has expanded. High unemployment rates imperil affirmative action sought by women's groups, or environmentalists' protection of national parks with mineral or timber exploitation possibilities. It is increasingly apparent that basic economic policies affect the well-being of these groups that formerly paid little attention to interest rates or the federal budget. The economy of local communities depends on national expansion and rising national tax revenues which can be passed along to localities. The growth of military expenditures – an economic as well as a strategic issue – drives out funding for social and other programs.

Many groups *fear* that even if recapitalist economic expansion were successful, it would not improve their conditions. Unemployment would remain high; tax dollars would go to business and not to declining communities; regulation of business to promote affirmative action, safety, or a clean environment is already sacrificed to decreasing costs and increasing productivity. These groups will not be the beneficiaries of recapitalization, but they will bear its costs.

A basic source of *weakness* is that no economic class dominates electoral politics, so that gaining the vote of the working or middle classes is not enough to determine the outcome of elections. Indeed, differences within classes, especially the working classes, are great. The electorate is very split and its attitudes and allegiances fluid, a condition that has been termed "political dealignment."

The abundance of single-interest organizations testifies to the variety of concerns, many non-economic, which are salient to people and propel them into fighting for this goal or preventing that action; e.g., nuclear waste, the threat of nuclear war, energy costs, environmental protection, battered women, occupational health. It is good that people are being drawn into activity on those issues close to them. On the other hand, only pockets of limited influence develop among these and the community groups that dot the political landscape. Very few have towering power. Most are politically weak or can win only minor concessions. Many have not thought of themselves as involved in politics. In the main, they are "agin" groups fighting off encroachments and dangers rather than "for" groups moving on to their deeper goals. Their political weakness could be overcome if their interests blended together in an effective political way. Many are beginning to envision that possibility.

The Democratic Party, then, has an *opportunity* to benefit from the groundswell of disappointment in and disapproval of harsh reactionary recapitalization. It could win the support of these diverse groups that have disdained national politics or were uninterested in or disapproving of the Democratic Party. It could provide an electoral home for those groups who now seek a national political influence as they recognize the penalties of recapitalization. These groups will not become constituents of a Democratic Party, although some of their members may. Their relationship to the Democratic Party is likely to take the form of that of the AFL-CIO, which maintains an independent position, role, and identity while affecting Democratic national policy at the national as well as at the local level.

The recapitalization difficulties of the early 1980s have made "coalition" a respectable and viable term for politicians and movement people. Groups that have not seen what they had in common joined together to fight the Reaganite propensity for increasing inequality, placing the burden of improving the economy on the most vulnerable groups, lifting the barriers to discrimination, consumer fraud, and environmental devastation while increasing the possibilities of war and burdening the economy with heavy military costs for a dubious expansion. The possibilities of a new coalition do exist even if its management will not be easy.

The 1930s vs. the 1980s

The emerging coalition contains many components of the liberal-labor, New Deal/Great Society Democratic Party coalition of the

1930s and 1960s, but with new elements which promise important changes.[1]

The national Democratic Party, big labor, loosely organized liberals, and big city Democratic machines were the base of the New Deal/Great Society coalitions. All of them have declined in electoral strength. Movements which were hardly noticeable in New Deal days have now become highly significant in the current scene and are important potential members of a progressive coalition.

Civil rights groups were small in the 1930s and mainly symbolically important rather than carrying a big political stick. In the 1960s, they became significant as blacks became pivotal voters in some big states and as street uprisings upset conventional politics. Blacks are now a significant voting bloc in many northern states and, for the first time since Reconstruction, in the South as well. Hispanics are also gathering political strength.

New to political prominence are the women's, environmental, anti-war, anti-nuke, consumer, and citizen action movements. The aging have also become a strongly organized political force. More people, according to sociologist Peter Dreier, are involved in some form of liberal-progressive movement than at any time since the New Deal.[2]

Small and medium-sized businesses have little to gain from most recapitalist measures. Since they are not involved very much if at all with exports, their interest is in a strong, vital domestic market. Low-growth policies to curb inflation kill off their domestic demand. They need different policies and conditions than does big business. As they learn the sad truth that their needs diverge from those of the multinationals and conglomerates, they may join in attacking many recapitalist policies. But economic interests do not always override ideology nor lead to organization. Small and medium businesses may continue to go along with, or at least not strongly oppose, pro-big business proposals and policies. The *potential* of their opposition is there. What happens depends not only on events but on efforts to win sectors of smaller enterprises to espouse their interests when different from recapitalizing big business.

Many movements are searching for a national agenda and an electoral platform. Although they remain "single-interest" activities, they understand that employment and social programs are important to the well-being of their adherents. They desire different kinds of social programs. They are beginning to be open to greater public guidance of the economy. The possibilities for a strong progressive coalition are great and beginning to emerge.

Reagan's election victory of 1980 swept the political center of the country toward the right. The Congressional Democrats in 1981 feared to battle with the radical right Reaganite tax program and indeed seemed aimed at going beyond Reaganism in eagerness to reduce business taxes. The experience of Reaganite recapitalization has, however, since moved the political center to the left, as shown by the 1982 Congressional elections, which heartened those who oppose Reaganism. For the extraordinary greed of big business and the military, the prolonged depression, the tears in the Reaganite "safety net," and the hardheartedness and elite style of the administration changed the mood of the country. The value of social programs began to be recognized once again; military expenditures and strategic concepts lost their expensive and dangerous "sacred cow" position; combating inflation is now seen as a poor road to jobs. These feelings promote a coalition, but its appearance is no sure matter.

Coalition cracks

The coalition of the 1980s will not only differ from that of the 1930s, but will have even more difficulty in keeping together. The national and local Democratic parties are far weaker than before. Weakness as well as strength may make them reluctant to embrace movements that are demanding and do not accept the traditional political discipline of "going along" in order to win elections. The movements can be seen by political operatives as too anti-mainstream in position and anti-moderate in style, threatening the Democrats' appeal to those in the center. Movements may spell too much trouble for those who seek to control party machinery.

Nor do the movements see themselves as forced to work within the Democratic Party. They reserve the right to work with Democrats on their terms at times that they deem appropriate. An unattractive Democratic candidate will not automatically win allegiance on the basis of party loyalty as often happened in the past. Many movement members feel that over the longer run they must create a new party like the Citizens' Party, competing with the Democrats and Republicans, or change the Democratic Party to more radical proposals and ideologies than it has embraced in the past. In the shorter run, the movements are not mainly tuned to national or even local politicking, lobbying, and electioneering. They often see confrontational, disruptive actions as essential to their gains and as a style of political work that is important in their attractiveness and well-being. In short, they are movements and mobilizations leaning toward a more conventional electoral role but seeking to maintain the vitality, independence, and militance of "the movement." They are not easy partners.

In the next years a sufficient number of issues can bring together elements of the New Deal coalition with those newer components. Chief among the cementing issues is increasing the number of jobs and protecting the vulnerable through social programs. Most components of the coalition also are oriented to empowerment, to increasing the capacity of citizens to make the important decisions and to carry out the important activities that affect them. While empowerment conflicts with some traditional ways of conducting social programs, as we discussed earlier, it should be possible to work out a *modus vivendi* which balances the need for centralization to raise revenues and to insure that effectiveness, non-discriminatory and other goals are maintained with the need for decentralization to promote empowerment.

The core, near-term difficulties in the coalitional agenda are likely to center around affirmative action and military policy. The differences are most likely to appear in relation to labor unions.

The labor question

As we have indicated in Chapter 6, recapitalization policies are about labor costs, not just physical productivity as their supporters usually contend. The pressure on wages is already visible in "givebacks" – the demand that unions renounce gains won in collective bargaining and detailed in corporation–union contracts. The calculated propaganda of recapitalists to define a full employment level as at least a 6 per cent unemployment rate is premised on the depressing effect that such a high rate of unemployment has on wages. Unions and workers as well as the transfer-dependent poor are the main targets of recapitalists. Strikes and the ballot box will be labor's response.

In the next years, such pressures will continue to make volatile the labor question. Make no mistake about it – a liberal-progressive coalition must involve the unions, though not necessarily all of them. How the other members of the coalition respond to the needs of labor will be central to the ability of the coalition to be effective. On macro-economic questions there is wide agreement of other groups with unions. And unions are likely to play a central role in contesting conservative and reactionary recapitalist policies – the very future of unions and their members is at stake.

The keeping of unions in a coalition is important not only for numbers and money but also because it modifies the class character of the coalition. Many of the newer movements, e.g., women's, peace, environmental, consumer, are largely middle class in membership and, to a large extent, in concerns. That has its virtues, for the middle classes are numerous and active, but it has the deficit of underweighing the needs of blue-collar workers and the convergence of many of their interests with those of the middle classes.

As in the 1930s, a cross-class alignment is needed to have electoral prowess and to influence ways of thought. Union members are not involved in many other organizational and political activities. They can only be addressed organizationally through their unions. A cross-class program and participation has political appeal. Further, much of the political energy to tame recapitalization will come from workers who are so threatened by it. As Alan Wolfe says, "Political coalitions need to tie themselves to a social class in order to have a purpose, even while trying to broaden their base to other classes in order to win elections."[3]

The two chief sources of immediate coalitional difficulties are affirmative action, which many unionists see as threatening their jobs in a declining labor market, and a peace/anti-military expenditures approach, which reduces jobs in defense industries and which, to many, appears to undermine American security in the world. Other issues like abortion rights and environmental protection are somewhat less important. A coalition will clearly have to learn how to live with significant differences.

It may be easier to work with individual unions, especially locals, than with the AFL-CIO, although there are signs of openness at the top there. For example, in its Solidarity Day mobilization of 1981, AFL-CIO president Lane Kirkland accepted the participation of groups in disagreement with official AFL-CIO policy on military and foreign policy and with policies of individual unions on energy, environmental, or other issues. While not going as far as Janos Kadar on ascending to power after the Hungarian Revolution of 1956 – "Anyone who is not an enemy is a friend" – the AFL-CIO made it clear that it was not insisting on its standards of ideological or political rectitude in the struggles against Reaganite recapitalization. Furthermore, the top AFL-CIO leadership, a staunch supporter of military strength, questioned the wisdom of the extraordinary expansion of defense expenditures which the Reagan Administration sought. Many unions recognize their isolation in American culture and accept the importance of connecting, at least politically, with other groups.

What would help coalition-building would be the recognition by the other partners that the AFL-CIO, despite oligarchy and corruption in some unions, has been at the forefront of major liberal and progressive legislation for decades. That legislation includes civil rights laws as well as anti-poverty programs. There is more flexibility and potential with the unions than many middle-class organizations and individuals have understood.

In turn, the AFL-CIO and its member unions have to build on their beginning awareness that they have much in common with groups with whom they disagree on foreign policy or other issues. Such sensitivity seems to be growing. It is important to realize that differences, indeed important differences, exist but that coalitional activity is still possible on the issues that join together different organizations and interests.

A coalition is joint action of groups that maintain their identity. Politics makes strange bedmates – perhaps no stranger matches have been consumated than the New Deal coalition which contained Southern Bourbons and civil rights believers. If that coalition could persist and make history, the coalition of the 1980s has real possibilities.

We have addressed the coalition issue from the point of view of the movements. What about the Democratic Party's receptivity to a coalition arrangement with the movements?

Democratic realignment?

The Democratic Party, if it is to be strong, must learn to live with and partially through the movements. It will have to countenance movements criticizing local, state, and national Democratic office-holders who fail to meet the movements' objectives. On many issues, the movements will be much less moderate than Democratic politicians and many Democratic voters. The movements will disturb established power-wielders in the party by seeking to share influence in determining platform and candidates.

If the Democratic Party resists connection with movements or engages in procedural steps that would severely limit their impact, it is unlikely to be able to attract supporters and voters in large numbers.

The Democratic Party as a party no longer has a great attraction for voters. It has an uncertain core epitomized by the gulf between neo-liberals and strong supporters of unions and the welfare state; its recent history has been checkered, at the least. The dealignment of traditional voting blocs, especially blue-collar workers, with the Democratic Party should force that party to reach out to realign support. It can make gains, likely to be temporary, because of reactions to Reaganite recapitalization. Or it can build a more basic realignment by weaving together the variety of liberal-progressive movements and moving to a more just and effective set of policies. (We doubt that neo-liberal recapitalization will attract many.) Political energy and attractiveness now characterize the movements; they do not characterize the pols (or the polls). What may open up the Democratic Party to the movements is the chance to improve enormously the chances for electoral victories.

If one threat to a coalition is in forging it, overcoming the differences among the participating groups, the other threat is in its success. For the achievement of the coalition may be a "least common denominator" gain, winning on issues that may lack depth or the ability to change things in profound ways. For example, the 1982 agreement of many groups to press for a public works program as a small way of reducing unemployment was important. But it did little to deal with root causes of unemployment, nor could it reduce unemployment, especially for non-construction workers, very much.

In the next two sections we deal with the issues of the backwardness of America and what happens after legislation is passed. Both conditions call for great vigilance and clarity by the coalition and the avoidance of least common denominator attitudes.

'After the ball'

Getting effective, progressive legislation and policies into place is necessary – but not enough. It is not only what is written into law or regulations at the beginning that is important but what happens over time. "The flies capture the flypaper," as has happened in many regulatory commissions where regulated businesses over time came to dominate their regulators.[4] (A marvellous Greek tragedy: Senator Burton Wheeler of Montana was the scourge of the regulatory commissions, characterizing them as the pawns of the regulated; in the next generation, his son is reputed to be one of the leading business lobbyists with regulatory commissions.) Or, consider the Humphrey-Hawkins law on full employment, requiring presidential action when unemployment rises above 4 per cent. A liberal-labor coalition involving many organizations struggled and compromised to achieve its passage. Their political weakness in stagflationary and then depression circumstances made Humphrey-Hawkins a dead requirement. The coalition was unable to generate sufficient political strength to compel enforcement of the law in the Carter as well as in the Reagan Administration.

Legislators, courts, and administrators read not only election returns but also the political *Zeitgeist*. Changes in political attitudes affect how policies are conducted. Policies are what happens in action, not what is written in law or history. Active political pressure is needed to keep good practices and policies from going bad and bad policies from getting worse. The details of legislation *and* of administrative practice are important. That is why, for example, we called for contestional planning in the previous chapter.

Vigilance is the price not only of liberty but of maintaining effective legislation. And some organized power too. That requires a different kind of politics than one that is narrowly oriented to elections. We shall return to this issue.

Backward America

The United States is known for its great variety of civic organizations, especially at the local levels. Few countries can match the number of its garden clubs, lodges, brotherhoods and sisterhoods, and associations. As de Tocqueville noted long ago, Americans are joiners. But the U.S. lacks public economic institutions which are now crucial to effective economic functioning and which exist among our competitors.

The United States does not have an agency which tries to influence the allocation of capital among enterprises as have Japan, France, and West Germany. It lacks an agency which attempts to project long-term trends and to direct industry toward promising possibilities. The United States does not require corporations to include worker representatives on their board of directors. The U.S. does not try to influence layoffs and plant shutdowns by requiring advance notice, termination pay, and efforts to prevent unemployment and shutdown.

These are examples of the absence in the U.S. of public institutions and governmental regulations which are widespread and important in other advanced capitalist countries. In short, the U.S. is backward in terms of governmental involvement in economic activity. And American big business strenuously resists efforts to extend the kind of activities that would aid economic functioning. The consequence is that liberals and neo-liberals as well as progressives have to work hard just to bring about economic institutions and public practices that are needed to "save" or improve capitalism, practices that are ongoing elsewhere. These measures remedy capitalist malfunctioning; they do not transform the capitalist system in a more progressive direction. Thus, a Reconstruction Finance Corporation which would provide capital to businesses without any strings requiring domestic investment and employment appears to be a very bold proposal in the American context. It is not bold in terms of greater equality, democracy, or even employment – it is "bold" only because the U.S. in practice and in ideology is so backward. In the U.S. less government is regarded as the key to business success, while elsewhere it is recognized that a government active in economic affairs is essential to business gains.

This American backwardness complicates politics. For improving business profitability takes precedence over other claims when business acts as stupidly and as inefficiently as American business often does. In the 1930s and 1940s, the unionization of American industry forced greater rationality and efficiency on union-fighting firms. Unions required job classifications, a clear pay structure, promotion channels, safety regulations, a grievance structure, layoff recall procedures – conditions of rationality and sensible procedures lacking in many concerns. Companies began to recognize the importance of worker attitudes and to respond in part to worker concerns. In the 1980s, those who do not imbibe the ideological stream which contends that governmental involvement is always negative will again have to push American business into acting rationally in terms of its own long-term interest and to accept government involvement. But the terms of that involvement are the key.

This situation of backwardness restricts and twists the political agenda. The need will be to tie efforts to promote these needed and lacking economic institutions to long-run social objectives of democratizing enterprises and promoting employment. The coalition should demand more than overcoming big business resistance to understanding and acting realistically in its own best interests.

Connected to this backwardness is the absence in the United States of a large mass-based socialist or even social democratic party. In most advanced capitalist countries a left or labor party or parties exist: The Labour Party in the U.K., the Communist and Socialist parties in France and Italy, the Social Democratic Party in West Germany. Sometimes they are the government, an element in governing, or a potential government. Their strong presence opens up issues for discussion; widens policy measures; and breaks through limited acceptable wisdom to force consideration of strong alternatives. In Europe, countries like Sweden have had corporatist policies that have won high public benefits and raised real wages for workers in a social contract which regulated business–labor–government relations.

The U.S. lacks this left perspective and mobilization. The range of debate is exceedingly narrow here, as well as the range of governmental activity. The hope that some express in the U.S. for a "social contract" that will replace the implicit social contract of the 1950s and 1960s built around economic growth requires agreement between strong partners of business and labor who can deliver their members. In a period of economic growth so low that it cannot overcome problems of the distribution of the economic pie and in conditions of weak labor–progressive institutions, a new social contract that would not harm workers and the poor will not be easily gained. It even has trouble getting much attention.

This narrowness of ideological and policy debate requires a different politics that can break beyond the bounds that now constrict American understanding and practice.

Politics as education

The coalition will have to move to broaden public debate, to make winnable issues out of new ways of thinking about the economy and society; for example, participation by government in investment decisions, democratization of enterprises, empowerment. If new doctrines, goals, and instruments do not become politically viable, policies will be stunted and ineffective. They will likely exacerbate inequalities, promote concentration of power, and worsen the quality of life.

Our understanding of this issue is influenced by the Italian Marxist Antonio Gramsci who recognized that a revolution in politics requires a revolution in thought. A transformation of society would not be accomplished by economic change alone but required that the prevailing ways of thinking – which he saw as functioning to support the capitalist ruling class – be overcome. "Ideological hegemony" was the term he employed for the prevailing modes of thought, and he saw that a long period would be needed for these dominating perspectives to be supplanted.[5]

One does not have to accept the place from which Gramsci

started or the destination at which he aimed, to see the importance of his emphasis on ideological or value or attitudinal outlooks (to use a series of words in descending order of the irritation that they provoke).

MIT political scientist Walter Dean Burnham has applied Gramsci's analysis to the United States:

Where there is no organized conflict over the fundamentals of collective existence in society or economy, what elsewhere would require ideological clarity for its defense tends to recede below the level of consciousness to become "prejudices" or "inarticulate major premises." . . . The crucial difference between the U.S. and most if not all other advanced industrial societies with democratic political regimes is that in this country alone (cultural) *hegemony has been effectively uncontested.*[6] (Italics in the original.)

To achieve electoral victories which begin to make possible structural changes will require the breaking up of the domination of ideas that only markets work and that they work best where government is least.

"Experience" alone will not assure the decompostion of the accepted wisdoms. Some believe that only the experience of crisis is likely to open up a society to the kind of progressive changes that are required to resolve economic difficulties and to lead it to more humanistic, democratic goals. But crisis alone is not enough. Gramsci's "ideological hegemony" is not inevitably broken and turned in a progressive direction by a crisis. How experience is interpreted is crucial and not necessarily dictated by the deep structure of the crisis. Indeed, Gramsci's emphasis was on the long period of development that is required to change basic perspectives, ways of seeing and interpreting experiences and events, before new humanitarian values and a sense of their possibilities emerge. How crises and other experiences are understood and which ways of moving beyond them seem palatable and possible influence what "experience teaches."

The implication, then, is that it is necessary to struggle to influence thought before, during, and after a crisis or strain. Tension itself does not free people from misleading views and outmoded attitudes, nor move them toward new possibilities and values.

A struggle for new ideas and understandings must accompany battles over electoral victories.

What can be done? The usual complaint is that the media and established institutions promote accepted wisdoms and are reluctant, indeed resistant, to making available alternative ways of thinking or, at least, to criticizing the received wisdoms. To bewail the outlook of the media and established institutions may lead to some changes in them. But it is exceedingly unlikely that they will be the locomotives pulling new, disturbing ideas into American consciousness.

What is available to the coalitional partners are their members, near-members, and potential members. While many people are restive about the current situation, they are not clear about the way to more effective alternatives. An educational job must be done. This requires the active involvement of members in their organizations. This involvement is important for other reasons as well. The movement element, the engaging of people in strongly felt activity, should not be lost in the important struggle for progressive electoral victories. Movements should educate as well as mobilize.

Where are the grass roots?[7]

Some of the potential components of the coalition are vital, creative, democratic institutions which engage the loyalty and participation of their members. Others are not "organizations" or "institutions" for they do not have a continuing organized life. To a large extent, that has been the case of the peace and anti-nuclear movements. Still others have an organizational structure, certainly a voice, a form to raise money, but they lack a major quality – active, participating, committed membership. Many civil rights organizations are "letterhead organizations," able to present an attractive board of directors or advisors, a nominal organizational structure of an executive director and a staff, some ability to raise money, but very little capacity to generate action among their potential constituencies. Similarly, many trade unions have compulsory checkoff through collective bargaining contracts which provide their source of income, a well-defined organizational and electoral structure, a variety of important activities, but little influence on the voting and political outlook of members; nor can they easily engage them in action.

In short, many organizations and movements have a voice but not a base. The need, then, is not only to weld and hold together a coalition but to revitalize its member movements and organizations by involving their grass roots in more attractive and effective ways and to organize the unorganized and unemployed. Obviously, these are important for electoral purposes. Many elections are determined by very small swings in votes or changes in the numbers who don't vote. Low-income people vote less than those of high income who are more likely to see advantages in recapitalist policies. Getting members to register and to vote for coalition candidates will be important for the success of the coalition. Each organization is likely to expand and to be more effective in its main activities if its members are involved and involving others.

Since the coalition is unlikely to have considerable sums that can be used in elections, while the supporters of recapitalization are likely to continue to have sizable financing, the coalition must depend on electoral activity by its members to offset the media exposure and other advantages of the opposition. People can substitute for money, especially where they are well organized and devoted.

Greater involvement of members and the revitalizing of organizations in terms of activity, agenda, and internal democracy offer another advantage. The best way to break through the prevailing ideological domination is through involvement in action. Fighting on rent or utility increases reveals some of the peculiarities of an unregulated market or the power of vested interests. More critical ideas develop. Long-held but unexamined attitudes and values can become unsettled. What once appeared outlandish, un-American, outside the acceptable consensus of what is right, now appears necessary and desirable. Old habits of thought are broken as members have new experiences and understandings. The ideological domination of recapitalist ways of thinking is most likely to be broken not by harangues but by involvements and experiences. They demonstrate the inadequacies of the acceptable interpretations of what is wrong and necessary in the American economy and the need for new goals and approaches.

It is day-to-day life and personal contact which shape attitudes. They are much more important than the vaunted media.[8] This situation is to the advantage of a progressive coalition. It should not be lost.

If one's organization is attractive and effective and one enjoys and benefits from democratic processes in the organization, then it is not a far jump to believe that greater democracy and effectiveness are appropriate for major economic and social institutions. The constituent organizations of the coalition are not only means; they can demonstrate what a transformed society might begin to look like.

A coalition at the top is important. It would be much more significant if there were a grass roots level that fed and was fed by the organizations in the coalitions. Indeed, without involvement of members in activities which are close to them, they are unlikely to maintain interest in broad, important, but remote national politics. An effective national coalition requires a base of involvement in local issues. In fact the great political energy in the U.S. is at the local level, not the national. Building on this energy and extending it is crucial.

The linking of local issues to national changes in an enduring way depends upon involvement at the local level. The tension occurs in making the connection to the national, so that the basic appeal of the organization is not lost. That appeal comes from dealing with immediate, personal hurts which can be remedied at the local level. Learning how to connect to national issues without losing the local or single interest is difficult for organizations attempting to go "glocal" – relating the local and special to the global.[9] Making that connection is vital.

Starting up theory

In this chapter and the preceding one, we have not offered a detailed program of action; rather we have discussed the broad outlines of an approach to economic and social issues and the making of a political formation. Partly we have moved in this way because many detailed proposals and platforms are now being offered. Many appear very good, but frequently lack a political appeal. Others have not been thought through adequately. But this situation is not disheartening, for it takes a while to have good ideas percolating. A look at the 1930s is encouraging and helps to explain why we do not feel remiss in not offering a list of concrete, short-run, action proposals.

Many view the New Deal's progressive measures (the social security programs; the Wagner Act) as ideas which suddenly emerged, newly hatched by people at the national level. This understanding is inadequate. States like Wisconsin and New York had already innovated unemployment insurance, old-age pensions, protection of union organizing. The New Deal took over and modified these policies and made them into national programs. The spark was not initially national. That local inspiration may be happening again today as communities throughout the United States discuss and sometimes accept plans to take over shutdown plants in worker-community buyouts, buy energy at reduced prices, promote empowerment activities by public housing tenants, seek to reorganize the industrial potential of the area, develop capital sources for new or old industry on the basis of *quid pro quos* about investment and jobs, organize crime patrols, and promote citizen involvement in decisions. Some of these ideas and approaches will develop into the common agenda of the emerging coalition.

Talent and energy are now widely diffused across the United States. As a consequence, progressive ideas and practices are "incubating," in Peter Dreier's phrase, in many places and will provide basic leads toward national platforms and policies.[10] Local initiatives often precede national efforts.

At the level of basic economic policies, a look at the 1930s is also instructive. The dismay at the breakdown of the growth policies of the 1960s should not lead to an anguished waiting for a new theory to suddenly appear.[11] The emergence of what came to be called "Keynesianism," a stress on the need to stimulate demand in order to overcome depression and to promote growth, influenced the policy development of the 1930s, although too timidly to speed up recovery. It became crucial to the economic growth of postwar advanced capitalist countries. The belief of many is that its progenitor, British economist John Maynard Keynes, first offered the theory and policy in his deeply influential 1936 book, *The General Theory of Employment, Interest and Money*. Not so. As early as 1925, Keynes recognized the dangers involved in the deflationary policies of the chancellor of the exchequer and excoriated them in his *The Economic Consequences of Mr. Churchill*, a play on Keynes's best-selling analysis (*The Economic Consequences of the Peace*) of the disastrous outcome that he foresaw in the Versailles Treaty. The General Strike of 1926 was one consequence of the Churchill policies. Later in the 1920s, Keynes strongly supported the expansionary policies advocated by Lloyd George, which contrasted with the deflationary policies then in vogue. Keynes's and George's policies failed to gather a following. *The General Theory* provided the theoretical foundations for policies that Keynes (and some others like the Columbia University economist John Maurice Clark) had long pushed. Of course, the expansionary policies followed by the Second New Deal after 1934 *preceded* Keynes's book.[12]

It is likely that policies will emerge during this long period of economic difficulty that at some point will be clarified by a theoretical analysis which explains why some policies are beneficial, thereby promoting their acceptance and expansion. As is usually the case, theory will follow practice and action, the involvements of ordinary people, rather than initially leading it. Once the theory helps explain the actions, then the actions may be shaped more effectively and modified.

This way of looking at the evolution of a theoretical approach is important to understand because we should not wait for a theory to emerge or to believe that it will come about independent of practical and political action.

We do not assume that there is an inexorable determinism that governs fate. Events and conjunctures are important, generally unpredictable in timing, and uncertain in outcome. But the outlines of a coalition are clearly there and the makings of a pro-jobs agenda beginning to be filled in. Recapitalist thinking is shifting to less extreme, perhaps neo-liberal forms, but still ones which do not adequately answer the questions of who gains, who pays, who decides?

Sea-changes are underway in the world economy and in the U.S. The United States more than most countries must learn to play different roles. Ordinary politics does not encourage such repositioning.

The French sociologist Alain Touraine and others assert that conventional electoral politics hobbles in its death embrace.[13] Movements cut across and around electoral politics; they disequilibrate political and governmental actions; they do not depend on traditional political processes as they organize, mobilize, confront, provoke, and demand. At the least, they challenge conventional political thinking and bring together under-represented people. While we believe the Touraine view is exaggerated, it does point to the need for a politics that moves in and outside conventional electoral politics. That possibility of breaking the boundaries of political debate and action seems to be growing, and offers a substantial chance of overcoming recapitalist pressures and promoting a more humane society.

Recapitalizing America is neither necessary nor inevitable. For an alternative industrial policy to supplant recapitalization active democratic attention must be paid to ends and means and particularly to who benefits.

Notes

Chapter 1 Accepted wisdoms

1 Among the best known of the neo-conservatives are Irving Kristol, Nathan Glazer, Peter Berger, and Norman Podhoretz. They can be found in publications such as *The Public Interest* and *Commentary*. An excellent introduction to the New Right can be found in Alan Crawford's *Thunder on the Right*, New York, Pantheon, 1980.

2 The striking similarity between the economic policies that Carter planned to pursue if re-elected and those Reagan did pursue can be found in the press releases and public statements of the Carter Administration in the fall of 1980. Particularly interesting are the August 28, 1980 release entitled *Economic Growth in the 1980's* and the testimony of Charles L. Schultze, then Chairman of Carter's Council of Economic Advisors, on September 8, 1980 before the Budget Committee of the House of Representatives.

3 A good example is the policy statement by the Business Roundtable (an elite political lobbying organization comprised of the chief executive officers of two hundred of the largest U.S. industrial corporations), "Policies necessary to reduce the rate of inflation," Washington, D.C., The Business Roundtable, June 1978.

4 Rohatyn's "liberal" approach to industrial/economic policy can be found in Felix Rohatyn, "A better way to bail out Chrysler," *New York Times*, January 13, 1980, p. 16f; "The older America; can it survive?," *New York Review of Books*, January 22, 1981, pp. 13–16. See also Senator Paul Tsongas, *The Road From Here*, New York, Vintage Books, 1982.

5 Interestingly, Ronald Reagan's political reaction to the 10.2 per cent U.S. unemployment rate in September of 1982 was to sign an export promotion bill.

6 The Reagan Administration explored methods to open international trade so as to increase U.S. exports of services.

7 Ernest Mandel, *Late Capitalism*, London, New Left Press, 1975. For a non-Marxist analysis of present economic difficulties that also uses the Kondratieff analysis, see W. W. Rostow, *The World Economy*, Austin, University of Texas Press, 1978.

8 Reagan's effort to expand swiftly military expenditures, while playing some role in stimulating the economy in the short-run version of supply-side economics, was not basic to the long-term concern with imports. It threatened the administration with loss of support from

big business as reduced tax receipts and government spending
ballooned the federal deficit.

9   At times, we lump the reactionary and moderate standpoints together
and label them "conservative."

10 Moderate business approaches were best exemplified in the early
1980s by people like Walter Wriston of Citibank who, while
generally agreeing with the Reagan approach to business,
government, and the poor, cautioned the administration to go slow
on military buildup. Neo-liberals include Democratic Senators Paul
Tsongas (Massachusetts), Gary Hart (Colorado), and Bill Bradley
(New Jersey), as well as financier and New York City bailout czar
Felix Rohatyn.

11 Most prominent among the liberals are the ex-Carter Administration
group that clusters around Ray Marshall, former Secretary of Labor.
Their liberal policy statement is: Ray Marshall and other prominent
economists, *An Economic Strategy for the 1980's; The Failure of
Reaganomics and the Full Employment Alternative*, Washington, D.C.,
Full Employment Action Council and National Policy Exchange,
1982. If there had been a second Carter Administration, its economic
policies would most likely have been somewhere between the liberal
and neo-liberal camps. The AFL-CIO is also in the liberal camp:
see, for example, "Kirkland urges 'coherent policy' for revival,"
Memo from Cope, January 26, 1981, AFL-CIO Labor Press.

12 We cannot overstress the importance of this change in the accepted
wisdom. Even though there is much controversy in the U.S. over
specific policies, the goal of increased international competitiveness,
through the mechanism of private-investment-fed productivity growth
and reduced government intervention in the economy, frames the
debate. Recapitalization as belief has ideological respectability; it
is the new accepted wisdom. For industry-generated data on the
general nature of the recapitalization ideology, see the results of a
survey of the economic beliefs of U.S. citizens, "The vital consensus;
American attitudes on economic growth," Union Carbide
Corporation, Spring 1980.

13 Two good examples of the necessitarian dictum which has been
attached to the recapitalization wisdom can be found in the *New
York Times*. The first is a full-page advertisement (July 28, 1980,
p. A7) in which academics, politicians, and corporate chief executives
responded to the question "How can the U.S. remain competitive?"
Their answers include: 1   change tax policy to accelerate investment;
2   expand exports; 3   reduce antitrust activity in order to
strengthen the U.S. as an international competitor; 4   deregulate

business "where necessary"; and finally (or primarily!) 5 develop a national consensus. The second example, a news story, was published two months later (August 18, 1980, pp. D1, D8), "U.S. industry seeking to restore competitive vitality to products." This major article analyzes the "loss" of U.S. international competitiveness and concludes that it is the product of low productivity, which in turn is the product of government regulation, over-taxation of business, and trade union protectionism.

Chapter 2 The Great Transformation

1 Military and economic dominance do generally coincide. It is unlikely, however, that lasting economic strength can be forged for the United States today in the furnace of military activity.
2 Alan Wolfe in *America's Impasse* (New York, Pantheon, 1981) explains why U.S. dominance of the world political economy was crucial for U.S. domestic policy. The affluence afforded by world dominance permitted a politics of growth in which social problems could be addressed through government spending instead of by attention to the structural basis of those problems. As world dominance wanes, growth politics is now too expensive. Thus, the drive for renewed world supremacy especially in the economic realm is a conservative longing for past political formulae as much as it is for productive efficiency.
3 In the early 1980s speculation on the probability of world-wide slumps (an euphemism for recessions that verge on depressions) began to crowd more traditional discussions of national recessions in the business pages of local newspapers. See, for example, "Next a global slump?," *New York Times*, March 16, 1980, p. D2; "World bank predicting global economic decline," *New York Times*, August 18, 1980, p. D1.
4 This is an important theoretical point for both academics and policy analysts. While the world economy has always lurked in the background of national economic analysis, the increased influence of international production, service, employment, and especially capital flows on U.S. economic activity demands that increased attention be paid to the international context. Sociologists Wolfe (op. cit.) and Fred Block (*The Origins of International Economic Disorder*, Berkeley, University of California Press, 1977) have put U.S. politics and monetary policy in the context of international trade. Economists Barry Bluestone and Bennett Harrison have addressed

the effect of international capital flows upon U.S. industrial
employment (Bluestone and Harrison, *The Deindustrialization of
America*, New York, Basic Books, 1982).

5 Immanuel Wallerstein, "The rise and future demise of the world
capitalist system," *Comparative Studies in Society and History*, 1974,
vol. 16, 4, pp. 387–415. The reason for decline in domestic control
of internationally oriented firms lies in the divergence of interest
between multinational firms and the U.S. government and people, as
U.S. domestic control of the world market is replaced by mere
participation in that market.

6 The debate over the efficacy of concentration revolves around the
deviation from American academic ideology that concentrated
wealth and power represent. In the economic formulation, monopoly
or oligopoly industries represent a retreat from the market, unfair
competition, and, perhaps worst of all, an undermining of
conventional economic theory. In the political formulation, the
political influence of the large corporation on U.S. government policy
represents an intolerable end-run around pluralist ideals of
representative democracy. Here the political theory of the American
democracy is threatened. As we will see, our approach is different.

7 For more on the similarity and connections between the Chrysler
bailout and the international debt problem, see Donald Tomaskovic-
Devey and John B. McKinlay, "Bailing out the banks," *Social Policy*,
January 1981.

8 These problems will be discussed at length in Chapter 5.

9 Thorstein Veblen, "The captains of finance and the engineers," *The
Engineers and the Price System*, New York, Viking, 1921, pp. 58–82.

10 Harry Brill writes that 88 per cent of U.S. Steel's profits come from
non-steel enterprises including banking, money markets, and oil
exploration; see his "The runaway steel industry," *The Nation*, Feb.
1980, pp. 138–9.

11 Robert Hayes and William Abernathy, "Managing our way to
economic decline," *Harvard Business Review*, July 1980, vol. 58, 4,
pp. 67–77.

12 Ezra Vogel, *Japan as Number One*, New York, Harper & Row,
1979, p. 253ff.

13 The first exception to the general trend of upward price movement
occurred in 1982 as a result of the deepest recession in the American
economy since the great Depression of the 1930s. This is the
exception that proves the rule – the economy had to be "dead in
the water" before upward price rises would slow. For Lester Thurow

on upward price shocks, see his *The Zero-Sum Society*, New York, Penguin, 1980, pp. 41–75.

14 Unionized workers' wages may contribute to inflation in two ways: the prices of the goods they produce may be important components of other products; the level of union wages affects non-union wages.

15 Bluestone and Harrison, op. cit. This is the best single source on deindustrialization and its importance for economic policy and employment.

16 Eli Ginzberg and George Vojta describe this trend in "The service sector of the U.S. economy," *Scientific American*, March 1981, vol. 244, 3, pp. 48–55. They point out the necessity of understanding the new importance of service industries when developing industrial policy.

17 Daniel Bell, *The Coming of Post-Industrial Society*, New York, Basic Books, 1974.

18 See Donald Tomaskovic-Devey, "The stratification consequences of U.S. industrial and occupational change," Ph.D. dissertation, Department of Sociology, Boston University, 1983.

19 David Birch, "The job generation process," Program in Neighborhood and Regional Change, MIT–Harvard Joint Center for Urban Studies, 1979. Also see Birch, "Who creates jobs?," *The Public Interest*, Fall 1981, 65, pp. 3–14. Bluestone and Harrison, op. cit., argue that the apparent strength of small business employment is by default; it is a residual growth, impressive only because of the deindustrialization process of large manufacturers. Although this seems unlikely due to the large number of service jobs generated by small businesses, we would agree with Bluestone and Harrison that the new jobs are of lower quality (in terms of income, stability, and promotion prospects) than the ones they replace.

20 Eli Ginzberg, "The job problem," *Scientific American*, November 1977, vol. 237, 5, pp. 43–51.

21 Many economists believe that labor shortages rather than unemployment will be the issue of the late 1980s and 1990s as the small cohorts of babies born in the 1960s and 1970s enter the labor market. The assumptions are that the female labor force will only slowly increase from now on, despite the rising need for two incomes to maintain an adequate standard of living, and that people will retire from the labor market at relatively younger ages despite the impact of inflation and recapitalization on pensions and savings. Demography is not always destiny.

22 Robert Heilbroner suggests that the transformation of the U.S. economy is of such a fundamental nature that existing ideologies

and institutions are no longer adequate. See Robert Heilbroner, "Does capitalism have a future?," *New York Times Magazine,* August 15, 1982, pp. 20–60.

Chapter 3 International trade: the *real* British Disease?

1 *Newsweek,* September 8, 1980, p. 58. Even before the Reagan election export expansion was an active policy objective; for example, see "Senate backs bill for trading companies," *New York Times,* September 4, 1980, p. D3.

2 Of course, the U.S. would do well to help other, weaker nations attain higher standards of living also. Our point is that the nationalist drive to be first is outmoded.

3 For one good example among many on the Japanese, see the special issue of *Business Week,* "Japan's strategy for the 80's," December 14, 1981.

4 *Economic Report of the President, 1982,* Washington, D.C., U.S. Government Printing Office, B-106, p. 352.

5 Ibid., B-1, p. 233; B-102, p. 348.

6 Ibid., Table B-102, p. 348; and *Statistical Abstract of the United States, 1981,* Table 1314, p. 732.

7 *Economic Report of the President, 1982,* B-84, p. 392.

8 Ibid., Table B-48, p. 287; and *Statistical Abstract of the United States, 1982,* Table 937, p. 551.

9 This calculation was made by multiplying the known exports of goods and services of the U.S. economy by the ratio of assets to sales of the *Fortune 1000* companies in 1980 to yield an approximation of the investment in productive assets that exports represent. The ratio of assets to sales for *Fortune 1000* in 1980 was 0.713. Total exports of goods and services were $345 billion (from *Statistical Abstract of the United States, 1982,* Table 923, p. 544). U.S. private assets abroad in 1980 were $513.3 billion (from *Economic Report of the President, 1982,* Table B-105, p. 351). This is an essentially conservative estimate. The *Fortune 1000* ratio of assets to sales is probably high because of the capital intensive structure of the largest corporations in the U.S.

10 The "comparative advantage" doctrine assumes that each nation concentrates production on what it does most efficiently and then trades for other products with nations similarly concentrating on their efficiently produced commodities.

11 *Economic Report of the President, 1982*, Table B-1, p. 233, and Table B-107, p. 353.

12 Similarly, when the dollar is strong or inflation high in the United States our exports drop and imports rise. See, for example, "Strong dollar, weak industry," *New York Times*, July 3, 1982, p. 27.

13 Ronald Müller, *Revitalizing America*, New York, Simon & Schuster, 1980, calls for revitalization through open international trade. He sees internationalization of production and investment as inevitable and urges the U.S. to run the race. Bluestone and Harrison, op. cit., are more cautious, advocating industrial policy to deal with the domestic dislocation caused by international trade and controls on private investment. Our analysis tends to agree with Bluestone and Harrison here.

14 Calculated from *Statistical Abstract of the United States, 1981*, Table 1422, p. 785.

15 In fact, the International Monetary Fund reports that national responses to the international recession of the early 1980s were to increase protectionist measures: "Slump in trade, sluggish economic conditions, rise in restrictive practices noted in study," *IMF Survey*, August 16, 1982, pp. 241–7.

16 Of course, this translates into a policy of beggaring the citizens of the U.S. in order to increase exports.

17 *The General Theory of Employment, Interest and Money*, New York, Harcourt Brace, 1936, pp. 382–3.

18 See S. M. Miller, "Notes on neo-capitalism," *Theory and Society*, 1975, vol. 2, 1, pp. 1–45, for a discussion of the importance of small and medium-sized firms in the U.S. economy.

19 U.S. corporate and private income from direct investments abroad has risen from about $4 billion in 1961, to $9 billion in 1971, to $18 billion in 1975, to over $40 billion in 1981. See "U.S. companies profit from investments they made years ago in plants overseas," *Wall Street Journal*, March 11, 1981, p. 56ff.

20 Some of the capital flows and the logic behind them are traced in Richard Barnet and Ronald Müller, *Global Reach*, New York, Simon & Schuster, 1974.

21 The leading liberal/conservative solution to the unemployment and low wages produced by the international mobility of capital is presently urban enterprize zones. The logic of these low-wage, low- or no-tax zones is to lure U.S. capitalists to invest in the U.S. William Goldsmith characterizes this solution as "Bringing the Third World home," *Working Papers*, March 1982, vol. 9, 2, pp. 24–31.

22 For one approach to negotiating world trade flows, see Willy Brandt

(Chairman), *North-South: A Program For Survival,* Report of the Independent Commission on International Development Issues, London, Pan, 1980.

Chapter 4 Productivity: producing confusion

1 "The U.S. productivity crisis," *Newsweek,* September 8, 1980, pp. 53–9. Similar analyses can be found in an important article in the *Wall Street Journal,* "Many culprits named in national slowdown in productivity gains," October 24, 1980, pp. 1, 24.
2 Official productivity statistics *did* decline in some quarters of 1979 through 1982. But we shall see that productivity data are complex and unreliable.
3 See "Productivity and inflation," Joint Economic Committee, Congress of the United States, April 24, 1980.
4 Gus Tyler, "Study cites unions as spur to U.S. lead in productivity," *AFL-CIO News,* October 18, 1980, p. 4. Gregory Schmid, "Productivity and reindustrialization: a dissenting view," *Challenge,* January 1981, vol. 23, 6, pp. 24–9, follows this analysis also.
5 The actual measurement of productivity is less simple and less reliable. The dollar value of output in a year is deflated by the rise in price level from the previous year and then divided by the size of the labor force. Monetary values are translated into physical changes – a most unsatisfactory procedure. This curious method of calculation should lead people to treat productivity estimates with great care. Unfortunately, skepticism about productivity figures is not widespread among economists.
6 *Statistical Abstract of the United States, 1981,* Table 1562, p. 883.
7 See Bruce Greek, "New measures bear out productivity drop," *Chemical and Engineering News,* September 1980, vol. 58, 35, pp. 12–14; and also the recent policy statement by the National Council on Employment Policy, *Labor Force and Productivity Measurements: Danger Ahead,* Washington, D.C., Labor Day 1982.
8 See, for example, Nicholas Bond, "The psychological component in productivity," *Wall Street Journal,* March 10, 1981.
9 Lestor Thurow, *The Zero-Sum Society,* New York, Penguin, 1980, pp. 80–2.
10 See Harry Brill, "Chrysler on welfare," *Social Policy,* 10, 5, March/April 1980, pp. 10–13.

11 *Statistical Abstract of the United States, 1980*, Table 700, p. 422. See also our Table 6.7, p. 110.

12 This surge in employment was accompanied by increasing unemployment which also keeps wages low as workers fear the loss of employment.

13 Thurow, op. cit., pp. 86–7; the editors, "Productivity slowdown: a false alarm," *Monthly Review*, June 1979, vol. 31, 2, pp. 1–12.

14 For data on OECD nations' decline in productivity growth see the *Economic Outlook*, Paris, OECD, 1979.

15 Thurow, op. cit., pp. 85–6; see also Bill Cunningham, "Productivity's link to economic growth," *AFL-CIO Federationist*, March 1978, pp. 1–5. This is an important observation for economic policy. Productivity, however measured, will not grow in the recession, no-growth, environment created by the conservative monetarist fight against inflation.

16 J. J. Servan-Schreiber, *The American Challenge*, New York, Atheneum, 1968.

17 The productivity growth–inflation equation can be found in "Productivity and inflation," Joint Economic Committee, op. cit., as well as in "Productivity's up and down," *New York Times*, November 12, 1980, p. A30. The productivity–wage–inflation analysis is present in two studies published by the Center for Democratic Policy: Daniel P. Mitchell, "Wage and Price Study 1" and Barry Bosworth, "Wage and Price Study 2," both in *Controlling Inflation: Studies in Wage/Price Policy*, Washington D.C., Center for Democratic Policy, 1981. A big-business analysis of the wage–inflation link can be found in "Policies necessary to reduce the rate of inflation," Washington, D.C., The Business Roundtable, June 1978.

18 *Statistical Abstract of the United States, 1980*, Table 700, p. 422.

19 This is, of course, exactly what is happening in the U.S. auto industry.

20 For the international nature of this contradiction between growth and inflation, employment and consumption see various issues of the *IMF Survey*. A few articles are cited here as examples, although the IMF as a world body spends much of its efforts manipulating this inflation–growth contradiction. "Very high priority is given to fight against inflation," *IMF Survey*, May 24, 1982, pp. 145, 159; "Severe problems facing world economy will be background to meetings in Helsinki," *IMF Survey*, April 19, 1982, pp. 113, 126; "Persistent structural rigidities must be tackled for industrial world to break grip of stagflation," February 8, 1982, pp. 33–6.

Chapter 5 Investment panacea

1 For energy comparisons see *Statistical Abstract of the United States, 1981*, Table 1565, pp. 886–7. For a comparison of governmental revenues as a percentage of Gross Domestic Product for six industrialized countries, see Ray Marshall, *An Economic Strategy for the 1980's*, Washington, D.C., Full Employment Action Council and National Policy Exchange, 1982, Table 2, p. 56.

2 *Statistical Abstract of the United States, 1980*, Table 700, p. 422. See also our Table 6.7, p. 110.

3 *Statistical Abstract of the United States, 1981*, Table 942, p. 553.

4 *Statistical Abstract of the United States, 1980*, Table 956, p. 569, and Table 957, p. 570.

5 *Economic Report of the President, 1981*, Table B-1, p. 233, and Table B-85, p. 330.

6 Calculated from *Statistical Abstract of the United States, 1981*, Table 420, p. 247.

7 The data for 1969 were calculated by then Congressman Charles Vanik, "Corporate federal tax payments and federal corporations for 1972," *Congressional Record*, House of Representatives, August 1, 1973. The 1977 data can be found in Richard Edwards, Michael Reich, and Thomas Weisskopf, *The Capitalist System*, New York, Prentice-Hall, 1978.

8 A good example can be found in Ralph Winter, "Many businesses blame government policies for productivity lag," *Wall Street Journal*, October 28, 1982, pp. 1, 22.

9 William K. Tabb, "Government regulations: two sides to the story," *Challenge*, November-December 1980. The original estimation of one hundred billion dollars was made by Murray Weidenbaum, briefly in the Reagan Administration. See also Frank Ackerman, "Regulation mythology," *Democratic Left*, April 1982.

10 The great political fallout between Reaganomics and big-business took place over this identification of the Reagan government's enormous deficits as potentially limiting private access to capital.

11 *Statistical Abstract of the United States, 1981*, Table 925, p. 546.

12 *Economic Report of the President, 1982*, Table B-1, p. 233, and *Statistical Abstract of the United States, 1981*, Table 926, p. 546.

13 *Statistical Abstract of the United States, 1981*, Table 925, p. 546.

14 *Ibid.*, Table 929, p. 547.

15 A. Rayner and I. M. Little, *Higgledy Piggledy Growth Again*, East Orange, N.J., Kelly, 1966.

16 Much has been made by business analysts and conventional economists

of the effect of uncertainty, particularly inflation, upon investment decisions. Very little attention has been paid to the implicit demands for political favors by private business. Why invest this year if not investing produces a special tax-cut "incentive" to invest next year?

17 *Statistical Abstract of the United States, 1980*, Table 1446, p. 812.

18 "Bumper crop of mergers last year," *San Francisco Chronicle*, January 14, 1982, p. 31. See also "Mergers climbed 27%, prices rose nearly 20% in 1981, surveys find," *Wall Street Journal*, January 14, 1982, p. 14.

19 Data for gross private domestic investment are from *Economic Report of the President, 1982*, Table B-2, p. 234.

20 Robert Hayes and William Abernathy, "Managing our way to economic decline," *Harvard Business Review*, July 1980, vol. 58, 4, pp. 67–77.

21 Michael Useem, "Corporations and the corporate elite," *Annual Review of Sociology*, vol. 6, pp. 41–77, 1980.

22 However, see Rosabeth Moss Kantor, *Men and Women of the Corporation*, New York, Basic Books, 1977.

23 Harry Braverman, *Labor and Monopoly Capital*, New York, Monthly Review Press, 1974. Others who discuss the accommodation of both profit and control include Richard C. Edwards, *Contested Terrain*, New York, Basic Books, 1979; Kathy Stone, "The origins of job structure in the steel industry," in Edwards et al. (eds), *Labor Market Segmentation*, Lexington, Mass., D. C. Heath, 1975; Steven Marglin, "What do bosses do? The origins and functions of hierarchy in capitalist production," *Review of Radical Political Economics*, vol. 6, pp. 60–112, 1974.

24 David Gordon, "Capital-labor conflict and the productivity slowdown," *American Economic Review*, vol. 71, 2, pp. 30–5, May 1981.

25 While the recapitalization analysis with its assumption of government and worker culpability was in full swing, a few commentators in the popular press were looking at management and business failures. Some of these include Sidney Blumenthal, "Whose side is business on, anyway?," *New York Times Magazine*, October 25, 1981, pp. 29–31, 94–6; and Steve Lohr, "Overhauling America's business management," *New York Times Magazine*, January 4, 1981, pp. 14–17, 42–5. A good deal of the attack on U.S. management has been by way of comparison with the Japanese. The latter's success in marketing cars, steel, and entertainment devices has led to an investigation of Japanese "management style" by U.S. journalists and academics. Books like William Ouchi's *Theory Z* (New York,

Addison-Wesley, 1981), and Richard Pascale and Anthony Athos's *The Art of Japanese Management* (New York, Simon & Schuster, 1981), are uncritical endorsements of the Japanese system, which they characterize as worker participation, lifetime employment, and a benevolent paternalism. As Robert Schrank pointed out in an unpublished review of these two books, the humanist tone of Japanese management was lifted from U.S. business schools, not from some superior cultural cohesion of the Japanese. In a comprehensive article, "Japanese management: myth or magic?" (*AFL-CIO American Federationist*, April 1982, pp. 3–12), James Ellenberger exposes the Japanese system as having extremely segmented labor markets (a minority of men and no women actually benefit from lifetime employment), and a definitely un-American system of cooperation in which suggestions from workers are courtesies within a rigid honor-bound class system. Paternalism is a misnomer – what is really going on is humiliation. Ellenberger concludes that what makes some Japanese exports extremely competitive is not so much worker–management cooperation as long-term industrial planning by both the Japanese government and businesses, and the acceptance of an extremely low (by American standards) profit rate of 1 to 2 per cent.

26 For more on corporate rationality see our paper "Business rationality and barriers to recapitalization," World Congress of Sociology, Mexico City, August 1982.

27 Hayes and Abernathy, op. cit.

28 This attitude can also be seen in General Motors management as described by De Lorean in J. Patrick Wright, *On a Clear Day You Can See General Motors*, New York, Avon, 1979. For a company coming to grips with this short-range mentality, see "GE's wizards turning from bottom line to share of the market," *Wall Street Journal*, July 12, 1982, pp. 1, 16. For the less enlightened activities of manufacturing companies looking like bankers and actors, see "Many firms are selling off acquisitions to clarify their image, lift their stock," *Wall Street Journal*, December 4, 1980, pp. 54–5.

29 Wright, op. cit.

30 When William Agee, then chairman of Bendix Corporation, attempted a "hostile" acquisition of Martin Marietta Corporation in the fall of 1982, the American public was treated to a clear view of the importance, and in this case dominance, of individual quests for power and prestige over the long-term needs of the firm. Here it became obvious that top managers may be working for themselves rather than for their corporation. If we return to our theoretical

orientation that these large firms are the institutionalized wealth of
the United States, personal quests for power and irrational firm
behavior become quite frightening. We do not think that Reagan's
Secretary of Commerce was too harsh when he called U.S.
management "fat, dumb, and happy." See "Baldridge lashes U.S.
management," *Boston Globe*, October 1, 1981, p. 47.

31 *Economic Report of the President, 1982*, Table B-48, p. 287; and
Statistical Abstract of the United States, 1982, Table 937, p. 551.
This calculation was made by multiplying the known exports of
goods and services of the U.S. economy by the ratio of assets to
sales of the *Fortune 1000* companies in 1980 to yield an
approximation of the investment in productive assets required for
exports. In 1980 the ratio of assets to sales for the *Fortune 1000*
firms was 0.713. Total exports of goods and services were $345
billion (from *Statistical Abstract of the United States, 1982*, Table
923, p. 544). U.S. private assets abroad in 1980 were $513.3 billion
(from *Economic Report of the President, 1982*, Table B-105, p. 351).
This is an essentially conservative estimate. The *Fortune 1000*'s
ratio of assets to sales is probably high because of the capital intensive
structure of the largest corporations in the U.S.

32 For an analysis of these laws, see Barry Bluestone and Bennett
Harrison, *The Deindustrialization of America*, New York, Basic
Books, 1982, and Richard Barnet and Ronald Müller, *Global Reach*,
New York, Simon & Schuster, 1974.

33 Our explanation for increased demand of services even in recessions
is threefold. The speculative activity of business increases in uncertain
or inflationary economic times, producing prosperity for accountants,
lawyers, and other business services. Service industries require less
capital investment than manufacturing and are attractive investments
for that reason. Since more members of the family must enter the
labor force as individual earnings decline, the demand for consumer
services like restaurants and dry cleaners also increases. This trend,
however, may falter if consumer demand is choked off by the upward
redistribution of income intended by most variants of
recapitalization.

34 "The Fortune 500," *Fortune Magazine*, May 3, 1982, pp. 84–110.

35 Motor vehicle investment picked up again in 1977. See *Statistical
Abstract of the United States, 1980*, Table 1447, p. 812; and
Statistical Abstract of the United States, 1981, Table 943, p. 553.

36 If current economic structures were altered, one might envision a
world in which nations voluntarily and equitably balance their exports
and imports rather than struggle to export their unemployment and

import other nations' wealth. Chapter 8 discusses some of these issues.

Chapter 6 Can recapitalization provide the jobs?

1 For discussions of the importance and development of corporate control functions in the center of otherwise stagnant urban centers, see John Mollenkopf, "The post-war politics of urban development," in William Tabb and Larry Sawers (eds), *Marxism and the Metropolis*, New York, Oxford University Press, 1978, pp. 117–52; Susan Fainstein and Norman Fainstein, "Production and welfare in American cities: changing functions and the consequences for inequality," presented at a conference on New Perspectives on the Urban Political Economy, Washington, D.C., The American University, May 1981; Donald Tomaskovic-Devey and S. M. Miller, "Recapitalization: the basic U.S. urban policy of the 1980's," in Susan Fainstein and Norman Fainstein (eds), *Urban Policy Under Capitalism*, Beverly Hills, Calif., Sage, 1982.

2 Emma Rothchild, "Reagan and the real America," *New York Review of Books*, February 1981.

3 *Economic Report of the President, 1980*, Table B-34, p. 242.

4 Daniel Bell, *The Coming of Post-Industrial Society*, New York, Basic Books, 1973.

5 *Employment and Training Report of the President, 1980*, Table C-3, p. 309.

6 Increasingly, semi-skilled middle-aged male workers who have been fired/laid off from the deindustrializing manufacturing industries have to settle for service jobs.

7 The dual-labor market literature is growing rapidly. Some of the central works are, Peter Doeringer and Michael Piore, *Internal Labor Markets and Manpower Analysis*, Lexington, Mass., D. C. Heath, 1971; Richard Edwards, *Contested Terrain*, New York, Macmillan, 1979; Richard Edwards, Michael Reich, and David Gordon (eds), *Labor Market Segmentation*, Lexington, Mass., D. C. Heath, 1975; Bennett Harrison, *Education and Training and the Urban Ghetto*, Baltimore, Johns Hopkins University Press, 1972.

8 David Birch, *The Job Generation Process*, MIT Program in Neighborhood and Regional Change, 1979.

9 The policy recommendation that follows from this analysis is not a simple one. On the one hand, high-productivity manufacturing investment produces few jobs. On the other hand, low-productivity

service investment produces many low-quality jobs. The result of manufacturing investment is unemployment, while the result of service investment is poor employment.

10 Interestingly, IBM, the granddaddy of the U.S. computer industry, launched an advertising campaign to increase investor awareness that they were indeed a "high-technology" company. See James White, "IBM is aggressively claiming widening lead in technology," *Wall Street Journal*, July 30, 1982, p. 21.

11 The development importance that has been attached to high technology by politicians and the media cannot be exaggerated. Liberals, like Tip O'Neill (Speaker of the House, Democrat, Massachusetts) and Ray Marshall (former Secretary of Labor under Carter), offered high-tech expansion as their alternative to Reaganomics. Reagan, in turn, attempted to appropriate the high-tech motif for himself. The Hi-Tech Council of Massachusetts (a political coalition of self-styled high-tech corporations) has played an aggressive and at times leading role in Massachusetts politics. See Eric Lundquist, "High tech in the hot seat," *Boston*, vol. 72, 2, pp. 78–80, 103–10, February 1981. For the international politics of high-tech see Julian Hollich, "A frank plan to go high-tech: using New England as a model, France woos computer firms," *Boston Globe*, June 23, 1981, pp. 49, 62; and Tod Loofburrow, "Japan and U.S. duel in robotics," *Harvard International Review*, November 1980, pp. 14–16.

12 We argue elsewhere (Tomaskovic-Devey and Miller, op. cit.) that with the failure of the radical recapitalization of Reaganomics to meet long-term structural problems, more targeted approaches to industrial policy will succeed those policies. As that happens, the corporation or industry that can successfully claim to be high-tech will be in a favorable position.

13 The "Sci-Tech" definition can be found in R. Vinson and P. Harrington, *Defining High-Technology Industries in Massachusetts*, Boston, Commonwealth of Massachusetts, Department of Manpower Development, 1979. The "R & D" definition can be found in U.S. Congress, Subcommittee on International Finance of the Committee on Banking, Housing and Urban Affairs, "Oversight of U.S. high technology exports," Washington, D.C., U.S. Government Printing Office, 1978. The "Mass." definition came from the Massachusetts Division of Employment Security, "High technology employment in Massachusetts and selected states," Boston, Commonwealth of Massachusetts, Labor Area Research Publications, 1981.

14 The data to support this orientation are sparse. Of course, the logical

outcome (as we have stressed throughout this book) of productivity increases in a slow-growth environment is the loss of jobs. The glamour of computers and robots notwithstanding, the primary reason firms introduce new or high technology into the workplace is to increase efficiency. Some evidence does exist on both the deskilling of computer workers, secretaries who use word processors, and on technological unemployment. Joan Greenbaum, *In the Name of Efficiency: A Study of Change in Data Processing Work*, Phil., Temple University Press, 1979; Ida Hoos, *Automation in the Office*, Washington, D.C., Public Affairs Press, 1960; Evelyn Glenn and Roslyn Feldberg, "Proletarianizing clerical work: technology and organizational control in the office," in Andrew Zimbalist (ed.), *Case Studies on the Labor Process*, New York, Monthly Review Press, 1979, pp. 51–72; Phillip Kraft, *Programmers and Managers: The Routinization of Computer Programmers in the United States*, New York, Springer Verlag, 1977. See also William Serrin, "Worry grows over upheaval as technology reshapes jobs," *New York Times*, February 4, 1982, p. 1; Colin Norman, "The menace of microelectronics," *New York Times*, October 5, 1980, p. D3.

15 Robert Howard, "Second class in silicon valley," *Working Papers*, vol. 8, 5, 1981, pp. 21–31.

16 Military booms produce their own dislocations, as skilled engineers and machinists are lured to work for high-wage, cost-plus military contractors, leaving manufacturers that produce socially useful products with realizable market values short of skilled workers.

17 See Paul Blumberg, *Inequality in an Age of Decline*, New York, Oxford University Press, 1980, for a useful discussion of widening inequality in U.S. society.

18 *Statistical Abstract of the United States, 1981*, Table 726, p. 436; and Table 646, p. 386.

19 For a preliminary analysis of the specific effects of the Reagan policies upon different groups and services in the United States, see Alan Gartner, Colin Greer, and Frank Riessman (eds), *What Reagan is Doing to Us*, New York, Harper & Row, 1982. Frances Fox Piven and Richard Cloward, in *The New Class War*, New York, Pantheon, 1982, present a brief analysis of the effects of Reagan's cutbacks on some specific social programs.

20 In late 1982 inflation-fighting tight-money policies were relaxed in the face of a "dead-in-the-water" U.S. economy and sparked the spurt in the stock market. These and other inflation-fighting, slow-growth policies will be revived as structural inflation heats up with economic growth. Douglas Hibbs, "Political parties and

macroeconomic policy," *American Political Science Review*, vol. 71, 4, pp. 1467–87, December 1977, concludes that cross-national comparisons of advanced industrial countries' economic policies indicate that fast-growth (low unemployment), high-inflation policies tend to produce declining inequalities, while slow-growth (high unemployment), low-inflation policies such as the U.S. and Great Britain are pursuing foster increased inequalities in society.

21 Piven and Cloward, op. cit.

22 Unless, of course, the American people refuse to acquiesce. See S. M. Miller, "Turmoil and/or acquiescence for the 1980s?," *Social Policy*, 11, 1, May 1980, pp. 22–5. Piven and Cloward (op. cit.) see confrontation as likely because of people's high expectations/ demands for government protection of their economic security.

Chapter 7 Old beginnings: contradictions and tensions in bureaucratic liberalism

1 For neo-liberals, see notes 1 and 4 to Chapter 1. For liberals, see Ray Marshall and other prominent economists, *An Economic Strategy for the 1980's: The Failure of Reaganomics and the Full Employment Alternative*, Washington, D.C., Full Employment Action Council and National Policy Exchange, 1982.

2 For political analysis, see Douglas Hibbs, "President Reagan's mandate from the 1980 elections: a shift to the right?," the *American Political Quarterly*, vol. 10, 4, October 1982, pp. 387–420.

3 Some assert that Carter was not re-elected because he had largely abandoned the liberal platform. When voters are faced with a choice between a conservative Democrat and a Republican, the argument contends, they will choose the latter as more authentic. Obviously, neo-liberals like Senator Paul Tsongas do not accept this interpretation.

4 Social security and unemployment insurance payments are not viewed in this light. But there is political and ideological pressure to lower benefits, to means-test them so only the "truly needy" receive them, and to demean them. The contest over what should be regarded as contributory insurance programs (social security pensions, unemployment insurance) is keen and is demonstrating support for some basic elements of the welfare state. None the less, a heavy price will be paid in the cutting of benefit levels and restrictions on eligibility.

5 S. M. Miller and Martin Rein, "Can income redistribution work?," *Social Policy*, 6, 1, May/June 1975, pp. 3–18.

6 *Wall Street Journal*, January 11, 1980, p. 20.
7 Walter Dean Burnham, "The 1980 earthquake: realignment, reaction, or what?," in Thomas Ferguson and Joel Rogers (eds), *The Hidden Election: Politics and Economics in the 1980 Presidential Campaign*, New York, Pantheon, 1981, p. 121.
8 This was the image. In fact, huge benefits went to corporations, the rich, and the better-off. But the conditions of a great many low-income people were improved.
9 See, for example, *Time*, January 1, 1982, and *Newsweek*, January 4, 1982.

Chapter 8 Progressive departures

1 For a popular discussion of this outlook, see John Eatwell, *Whatever Happened to Britain?*, London, Duckworth and BBC, 1982.
2 Marion Anderson, "The empty pork barrel: unemployment and the Pentagon budget," 1981; and "Converting the work force: where the jobs would be," 1982, Lansing, Michigan, Employment Research Associates.
3 Barry Bluestone's testimony before the Joint Economic Committee of Congress, May 18, 1982.
4 We do not take the threat of repression lightly. Great and widening inequalities make democratic representation difficult.
5 The counter-argument is that higher productivity will lead to lower prices. That contention assumes that consumers rather than stockholders, managers, and employees will be the primary beneficiaries of lowered costs of production. Sometimes that may be true, but it does not seem to have been the case in many major industries.
6 Kirk Scharfenberg, "The community as bank examiner," *Working Papers*, September/October, 1980, pp. 30–5.
7 Gösta Rehn, "Employment premiums in economic policy," Center for Public Policy, University of California, Berkeley, 1979.
8 *New York Times*, May 31, 1982, p. 84.
9 Alfred J. Watkins, "Felix Rohatyn's biggest deal," *Working Papers*, vol. 8, 5, 1981, pp. 44–52.
10 The classic treatment of the hidden values of economics remains Gunnar Myrdal's *The Political Element in the Development of Economic Theory*, Cambridge, Mass., Harvard University Press, 1954.
11 Of course, pro-labor politics in the U.S. is itself problematic. Organized labor represents only about 20 per cent of U.S. workers,

and an even smaller percentage of women and minorities. The participation of organized labor in government planning bodies does not assure that all working Americans are represented. On the other hand, the AFL-CIO has a very good record when it comes to promoting general pro-worker legislation in terms of wages, benefits, transfer programs, and anti-poverty social legislation.

12 The French phrase for this role in planning bodies is "contestational." See Stephen Cohen, *Modern Capitalist Planning: The French Model*, Los Angeles, University of California Press, 1977.

13 Martin Carnoy and Derek Shearer, *Economic Democracy*, White Plains, M. E. Sharpe, 1980.

14 One could argue that a partial explanation for the failure of Soviet-style command planning has been the absence of democratic politics and discourse over the goals and means of economic policy and development, coupled with the dominance of a new technocratic elite.

15 GM successfully refused to accept this condition in their 1982 giveback negotiation with the UAW.

16 David Gordon, at a symposium of the Institute for Democratic Socialism, Washington, D.C., December 1980.

17 Despite the popularity of such proposals as national health insurance, presently the general tendency is in the other direction of reprivatization, increased reliance on work-connected rather than public, universal benefits for all. The result is that a small percentage of the labor force in strong companies does comparatively well while the majority of employees fare badly in basic protections against the insecurities of ill health and retirement.

18 Harry Boyte, *Backyard Revolution*, Phil., Temple University Press, 1981.

19 The Boston Women's Health Collective is an example of the self-help movement. Particularly well received and influential has been their women's health primer, *Our Bodies, Our Selves*, New York, Simon & Schuster, 1971. Local self-help groups are active in many areas in addition to health. Charas, for example, is a Puerto Rican alternate energy and community organizing group on the Lower East Side of Manhattan.

20 Ronald Dworkin, *Taking Rights Seriously*, Cambridge, Mass., Harvard University Press, 1977.

Chapter 9 Breaking political boundaries

1 Discussions with Roy Bennett, former American correspondent for the London *Tribune*, have influenced the analysis in this section.
2 Peter Dreier, "Socialist incubators," *Social Policy*, 11, 1, May 1980, pp. 29–34.
3 Alan Wolfe, *America's Impasse: The Rise and Fall of the Politics of Growth*, New York, Pantheon, 1981, p. 244.
4 There are many studies documenting the relationship between regulators and the regulated. We provide a sampling: A. Lee Fritschler, *Smoking and Politics: Policymaking and the Federal Bureaucracy*, Englewood Cliffs, N.J., Prentice-Hall, 1975; Robert Fellmeth, *The Interstate Commerce Commission*, New York, Grossman, 1970; Beverly C. Moore, "The FCC: competition and communications," in Mark Green (ed.), *The Monopoly Makers*, New York, Grossman, 1973; K. G. J. Pillar, "The CAB as travel regulator," in Mark Green, op. cit; David L. Serber, "Regulating reform: the social organization of insurance regulation," *Insurgent Sociologist*, vol. 5, spring 1975, pp. 83–105.
5 Antonio Gramsci, *Selections From the Prison Notebooks*, New York, International Publishers, 1971.
6 Walter Dean Burnham, "The 1980 earthquake: realignment, reaction or what?," in Thomas Ferguson and Joel Rogers (eds), *The Hidden Election: Politics and Economics in the 1980 Presidential Campaign*, New York, Pantheon, 1981, pp. 119–21.
7 Several friendly arguments with Mike Miller of Organize Training Center in San Fransico have influenced this section.
8 Left groups, old and new, have stressed media control of attitudes and values. Almost every study of influences on attitudes rate personal contacts and experience as much more important than the media. See Elihu Katz, "Diffusion: interpersonal influence," *International Encyclopedia of the Social Sciences*, David L. Sills (ed.), vol. 4, 1968, pp. 178–85; also Joseph Klapper, "The effects of mass communication," in ibid., vol. 3, pp. 81–9. Left analyses stress the gullibility and permeability but underestimate the fluidity of opinion and the impact of the experiences and contacts that people have.
9 "Glocal" has an uncertain parentage. The term was passed on to us by Mike Miller of organizing fame. René Dubos has recommended thinking globally and acting locally.
10 Peter Dreier, op. cit.
11 The following discussion is based on S. M. Miller, "Economic Inventions," *Challenge*, May-June, 1977.

12 Our reference to the Second New Deal follows the analysis of the neglected, useful *The History of the New Deal, 1933–1938*, (New York, Creative Age Press, 1944) by Basil Rauch. It divides the New Deal very differently than does Arthur Schlesinger, Jr. in his analysis of the break in Roosevelt policies in the early years (*The Coming of the New Deal*, Boston, Houghton Mifflin, 1954). Rauch's Second Deal moves away from the First New Deal's pro-business position of the National Recovery Administration and the Agricultural Adjustment Act to pro-consumption measures like the social security program, Works Progress Administration (WPA), and the like. Schlesinger sees the first New Deal as dominated by the Roscoe Tugwell planning faction, then supplanted by the Brandeis anti-big business supporters to form the Second New Deal.

13 Alain Touraine on social movements undermining political parties and institutions can be found in *The Voice and the Eye: an Analysis of Social Movements*, New York, Cambridge University Press, 1981.

Index

Abernathy, W., 24, 81, 83–4, 187, 194–5
Ackerman, F., 193
AFDC, *see* Aid to Families, etc.
AFL-CIO, 30, 33, 119, 146, 166, 171, 185
Agee, W., 195
Aid to Families with Dependent Children, 111, 122, 125, 158
American Productivity Center, 55, 57
American Telephone and Telegraph, 82, 86
Anderson, M., 201
Argentina, 47
assets, 20, 38–9
Athos, A., 195
ATT, *see* American Telephone, etc.
Australia, 47
automobile industry, 139; decline, 29; and demand, 64; employment in, 41; innovation, lack of, 84–5; in Japan, 16, 19, 28, 56, 87; labor costs, 63; non-investment in, 75, 85, 87; power of, 21–2; profits, 114; robots in, 114; wages in, 28; worker representation in, 147
awareness and coalition, 165

backward America, 174–6
balance of payments, 38–40
Bank for International Settlements, 43
banks, 20–1, 88–90, 141, 148
Barnet, R., 190, 196
Bell, D., 30, 96, 188, 197
Bennett, R., 203
big business: employment in, 137; exports and, 45–6; independence, 121; investment by, 22–3, 38–9, 48–9, 74–92 *passim,* 121; legislation and, 174–5; management in, 24, 59, 61, 81–7, 140–1; opposition to, 167; and profits, 68, 112–13; takeovers and mergers, 76–7, 79; and unemployment, 44; *see also* business; multinationals
Birch, D., 97, 188, 197
Block, F., 186
Bluestone, B., 29, 135, 186–8, 196, 201
Blumberg, P., 199
Blumenthal, S., 194
Boston Peace Budget, 135
Boston Women's Health Collective, 202
Bosworth, B., 192
Boyte, H., 152, 202

Brandt, W., 190–1
Braverman, H., 81, 194
Brazil, 16–17, 19, 21
Brill, H., 187, 191
Britain: alternate trade policy,
133–201; British Disease,
46–50; expansionary policies,
182; investment by, 47; left
politics, 175; nationalization in,
148; productivity and trade, 5,
7, 12, 16, 19, 132–3
budget deficits, 63, 73–4
bureaucracy: direction without,
139–42; unpopular, 123, 141
bureaucratic liberalism, 119–28
Burnham, W. D., 177, 201, 203
business, relegitimated, 11–12
Business Roundtable, 189, 192
business, wickedness of, 74–92;
investment lures, 88–92;
managerial incompetence, 81–7;
non-productive investments,
77–81; non-rational market,
86–8, 90; profits and
investments, 76–7; uneven
investment, 74–6; see also big
business; small firms

Cambridge Economic Policy
Group, 133
Canada, 47, 53, 153
capital: available, 78; crowding,
73–4; independence of, 45–6,
48; labor substituted for, 59;
mobility, 16, 22, 29; unit,
output per, 55, 57
capitalism, crisis of, 6–7; see also
recapitalization
caring, 160–2
Carnoy, M., 146, 202
Carter, President J., 4, 7–8, 109,
120, 126, 132, 173, 184
CETA programs, 134

changes: corporate, 20–5;
industrial, 28–34; inflation,
26–8; political, 33–4; power
and trade, 14–20
Charas, 202
Chase Manhattan Bank, 18, 45
China, 15
Chrysler, 21, 114, 147
Cincotta, G., 141
Citibank, 89
Clark, J. M., 182
class: cross-, program, 170;
differences, 160, 165
Cloward, R., 114, 160, 199–200
coalition, political, 165–83
Cohen, S., 202
commodity investment, 79–80
Community Reinvestment Act,
141
compassion, 155–7
competition, international, 16–17,
34, 36–7, 39, 43, 45, 49; and
inflation, 27–8; and investment,
66–7; and productivity, 52–5,
62; and service industries, 30–1
computers, see high technology
concentration of industry, 20–2
conglomerates, see big business;
multinationals
construction industry, 60
consumer goods deficit, 38–41
Consumer Price Index, 11
control, see government;
management
cooperation: industrial, 82, 148;
local, 153
corporate changes, 20–5
corporations, see big business;
multinationals; taxation
"corporatism," 144–5
"cost-effectiveness," 136
"cost-free game," 51
Crawford, A., 184

creativity, politics of, 162–3
credit increase, 25
crisis of capitalism, 6–7; *see also* recapitalization
cultural differences, 157–60
Cunningham, B., 191
current accounts, international, 39–40

debts, federal, 73–4
decline: exports, 16–17; industrial, 16–17, 28–30, 89; productivity, myth of, 51–8
deficits, 38–41, 63, 73–4
deindustrialization, 28–30, 89
De Lorean, J., 84–5, 195
democracy, 127–8; alignment and coalition, 172–3; economic, 146
Democratic Party, 33, 119–20, 128, 134, 144, 156, 164, 166–9, 172
Denmark, 7
dependence, economic, 17–19, 41, 47–9
destablizing effect of world trade, 49
De Tocqueville, A., 174
devaluation, 132
development policy, need for, 133–4
direction without bureaucracy, 139–42
disinvestment, 58
Doeringer, P., 197
dominance, American, loss of, 14–16, 35, 121–2
Dreier, P., 167, 181, 203
Dworkin, R., 162, 202

earnings, *see* wages
Eatwell, J., 201
economic guidance agencies, 145
education, politics as, 176–8

Edwards, R., 193, 194, 197
elections, 119–20, 156, 168, 172, 179
electronics industry, *see* high technology
Ellenberger, J., 195
El Salvador, 17
Employee Stock Ownership Plan, 149
employment, *see* jobs
empowerment, 153–4
environmental measures, 63, 72
equality, 149, 161–2
Europe: labor costs, 55; left politics, 175; loans to, 21; productivity, 7, 11, 15, 53–4, 60–1, 64–7; protectionism, 132; tax and wages, 142; trade, 18–19, 39–41, 43, 45, 132; worker participation, 149
exchange, foreign, 44–5
expenditure, government, 69–71; military, 12, 16, 73, 135, 151, 165
exports, 35–50 *passim;* and big business, 45–6; decline, 16–17; and employment, 42, 113; increase, 5–6, 10, 36, 39–40; and productivity, 64; progressive ideas on, 132–4; and small firms, 134; stagnation, 47; of unemployment, 43; *see also* trade
Exxon, 18, 46, 115

Fainstein, S. and N., 197
fear, 156–7, 165
Federal Reserve System, 25, 43, 73, 79
Feldberg, R., 199
Fellmeth, R., 203
Ford Motor Company, 22, 63

foreign exchange, 44–5
foreign investment, *see* investment, overseas
France, 53–5, 123, 148, 175
Franklin National Bank, 22
Fritschler, A. L., 203

General Motors, 63, 82, 84–7, 114, 139
Germany, *see* West Germany
Ginzberg, E., 188
"give-backs," 147, 169
Glenn, E., 199
GNP, *see* gross national product
Goldsmith, W., 190
Gordon, D., 81–2, 148, 194, 197, 202
government, 67–74; capital crowding, 73–4; deficits 73–4; as dinosaur, 11; regulation, 6, 71–2, 135, 140; *see also* expenditure; legislation; political; taxation
Grace, W. R., 45
Gramsci, A., 176–7, 203
Grand Cayman Islands, 48
grass roots and coalition, 178–80
Great Society, *see* New Deal
Great Transformation, 14
Greek, B., 191
Greenbaum, J., 199
gross national product, 131; and employment, 136; and government expenditure, 69–71; and investment, 74, 91; measurement of, 138–9; new, 138–9; in 1950, 15; in 1960, 36; from 1960–80, 110; from 1970–80, 68; and productivity, 60–1; and profits, 68; and trade, 17; and wages, 110

Harrison, B., 29, 186–8, 196

Hart, G., 5, 119, 185
Hayes, R., 24, 81, 83–4, 187, 194–5
health standards, 63, 72
Heath, E., 77
Heilbroner, R., 188–9
Hibbs, D., 120, 200
high technology firms, 16–17, 28, 31, 60, 98–108, 121; definitions, 99–101, 198
Hong Kong, 16
Hoos, I., 199
Hoover, H., 143
housing, 136–7
Howard, R., 105, 199
Humphrey-Hawkins law, 173

IBM, 18, 45, 82, 86
ideological hegemony, 176–7
idle capacity, 59–61
imports: and domestic industry 11, 16–19, 28, 30, 52–3, 87; increase, 37–42; oil, 37–41, 44; *see also* trade
incentives, 141–2
income, *see* wages
incompetence, managerial, 81–7
independence of capital, 45–6, 48
indices of production, 53, 55, 57
Individual Retirement Accounts, 141
individuals, managers as, 83, 85
industrial changes 28–34
industrial policy, 3–4, 65, 91, 119, 135, 143, 163, 183
industry: concentration of, 20–2; decline of, 16–17, 19, 28–30, 51–8, 89; type and employment, 31
inequalities, 11–12, 109, 114, 120, 123–4, 127, 154
inflation, 25–8, 123; and employment, 64, 94, 137; and

investment, 88; and prices, 27–8; and productivity, 59–64; reduction of 5, 8–9; and wages, 28; worldwide, 19

infrastructure, buildings, 9–10, 119, 134

instability, 19, 31

insurance companies, 141

interdependence, international, 17–19, 41, 47–9

interest groups, *see* organizations

interest rates, 18, 23–4, 131–2

internationalization, *see* interdependence

International Monetary Fund, 20, 43, 192

international trade, *see* trade

intervention, *see* government

investment: banks, 21, 89–90, 141; big business, 22–5, 38–9, 48–9, 88, 121; by Britain, 47; commodity, 79–80; and competition, 66–7; control, 49; and GNP, 74, 91; and inflation, 88; lures, 88–92; in non-productive industries, 75, 77–81, 88; overseas, 21–3, 38–9, 47–9, 88, 121; panacea, 66–92, 193–7; private, 4–5, 8, 12; in productive industries, 61, 64, 75–6, 89, 91; and profits, 67–9, 76–7, 86–90; in service industries 88; and taxation, 67–9, 73, 88, 91; uneven, 74–6

invisible taxation, 150–1

Iran, 15

Italy, 7, 19, 175

ITT, 69, 115

Japan: attitude to work, 25; car industry, 16, 19, 28, 56, 87; imports from, 11, 16, 28, 52–3, 87; management, 56, 82, 147;

productivity and trade, 7, 15, 36, 39–45, 49, 52–6, 59–60, 64, 132, 174

job-centered growth, 134–8, 152

job creation, 95–8, 101–6, 134–5, 169

job effectiveness, 136

jobless growth, 32–3, 65, 121, 134

jobs, 93–115, 197–200; and big business, 137; and coalition, 169–72; creation of, 95–8, 101–6, 134–5, 169; decline, 102; and exports, 42, 113; and GNP, 136; in high technology, 28, 98–108, 121; increase, 10, 59–60, 93, 101–3; and inflation, 64, 94, 137; and productivity, 64–5; prospects, dim, 112–15; by sector, 31; in service industries, 28, 30–3, 95–7; in small firms, 97–8, 137; upward redistribution, 108–12; *see also* unemployment

Johnson, President L., 126, 156

Kadar, J., 171

Kantor, R. M., 196

Katz, E., 203

Kennedy, J. F., 126–7

Keynes, J. M. and Keynesianism, 10, 12, 26, 33, 43, 122, 125–6, 130, 138, 181–2

Kirkland, L., 171

Kondratieff business cycle, 7, 185

Kraft, P., 199

Kristol, I., 124

labor costs, 48–9, 55, 63, 169; and productivity, 55–8, 75

labor force, *see* jobs

labor substitution, 59

Lance, B., 25

large firms, *see* big businesses
left politics, 46, 128, 175–6
legislation, 141, 147, 174–6, 181
liberalism, 9–10, 91, 143–4, 147;
    beyond, 155–62, 200–1;
    bureaucratic, 119–28, *see* New
    deal/Great Society liberalism;
    neo-liberalism
List, F., 133
Little, I. M., 76, 193
Lloyd George, D., 182
localism, 152–5, 165, 174
Lohr, S., 194
Loofburrow, T., 198

McKinlay, J. B., 187
macro-micro, 130–1
management, 61; financial
    background, 24; incompetence,
    81–7; and investment, 59,
    81–7; Japanese, 56, 82, 147;
    and productivity, 81–2; and
    profits, 81, 83–5; progressive,
    140–1
Mandel, E., 7, 184
manufacturing industry, 16–19,
    28–9; high technology, 98–108;
    investment in, 61, 64, 75–6, 89,
    91; *see also* car industry; steel
    industry
Marglin, S., 194
Marshall, R., 119, 185, 193, 198,
    200
Marx, K. and Marxism, 87, 176,
    185
Massachusetts Division of
    Employment Security definition
    of high technology, 99–101,
    103–4
measurement of productivity,
    138–9
Medicaid and Medicare, 122
mergers, 76–7, 79

Mexico, 19, 21
micro-electronics, *see* high
    technology
military expenditure, 12, 16, 73,
    135, 151, 165
Miller, G. W., 79
Miller, S. M., 190, 195, 197, 198,
    200, 203
mining, 60
minorities, employment of, 105,
    114
Mitchel, D. P., 192
mobility, capital, 16, 22, 29
Mobil Oil, 46, 69
Mollenkopf, J., 197
money supply, control of, 47
monopolies, 86, 151
Moore, B. C., 203
moral majorities, 157–60
Motorola, 82
movements, *see* organizations
Mueller, R., 190, 195
multinational firms: banks, 20;
    and exports, 45–6; investment
    by, 22–3; investment overseas,
    38–9, 48–9, 88, 121;
    proliferation, 16, 18, 20; *see
    also* big business
Myrdal, G., 201
myth of productivity decline, 51–8

nationalization, 148, 151
National Labour Relations Act,
    147
National Peoples' union, 141
neo-conservatism, 3, 124
neo-liberalism, 9–10, 91, 119,
    143–4
New Deal, 181–2
New Deal/Great Society liberalism,
    122, 146, 151–2, 156, 160–2,
    166–71

New International Economic
  Order, 49, 134
new jobs, 95–8, 101–6, 134–5
new politics, 164, 169
New York Public Interest
  Research Group, 152
New York Stock Exchange, 79
non-productive industries, 75–81,
  88; *see also* service industries
non-rationality, 85–8, 90

OECD, *see* Organization for
  Economic Co-operation and
  Development
O'Neil, T., 198
oil: imports, 37–41, 44; industry,
  nationalization of, 148; prices,
  3, 17–19, 26, 37–41, 44
old people, 159
oligopoly power, 86
OPEC, *see* Organization of
  Petroleum Exporting Countries
opportunity and coalition, 165–6
Organization for Economic Cooperation and Development, 20,
  33, 39–40, 132
organizations and movements,
  single-interest, 127, 165, 167–8,
  172, 178–80
Organization of Petroleum
  Exporting Countries, 17, 37,
  40–1, 46, 87
Ouchi, W., 194–5
output per worker hour, 52, 54–5;
  see also productivity
overseas investment, *see*
  investment
overselling productivity, 54–5

panacea: investment, 66–92,
  193–7; productivity as, 10–11,
  99
Pascale, R., 195

PATCO, 49
Piller, K. G. J., 203
Piore, M., 197
Piven, F. F., 114, 160, 199–200
planning, 143–6
plant closings, 58, 60
Poland, 17, 19, 21
policy, industrial, versus
  Keynesianism, 125–6
political: boundaries, breaking,
  164–8, 203–4; changes, 33–4;
  importance of productivity, 99;
  mood, bureaucratic liberalism,
  126–8
politics: of creativity, 162–3; as
  education, 176–8; left, 46, 128;
  175–6; planning as, 143–6; of
  productivity, 56–8; right,
  126–7, 168
power and trade, 14–22
prices: and inflation, 27–8; of oil,
  3, 17–19, 26, 37–41, 44; and
  production, 62, 64; and wages,
  143, 145
private investment, 4–5, 8, 12
productive industries, *see*
  manufacturing
productivity, 51–65, 191–2; in
  Britain, 52–3; comparative,
  53–4; and competition, 52–5,
  62; decline, myth of, 51–8;
  diagnosis, better, 59–65; and
  unemployment, 64–5; in
  Europe, 7, 11, 53–4, 60–1,
  64–7; and exports, 64; and
  GNP, 60–1; growth of, 3–4, 6,
  52–4, 60; and inflation, 59–64;
  and investment, 76, 91; and
  labor costs, 55–8, 75; and
  management, 81–2;
  measurement of, 138–9; and
  non-rationality, 87; as panacea,
  10–11, 99; politics of, 56–8;

and prices, 62, 64; producing confusion, 51–65; in service industries, 60; transformation in, 22; and unemployment, 58, 65; and wages, 59–64
product mix, 59–60
profits: big business, 68, 112–13; car industry, 85; and GNP, 68; importance of, 175; and investment, 67–9, 76–7, 86–90; and management, 81, 83–5
progressive departures, 129–63, 201–2; direction without bureaucracy, 139–42; GNP, towards new, 138–9; job-centred growth, 134–8; liberalism, beyond, 155–62; macro-micro, 130–1; planning as politics, 143–6; politics of creativity, 162–3; social sector, participating, 152–5; taxation and revenues, 150–2; trade, international, 131–4; work relations, 146–9
property boom, 77
prospects, dim, for employment, 112–15
protectionism, 132–3
public works program, 9–10, 151

racism, 158
Radical Right, 3
"R and D" definition of high technology, 99–101, 103–4
Rauch, B., 204
Rayner, A., 76, 193
Reagan, R. and Reaganomics, 3, 86; beyond, 118–83, 200–4; and deficits, 73–4; and military expenditure, 73, 135; and productivity, 52; reformulation, 5–6; and social service cuts, 47, 152, 154, 157, 159, 161; and

supply-side economics, 4, 7–9, 12; and tax cuts, 47, 69, 73, 119–20, 124, 140, 151, 157, 168; and unemployment, 184; and urban enterprise zones, 94, 142
recapitalization: beyond Reaganism and liberalism, 119–84, 200–4; defined, 4–5, 7–10; investment panacea, 66–92; jobs, 93–115; productivity, 51–65; trade, international, 35–50; transformation, great, 14–34
reciprocity, 156–7
Reconstruction Finance Corporation, 9, 143, 167, 174
redistribution, upward, 108–12
regional: changes, 29; differences in employment, 94, 106–7, 114; planning, 141, 146
regulation: government, 6, 71–2, 135, 140; social, 71–2
Rehn, G., 142, 201
Reich, M., 193
Rein, M., 200
reindustrialization, 3–4, 7, 11
reprivatization, 154
Republicans, 144, 169
retail trade, 60, 96; see also service industries
revitalization, 3, 7
RFC, see Reconstruction Finance Corporation
Ricardo, D., 39
right politics, 3, 126–7, 168
Rockefeller, D., 4
Rohatyn, F., 5, 143, 184, 185
Roosevelt, F. D., 143
Rostow, W., 184
Rothchild, E., 95, 197

safety measures, 63, 72

Saudi Arabia, 44
savings, 141, 157, 159–60
Scharfenberg, K., 201
Schlesinger, A., 204
Schmid, G., 191
Schrank, R., 195
Schultz, C., 184
"Sci-Tech" definition of high technology, 99–101, 103–4
self-help, 153–5
Serber, D. L., 203
Servan-Schreiber, J.-J., 61, 192
service industries: and competition, 30–1; employment in, 28, 30–3, 95–7; growth of, 96; investment in, 88; and productivity, 60; wages in, 32, 94; see also small firms
sexism, 158
sharing and caring, 160–2
Shearer, D., 146, 202
SIC, see Standard Industrial Classification
Sills, D. L., 203
Singapore, 48
small firms, 130–1; and coalition, 167; employment in, 97–8, 137; and exports, 134; see also service industries
Smith, A., 7
social contract, 176
socialism, 46, 128, 175–6
social sector, participatory, 152–5
social services: Britain, 47; and bureaucratic liberalism, 122–5; and coalition, 169, 181; cuts in, 3–5, 11–12, 47, 111–14, 152, 154, 157, 159, 161; growth in, 70–1; and liberals, 119–20
South Korea, 16, 19
speculation, 23–5, 28, 77–80, 121
spending, see expenditure
stagnation, 19, 47

Standard Industrial Classification, 102–3
standard of living, 49; see also inflation
steel industry: decline of, 29; and imports, 16–17; investment by, 24, 89; non-investment in, 75, 87; power of, 22
stock exchange, 79
Stone, K., 194
Strategic Oil Reserve, 44
style-of-life tensions, 157–8
supply-side economics, 3–4, 7–9, 12, 65, 91, 123
Sweden, 7, 175

Tabb, W. K., 72, 193
takeovers, 76–7, 79
"targeting," 91, 135, 140
taxation: in Britain, 47–8; corporation, cuts in, 4–5, 8–9, 12, 47, 69, 73, 119–20, 124, 140, 151, 157, 168; indexed, 124; inequalities after, 123–4; and investment, 67–9, 73, 88, 91; invisible, 150–1; progressive, 150–2; psychology of transfers, 122–5, 134; and wages, 142
tax-based incomes policy, 142
"tax revolts," 150
Tax Savers, 141, 159
tax shelters, 48
technology, see high technology
tertiary industries, see service industries
textile industry, 29
Thatcher, M., 47
theory, starting up, 180–3
Third World: intervention and aid, 15, 21, 25; trade with, 16–19, 43–5, 49, 134

Thurow, L., 27, 58, 60–1, 187, 191–2
Tomaskovic-Devey, D., 187, 188, 195, 197
Touraine, A., 183, 204
trade barriers, 49
trade, international, 35–50, 131–4, 189–91; balance of payments, 38–40; British disease, real, 46–50; destabilizing effect of, 122; and GNP, 17; increase, 16–19; and inflation, 26; and power, 14–20; progressive, 131–4; *see also* exports; imports
trade unions, *see* unions
transfers, 122–5, 134
transformation, great, 14–34, 186–9; corporate changes, 20–5; industrial changes, 28–34; inflation, 26–8; political changes, 33–4; power and trade, 14–20
transport system, 136–40
Tsongas, P., 4, 119, 184, 185, 200
Tyler, G., 53, 191

UAW, *see* United Auto Workers
UDAG, 142
undeserving poor, 159
unemployment, 32–3, 122; and big business, 44; export of, 43; and high technology, 105–7, 114; and productivity, 58, 65; and wages, 10–11, 170; *see also* jobs unions, 63, 143, 147–8; and coalition, 169–71, 175, 178; lack of, 96, 114; power of, 10–11, 46
Union Carbide, 185
United Auto Workers, 63, 147
United Nations, 15

Urban Development Action Grant, 142
Urban enterprise zones, 94, 142
Useem, M., 194
US Steel, *see* steel industry
utility industries, 60

Vanik, C., 193
Veblen, T., 24, 139, 187
Vietnam, 15, 103
Vogel, E., 187
Vojta, G., 188
Volcker, P., 79
voting, *see* elections

wages: in car industry, 28; and coalition, 169, 179; and GNP, 110; increases dampened, 6, 8–12; and inflation, 28; and investment, 67; low, 96–7, 109–11, 113, 136; and political changes, 33; and prices, 143, 145; and productivity, 59–64; and "property boom", 77; in service industries, 32, 94; and taxation, 142; and unemployment, 10–11, 170
Wagner Act, 181
Wallerstein, I., 18, 187
Watkins, A. J., 201
weakness, political, 165–6, 168
Weidenbaum, M., 193
Weisskopf, T., 193
welfare, *see* social services
West Germany, 7, 18; labor costs in, 55; left politics in, 175; productivity, 15, 53–4, 60, 64, 66–7; trade, 19, 39–41, 43
Wheeler, B., 173
wisdoms, accepted, 3–13, 184–6
Wolfe, A., 186, 203
women, employment of, 96, 105, 111, 114

worker: hour, output per, 52, 54–5; participation, 147–9; relations, progressive, 146–9; *see also* jobs

world trade, *see* trade

Wright, J. P., 195

young people, 96, 159

DATE DUE
